Just The facts101

Textbook Key Facts

Romania Economic & Development Handbook

by cram101
Texbook NOT Included

Table of Contents

Just The Facts101

Exam Prep for

Romania Economic & Development Strategy Handbook

Just The Facts101 Exam Prep is your link from
the texbook and lecture to your exams.

Just The Facts101 Exam Preps are unauthorized and comprehensive reviews of your textbooks.

Textbook publishers and textbook authors do not particpate in or contribute to these reviews.

Just The Facts101 Exam Prep

eAIN 448915

Foundations of Business

A business, also known as an enterprise, agency or a firm, is an entity involved in the provision of goods and/or services to consumers. Businesses are prevalent in capitalist economies, where most of them are privately owned and provide goods and services to customers in exchange for other goods, services, or money.

:: Marketing analytics ::

__________ is a long-term, forward-looking approach to planning with the fundamental goal of achieving a sustainable competitive advantage. Strategic planning involves an analysis of the company`s strategic initial situation prior to the formulation, evaluation and selection of market-oriented competitive position that contributes to the company`s goals and marketing objectives.

Exam Probability: **Medium**

1. *Answer choices:*

(see index for correct answer)

- a. Mission-driven marketing
- b. Marketing effectiveness
- c. Marketing strategy
- d. Marketing performance measurement and management

Guidance: level 1

:: Competition regulators ::

The ________ is an independent agency of the United States government, established in 1914 by the ________ Act. Its principal mission is the promotion of consumer protection and the elimination and prevention of anticompetitive business practices, such as coercive monopoly. It is headquartered in the ________ Building in Washington, D.C.

Exam Probability: **Medium**

2. *Answer choices:*

(see index for correct answer)

- a. Federal Trade Commission
- b. Directorate-General for Competition
- c. Federal Antimonopoly Service
- d. Federal Cartel Office

Guidance: level 1

:: Insolvency ::

________ is a legal process through which people or other entities who cannot repay debts to creditors may seek relief from some or all of their debts. In most jurisdictions, ________ is imposed by a court order, often initiated by the debtor.

Exam Probability: **High**

3. *Answer choices:*

(see index for correct answer)

- a. George Samuel Ford
- b. Debt consolidation
- c. Official Committee of Equity Security Holders
- d. Bankruptcy

Guidance: level 1

:: Actuarial science ::

_________ is the possibility of losing something of value. Values can be gained or lost when taking _________ resulting from a given action or inaction, foreseen or unforeseen . _________ can also be defined as the intentional interaction with uncertainty. Uncertainty is a potential, unpredictable, and uncontrollable outcome; _________ is a consequence of action taken in spite of uncertainty.

Exam Probability: **High**

4. *Answer choices:*
(see index for correct answer)

- a. Age stratification
- b. Risk parity
- c. Risk
- d. Fictional actuaries

Guidance: level 1

:: Television commercials ::

_________ is a phenomenon whereby something new and somehow valuable is formed. The created item may be intangible or a physical object .

Exam Probability: **Medium**

5. *Answer choices:*
(see index for correct answer)

- a. Blue Velvet
- b. Spongmonkeys
- c. Birds
- d. Creativity

Guidance: level 1

:: Information systems ::

_________ are formal, sociotechnical, organizational systems designed to collect, process, store, and distribute information. In a sociotechnical perspective, _________ are composed by four components: task, people, structure , and technology.

Exam Probability: **High**

6. *Answer choices:*

(see index for correct answer)

- a. Information systems
- b. Process development execution system
- c. Information Processes and Technology
- d. Policy appliances

Guidance: level 1

:: ::

Business is the activity of making one`s living or making money by producing or buying and selling products . Simply put, it is "any activity or enterprise entered into for profit. It does not mean it is a company, a corporation, partnership, or have any such formal organization, but it can range from a street peddler to General Motors."

Exam Probability: **Low**

7. *Answer choices:*

(see index for correct answer)

- a. surface-level diversity
- b. Sarbanes-Oxley act of 2002
- c. process perspective
- d. personal values

Guidance: level 1

:: Marketing ::

__________ comes from the Latin neg and otsia referring to businessmen who, unlike the patricians, had no leisure time in their industriousness; it held the meaning of business until the 17th century when it took on the diplomatic connotation as a dialogue between two or more people or parties intended to reach a beneficial outcome over one or more issues where a conflict exists with respect to at least one of these issues. Thus, __________ is a process of combining divergent positions into a joint agreement under a decision rule of unanimity.

Exam Probability: **Low**

8. *Answer choices:*

(see index for correct answer)

- a. Negotiation
- b. Branding national myths and symbols
- c. Merchandise Mart
- d. Competitor indexing

Guidance: level 1

:: Rhetoric ::

_________ is the pattern of narrative development that aims to make vivid a place, object, character, or group. _________ is one of four rhetorical modes , along with exposition, argumentation, and narration. In practice it would be difficult to write literature that drew on just one of the four basic modes.

Exam Probability: **Low**

9. *Answer choices:*

(see index for correct answer)

- a. Rhetorical exercises
- b. Epideictic
- c. Facilitas
- d. Procatalepsis

Guidance: level 1

:: Public relations ::

_________ is the public visibility or awareness for any product, service or company. It may also refer to the movement of information from its source to the general public, often but not always via the media. The subjects of _________ include people , goods and services, organizations, and works of art or entertainment.

Exam Probability: **Medium**

10. *Answer choices:*

(see index for correct answer)

- a. Publicity
- b. Lawfare
- c. Public diplomacy
- d. Public affairs

Guidance: level 1

:: Industrial design ::

In physics and mathematics, the _________ of a mathematical space is informally defined as the minimum number of coordinates needed to specify any point within it. Thus a line has a _________ of one because only one coordinate is needed to specify a point on it for example, the point at 5 on a number line. A surface such as a plane or the surface of a cylinder or sphere has a _________ of two because two coordinates are needed to specify a point on it for example, both a latitude and longitude are required to locate a point on the surface of a sphere. The inside of a cube, a cylinder or a sphere is three- _________ al because three coordinates are needed to locate a point within these spaces.

Exam Probability: **Low**

11. *Answer choices:*

(see index for correct answer)

- a. Junker test
- b. Industrial Designers Society of America
- c. Radiogram
- d. Dimension

Guidance: level 1

:: Logistics ::

_________ is generally the detailed organization and implementation of a complex operation. In a general business sense, _________ is the management of the flow of things between the point of origin and the point of consumption in order to meet requirements of customers or corporations. The resources managed in _________ may include tangible goods such as materials, equipment, and supplies, as well as food and other consumable items. The _________ of physical items usually involves the integration of information flow, materials handling, production, packaging, inventory, transportation, warehousing, and often security.

Exam Probability: **High**

12. *Answer choices:*

(see index for correct answer)

- a. G-Log
- b. StarShipIt
- c. The Institute of Transport Management
- d. Serial shipping container code

Guidance: level 1

:: International trade ::

__________ involves the transfer of goods or services from one person or entity to another, often in exchange for money. A system or network that allows __________ is called a market.

Exam Probability: **High**

13. *Answer choices:*

(see index for correct answer)

- a. Team Canada Mission
- b. Agreement on the Application of Sanitary and Phytosanitary Measures
- c. Trans-Atlantic trade
- d. Bilateral trade

Guidance: level 1

:: Stock market ::

A shareholder is an individual or institution that legally owns one or more shares of stock in a public or private corporation. __________ may be referred to as members of a corporation. Legally, a person is not a shareholder in a corporation until their name and other details are entered in the corporation`s register of __________ or members.

Exam Probability: **Medium**

14. *Answer choices:*

(see index for correct answer)

- a. Matchbook FX
- b. Direct finance
- c. Shareholders
- d. Chip

Guidance: level 1

:: Marketing ::

A _________ is an overall experience of a customer that distinguishes an organization or product from its rivals in the eyes of the customer. _________ s are used in business, marketing, and advertising. Name _________ s are sometimes distinguished from generic or store _________ s.

Exam Probability: **High**

15. *Answer choices:*

(see index for correct answer)

- a. Demand generation
- b. Grand cru
- c. Beat-sheet
- d. Landing page

Guidance: level 1

:: Property ::

The right to property or right to own property is often classified as a human right for natural persons regarding their possessions. A general recognition of a right to private property is found more rarely and is typically heavily constrained insofar as property is owned by legal persons and where it is used for production rather than consumption.

Exam Probability: **High**

16. *Answer choices:*

(see index for correct answer)

- a. The Great Transformation
- b. Gross annual value
- c. Property premium
- d. Rack-rent

Guidance: level 1

:: Auditing ::

_________ , as defined by accounting and auditing, is a process for assuring of an organization`s objectives in operational effectiveness and efficiency, reliable financial reporting, and compliance with laws, regulations and policies. A broad concept, _________ involves everything that controls risks to an organization.

Exam Probability: **High**

17. *Answer choices:*

(see index for correct answer)

- a. Sales tax audit
- b. Software licensing audit
- c. Detection risk
- d. Internal control

Guidance: level 1

:: Non-profit technology ::

Instituto del Tercer Mundo is a Non-Governmental Organization that performs information, communication and education activities. _________ , which was established in 1989, shares the same secretariat and coordinating personnel as Social Watch and is based in Montevideo, Uruguay.

Exam Probability: **High**

18. *Answer choices:*

(see index for correct answer)

- a. The Planetary Society
- b. Action for Global Information Sharing
- c. Integration Consortium
- d. PledgeBank

Guidance: level 1

:: Market research ::

_________ is an organized effort to gather information about target markets or customers. It is a very important component of business strategy. The term is commonly interchanged with marketing research; however, expert practitioners may wish to draw a distinction, in that marketing research is concerned specifically about marketing processes, while _________ is concerned specifically with markets.

Exam Probability: **High**

19. *Answer choices:*

(see index for correct answer)

- a. Market research and opinion polling in China
- b. Market research
- c. Computer-assisted telephone interviewing
- d. Market analysis

Guidance: level 1

:: National accounts ::

_________ is a monetary measure of the market value of all the final goods and services produced in a period of time, often annually. GDP per capita does not, however, reflect differences in the cost of living and the inflation rates of the countries; therefore using a basis of GDP per capita at purchasing power parity is arguably more useful when comparing differences in living standards between nations.

Exam Probability: **Low**

20. *Answer choices:*

(see index for correct answer)

- a. Gross domestic product
- b. Fixed capital
- c. National Income

Guidance: level 1

:: ::

A __________ is any person who contracts to acquire an asset in return for some form of consideration.

Exam Probability: **Low**

21. *Answer choices:*

(see index for correct answer)

- a. Sarbanes-Oxley act of 2002
- b. Buyer
- c. functional perspective
- d. surface-level diversity

Guidance: level 1

:: Management ::

A __________ is a method or technique that has been generally accepted as superior to any alternatives because it produces results that are superior to those achieved by other means or because it has become a standard way of doing things, e.g., a standard way of complying with legal or ethical requirements.

Exam Probability: **High**

22. *Answer choices:*

(see index for correct answer)

- a. Industrial forensics
- b. Best practice
- c. Process management
- d. Process-based management

Guidance: level 1

:: Business ::

__________ is the activity of making one`s living or making money by producing or buying and selling products . Simply put, it is "any activity or enterprise entered into for profit. It does not mean it is a company, a corporation, partnership, or have any such formal organization, but it can range from a street peddler to General Motors."

Exam Probability: **High**

23. *Answer choices:*

(see index for correct answer)

- a. Counter trade
- b. Business
- c. Business partnering
- d. Business idea

Guidance: level 1

:: Real estate valuation ::

_________ or OMV is the price at which an asset would trade in a competitive auction setting. _________ is often used interchangeably with open _________, fair value or fair _________, although these terms have distinct definitions in different standards, and may or may not differ in some circumstances.

Exam Probability: **High**

24. *Answer choices:*

(see index for correct answer)

- a. Market value
- b. PropertyShark
- c. Chartered Surveyor
- d. Rate base

Guidance: level 1

:: Marketing ::

_________ is based on a marketing concept which can be adopted by an organization as a strategy for business expansion. Where implemented, a franchisor licenses its know-how, procedures, intellectual property, use of its business model, brand, and rights to sell its branded products and services to a franchisee. In return the franchisee pays certain fees and agrees to comply with certain obligations, typically set out in a Franchise Agreement.

Exam Probability: **High**

25. *Answer choices:*

(see index for correct answer)

- a. Franchising
- b. European Information Technology Observatory
- c. Pricing strategies
- d. Marchitecture

Guidance: level 1

:: Social security ::

_________ is "any government system that provides monetary assistance to people with an inadequate or no income." In the United States, this is usually called welfare or a social safety net, especially when talking about Canada and European countries.

Exam Probability: **High**

26. *Answer choices:*
(see index for correct answer)

- a. Mahatma Gandhi Pravasi Suraksha Yojana
- b. Social security
- c. Total Social Security Accounts
- d. Child benefit

Guidance: level 1

:: International trade ::

_________ or globalisation is the process of interaction and integration among people, companies, and governments worldwide. As a complex and multifaceted phenomenon, _________ is considered by some as a form of capitalist expansion which entails the integration of local and national economies into a global, unregulated market economy. _________ has grown due to advances in transportation and communication technology. With the increased global interactions comes the growth of international trade, ideas, and culture. _________ is primarily an economic process of interaction and integration that`s associated with social and cultural aspects. However, conflicts and diplomacy are also large parts of the history of _________, and modern _________ .

Exam Probability: **High**

27. *Answer choices:*

(see index for correct answer)

- a. Foreign Agricultural Service
- b. Globalization
- c. Trade route from the Varangians to the Greeks
- d. Swiss Formula

Guidance: level 1

:: Business ::

A _________ is a mathematical object used to count, measure, and label. The original examples are the natural _________ s 1, 2, 3, 4, and so forth. A written symbol like "5" that represents a _________ is called a numeral. A numeral system is an organized way to write and manipulate this type of symbol, for example the Hindu–Arabic numeral system allows combinations of numerical digits like "5" and "0" to represent larger _________ s like 50. A numeral in linguistics can refer to a symbol like 5, the words or phrase that names a _________, like "five hundred", or other words that mean a specific _________ , like "dozen". In addition to their use in counting and measuring, numerals are often used for labels , for ordering , and for codes . In common usage, _________ may refer to a symbol, a word or phrase, or the mathematical object.

Exam Probability: **Low**

28. *Answer choices:*

(see index for correct answer)

- a. Business mileage reimbursement rate
- b. Relationship Science
- c. Business tourism
- d. Number

Guidance: level 1

:: Credit cards ::

The _________ Company, also known as Amex, is an American multinational financial services corporation headquartered in Three World Financial Center in New York City. The company was founded in 1850 and is one of the 30 components of the Dow Jones Industrial Average. The company is best known for its charge card, credit card, and traveler`s cheque businesses.

Exam Probability: **Low**

29. *Answer choices:*

(see index for correct answer)

- a. Centurion Card
- b. BC Card
- c. Revolution Money
- d. American Express

Guidance: level 1

:: ::

__________ is the production of products for use or sale using labour and machines, tools, chemical and biological processing, or formulation. The term may refer to a range of human activity, from handicraft to high tech, but is most commonly applied to industrial design, in which raw materials are transformed into finished goods on a large scale. Such finished goods may be sold to other manufacturers for the production of other, more complex products, such as aircraft, household appliances, furniture, sports equipment or automobiles, or sold to wholesalers, who in turn sell them to retailers, who then sell them to end users and consumers.

Exam Probability: **Medium**

30. *Answer choices:*

(see index for correct answer)

- a. Manufacturing
- b. empathy
- c. functional perspective
- d. hierarchical

Guidance: level 1

:: Information science ::

A __________ is a written, drawn, presented, or memorialized representation of thought. a __________ is a form, or written piece that trains a line of thought or as in history, a significant event. The word originates from the Latin __________ um, which denotes a "teaching" or "lesson": the verb doceo denotes "to teach". In the past, the word was usually used to denote a written proof useful as evidence of a truth or fact. In the computer age, " __________ " usually denotes a primarily textual computer file, including its structure and format, e.g. fonts, colors, and images. Contemporarily, " __________ " is not defined by its transmission medium, e.g., paper, given the existence of electronic __________ s. " __________ ation" is distinct because it has more denotations than " __________ ". __________ s are also distinguished from "realia", which are three-dimensional objects that would otherwise satisfy the definition of " __________ " because they memorialize or represent thought; __________ s are considered more as 2 dimensional representations. While __________ s are able to have large varieties of customization, all __________ s are able to be shared freely, and have the right to do so, creativity can be represented by __________ s, also. History, events, examples, opinion, etc. all can be expressed in __________ s.

Exam Probability: **High**

31. *Answer choices:*

(see index for correct answer)

- a. Bibliometrician
- b. Paper with delayed recognition
- c. Document
- d. Education informatics

Guidance: level 1

:: ::

An __________ is a contingent motivator. Traditional __________ s are extrinsic motivators which reward actions to yield a desired outcome. The effectiveness of traditional __________ s has changed as the needs of Western society have evolved. While the traditional __________ model is effective when there is a defined procedure and goal for a task, Western society started to require a higher volume of critical thinkers, so the traditional model became less effective. Institutions are now following a trend in implementing strategies that rely on intrinsic motivations rather than the extrinsic motivations that the traditional __________ s foster.

Exam Probability: **Medium**

32. *Answer choices:*

(see index for correct answer)

- a. corporate values
- b. Incentive
- c. open system
- d. similarity-attraction theory

Guidance: level 1

:: Consumer theory ::

__________ is the quantity of a good that consumers are willing and able to purchase at various prices during a given period of time.

Exam Probability: **Low**

33. *Answer choices:*

(see index for correct answer)

- a. Lexicographic preferences
- b. Consumer sovereignty
- c. Demand
- d. Rational addiction

Guidance: level 1

:: Marketing ::

A __________ is the quantity of payment or compensation given by one party to another in return for one unit of goods or services.. A __________ is influenced by both production costs and demand for the product. A __________ may be determined by a monopolist or may be imposed on the firm by market conditions.

Exam Probability: **Medium**

34. *Answer choices:*

(see index for correct answer)

- a. MWW
- b. Personalized marketing
- c. Audience segmentation
- d. Price

Guidance: level 1

:: Financial markets ::

A __________ is a financial market in which long-term debt or equity-backed securities are bought and sold. __________ s channel the wealth of savers to those who can put it to long-term productive use, such as companies or governments making long-term investments. Financial regulators like the Bank of England and the U.S. Securities and Exchange Commission oversee __________ s to protect investors against fraud, among other duties.

Exam Probability: **Medium**

35. *Answer choices:*

(see index for correct answer)

- a. STAMP
- b. Future Trading Act
- c. National best bid and offer
- d. Capital market

Guidance: level 1

:: Management ::

In organizational studies, __________ is the efficient and effective development of an organization`s resources when they are needed. Such resources may include financial resources, inventory, human skills, production resources, or information technology and natural resources.

Exam Probability: **Low**

36. *Answer choices:*

(see index for correct answer)

- a. Operations management
- b. Mushroom management
- c. Resource management
- d. Meeting

Guidance: level 1

:: Environmental economics ::

__________ is the process of people maintaining change in a balanced environment, in which the exploitation of resources, the direction of investments, the orientation of technological development and institutional change are all in harmony and enhance both current and future potential to meet human needs and aspirations. For many in the field, __________ is defined through the following interconnected domains or pillars: environment, economic and social, which according to Fritjof Capra is based on the principles of Systems Thinking. Sub-domains of sustainable development have been considered also: cultural, technological and political. While sustainable development may be the organizing principle for __________ for some, for others, the two terms are paradoxical . Sustainable development is the development that meets the needs of the present without compromising the ability of future generations to meet their own needs. Brundtland Report for the World Commission on Environment and Development introduced the term of sustainable development.

Exam Probability: **Medium**

37. *Answer choices:*

(see index for correct answer)

- a. Land Economics
- b. Sustainability
- c. Eco-social market economy
- d. Carbon accounting

Guidance: level 1

:: Corporate crime ::

_________ LLP, based in Chicago, was an American holding company. Formerly one of the "Big Five" accounting firms , the firm had provided auditing, tax, and consulting services to large corporations. By 2001, it had become one of the world`s largest multinational companies.

Exam Probability: **Low**

38. *Answer choices:*

(see index for correct answer)

- a. Arthur Andersen
- b. Arthur Andersen LLP v. United States
- c. backdating
- d. New England Compounding Center

Guidance: level 1

:: Generally Accepted Accounting Principles ::

In accounting, _________ is the income that a business have from its normal business activities, usually from the sale of goods and services to customers. _________ is also referred to as sales or turnover.Some companies receive _________ from interest, royalties, or other fees. _________ may refer to business income in general, or it may refer to the amount, in a monetary unit, earned during a period of time, as in "Last year, Company X had _________ of $42 million". Profits or net income generally imply total _________ minus total expenses in a given period. In accounting, in the balance statement it is a subsection of the Equity section and _________ increases equity, it is often referred to as the "top line" due to its position on the income statement at the very top. This is to be contrasted with the "bottom line" which denotes net income .

Exam Probability: **High**

39. *Answer choices:*

(see index for correct answer)

- a. Operating income
- b. Revenue

- c. Trial balance
- d. Net income

Guidance: level 1

:: Critical thinking ::

In psychology, _________ is regarded as the cognitive process resulting in the selection of a belief or a course of action among several alternative possibilities. Every _________ process produces a final choice, which may or may not prompt action.

Exam Probability: **High**

40. *Answer choices:*

(see index for correct answer)

- a. Ad hoc hypothesis
- b. Prudence
- c. Decision-making
- d. Rigour

Guidance: level 1

:: Loans ::

In finance, a _________ is the lending of money by one or more individuals, organizations, or other entities to other individuals, organizations etc. The recipient incurs a debt, and is usually liable to pay interest on that debt until it is repaid, and also to repay the principal amount borrowed.

Exam Probability: **Medium**

41. *Answer choices:*

(see index for correct answer)

- a. Loan sale
- b. Participation loan
- c. Government-backed loan
- d. Loan

Guidance: level 1

:: Debt ::

_________ is the trust which allows one party to provide money or resources to another party wherein the second party does not reimburse the first party immediately , but promises either to repay or return those resources at a later date. In other words, _________ is a method of making reciprocity formal, legally enforceable, and extensible to a large group of unrelated people.

Exam Probability: **Medium**

42. *Answer choices:*

(see index for correct answer)

- a. Credit
- b. Extendible bond
- c. Least developed country
- d. Phantom debt

Guidance: level 1

:: Infographics ::

A _________ is a symbolic representation of information according to visualization technique. _________ s have been used since ancient times, but became more prevalent during the Enlightenment. Sometimes, the technique uses a three-dimensional visualization which is then projected onto a two-dimensional surface. The word graph is sometimes used as a synonym for _________ .

Exam Probability: **Medium**

43. *Answer choices:*

(see index for correct answer)

- a. schematic diagram
- b. Glyph
- c. U.S. Route shield
- d. Diagram

Guidance: level 1

:: Security compliance ::

A __________ is a communicated intent to inflict harm or loss on another person. A __________ is considered an act of coercion. __________s are widely observed in animal behavior, particularly in a ritualized form, chiefly in order to avoid the unnecessary physical violence that can lead to physical damage or the death of both conflicting parties.

Exam Probability: **High**

44. *Answer choices:*
(see index for correct answer)

- a. Federal Information Security Management Act of 2002
- b. Nikto Web Scanner
- c. Information assurance vulnerability alert
- d. Threat

Guidance: level 1

:: Derivatives (finance) ::

__________ is any bodily activity that enhances or maintains physical fitness and overall health and wellness. It is performed for various reasons, to aid growth and improve strength, preventing aging, developing muscles and the cardiovascular system, honing athletic skills, weight loss or maintenance, improving health and also for enjoyment. Many individuals choose to __________ outdoors where they can congregate in groups, socialize, and enhance well-being.

Exam Probability: **Medium**

45. *Answer choices:*
(see index for correct answer)

- a. Quality spread differential
- b. EFETF
- c. Swap ratio
- d. Options arbitrage

Guidance: level 1

:: Economic globalization ::

_________ is an agreement in which one company hires another company to be responsible for a planned or existing activity that is or could be done internally,and sometimes involves transferring employees and assets from one firm to another.

Exam Probability: **Medium**

46. *Answer choices:*
(see index for correct answer)

- a. Outsourcing
- b. reshoring

Guidance: level 1

:: Costs ::

In microeconomic theory, the _________ , or alternative cost, of making a particular choice is the value of the most valuable choice out of those that were not taken. In other words, opportunity that will require sacrifices.

Exam Probability: **Medium**

47. *Answer choices:*
(see index for correct answer)

- a. Total cost
- b. Opportunity cost
- c. Cost overrun
- d. Repugnancy costs

Guidance: level 1

:: Money ::

In economics, _________ is money in the physical form of currency, such as banknotes and coins. In bookkeeping and finance, _________ is current assets comprising currency or currency equivalents that can be accessed immediately or near-immediately . _________ is seen either as a reserve for payments, in case of a structural or incidental negative _________ flow or as a way to avoid a downturn on financial markets.

Exam Probability: **Low**

48. *Answer choices:*

(see index for correct answer)

- a. Plutus
- b. Cash
- c. History of money
- d. European Monetary System

Guidance: level 1

:: Information technology ::

_________ is the use of computers to store, retrieve, transmit, and manipulate data, or information, often in the context of a business or other enterprise. IT is considered to be a subset of information and communications technology . An _________ system is generally an information system, a communications system or, more specifically speaking, a computer system – including all hardware, software and peripheral equipment – operated by a limited group of users.

Exam Probability: **High**

49. *Answer choices:*

(see index for correct answer)

- a. Information Technology Institute
- b. Software-defined storage
- c. Information society
- d. Information technology

Guidance: level 1

:: ::

_________ is an abstract concept of management of complex systems according to a set of rules and trends. In systems theory, these types of rules exist in various fields of biology and society, but the term has slightly different meanings according to context. For example.

Exam Probability: **Medium**

50. *Answer choices:*

(see index for correct answer)

- a. Regulation
- b. cultural
- c. open system
- d. Character

Guidance: level 1

:: Business law ::

A __________ is an arrangement where parties, known as partners, agree to cooperate to advance their mutual interests. The partners in a __________ may be individuals, businesses, interest-based organizations, schools, governments or combinations. Organizations may partner to increase the likelihood of each achieving their mission and to amplify their reach. A __________ may result in issuing and holding equity or may be only governed by a contract.

Exam Probability: **Low**

51. *Answer choices:*

(see index for correct answer)

- a. Security interest
- b. Partnership
- c. Chattel mortgage
- d. Retained interest

Guidance: level 1

:: Basic financial concepts ::

__________ is a sustained increase in the general price level of goods and services in an economy over a period of time.When the general price level rises, each unit of currency buys fewer goods and services; consequently, __________ reflects a reduction in the purchasing power per unit of money a loss of real value in the medium of exchange and unit of account within the economy. The measure of __________ is the __________ rate, the annualized percentage change in a general price index, usually the consumer price index, over time. The opposite of __________ is deflation.

Exam Probability: **High**

52. *Answer choices:*

(see index for correct answer)

- a. Financial transaction
- b. Maturity date
- c. Present value of costs
- d. Short interest

Guidance: level 1

:: Human resource management ::

_________ are the people who make up the workforce of an organization, business sector, or economy. "Human capital" is sometimes used synonymously with " _________ ", although human capital typically refers to a narrower effect . Likewise, other terms sometimes used include manpower, talent, labor, personnel, or simply people.

Exam Probability: **Low**

53. *Answer choices:*

(see index for correct answer)

- a. Job sharing
- b. Induction programme
- c. Individual development plan
- d. Human resources

Guidance: level 1

:: Statistical terminology ::

_________ es can be learned implicitly within cultural contexts. People may develop _________ es toward or against an individual, an ethnic group, a sexual or gender identity, a nation, a religion, a social class, a political party, theoretical paradigms and ideologies within academic domains, or a species. _________ ed means one-sided, lacking a neutral viewpoint, or not having an open mind. _________ can come in many forms and is related to prejudice and intuition.

Exam Probability: **Low**

54. *Answer choices:*

(see index for correct answer)

- a. Standard normal deviate
- b. P-value
- c. Kurtosis risk

- d. Bias

Guidance: level 1

:: Management ::

The __________ is a strategy performance management tool – a semi-standard structured report, that can be used by managers to keep track of the execution of activities by the staff within their control and to monitor the consequences arising from these actions.

Exam Probability: **Medium**

55. *Answer choices:*

(see index for correct answer)

- a. manager's right to manage
- b. Manager Tools Podcast
- c. Balanced scorecard
- d. Business-oriented architecture

Guidance: level 1

:: Management ::

The term __________ refers to measures designed to increase the degree of autonomy and self-determination in people and in communities in order to enable them to represent their interests in a responsible and self-determined way, acting on their own authority. It is the process of becoming stronger and more confident, especially in controlling one`s life and claiming one`s rights. __________ as action refers both to the process of self- __________ and to professional support of people, which enables them to overcome their sense of powerlessness and lack of influence, and to recognize and use their resources. To do work with power.

Exam Probability: **Low**

56. *Answer choices:*

(see index for correct answer)

- a. Responsible autonomy
- b. Main Street Manager
- c. Energy monitoring and targeting
- d. Fall guy

Guidance: level 1

:: Electronic feedback ::

_________ occurs when outputs of a system are routed back as inputs as part of a chain of cause-and-effect that forms a circuit or loop. The system can then be said to feed back into itself. The notion of cause-and-effect has to be handled carefully when applied to _________ systems.

Exam Probability: **Low**

57. *Answer choices:*

(see index for correct answer)

- a. Positive feedback
- b. feedback loop

Guidance: level 1

:: Semiconductor companies ::

_________ Corporation is a Japanese multinational conglomerate corporation headquartered in Konan, Minato, Tokyo. Its diversified business includes consumer and professional electronics, gaming, entertainment and financial services. The company owns the largest music entertainment business in the world, the largest video game console business and one of the largest video game publishing businesses, and is one of the leading manufacturers of electronic products for the consumer and professional markets, and a leading player in the film and television entertainment industry. _________ was ranked 97th on the 2018 Fortune Global 500 list.

Exam Probability: **Low**

58. *Answer choices:*

(see index for correct answer)

- a. Arteris
- b. Suzhou Oriental Semiconductor
- c. Sony
- d. Inotera

Guidance: level 1

:: Statistical terminology ::

__________ is the ability to avoid wasting materials, energy, efforts, money, and time in doing something or in producing a desired result. In a more general sense, it is the ability to do things well, successfully, and without waste. In more mathematical or scientific terms, it is a measure of the extent to which input is well used for an intended task or function . It often specifically comprises the capability of a specific application of effort to produce a specific outcome with a minimum amount or quantity of waste, expense, or unnecessary effort. __________ refers to very different inputs and outputs in different fields and industries.

Exam Probability: **Low**

59. *Answer choices:*

(see index for correct answer)

- a. Degrees of freedom
- b. Marginal distribution
- c. Percentile rank
- d. Efficiency

Guidance: level 1

Management

Management is the administration of an organization, whether it is a business, a not-for-profit organization, or government body. Management includes the activities of setting the strategy of an organization and coordinating the efforts of its employees (or of volunteers) to accomplish its objectives through the application of available resources, such as financial, natural, technological, and human resources.

:: ::

_________ is the process of two or more people or organizations working together to complete a task or achieve a goal. _________ is similar to cooperation. Most _________ requires leadership, although the form of leadership can be social within a decentralized and egalitarian group. Teams that work collaboratively often access greater resources, recognition and rewards when facing competition for finite resources.

Exam Probability: **High**

1. *Answer choices:*

(see index for correct answer)

- a. personal values
- b. Collaboration
- c. functional perspective
- d. levels of analysis

Guidance: level 1

:: ::

_________ , known in Europe as research and technological development , refers to innovative activities undertaken by corporations or governments in developing new services or products, or improving existing services or products. _________ constitutes the first stage of development of a potential new service or the production process.

Exam Probability: **Medium**

2. *Answer choices:*

(see index for correct answer)

- a. Sarbanes-Oxley act of 2002
- b. information systems assessment
- c. Research and development
- d. imperative

Guidance: level 1

:: ::

A _________ is a fund into which a sum of money is added during an employee`s employment years, and from which payments are drawn to support the person`s retirement from work in the form of periodic payments. A _________ may be a "defined benefit plan" where a fixed sum is paid regularly to a person, or a "defined contribution plan" under which a fixed sum is invested and then becomes available at retirement age. _________ s should not be confused with severance pay; the former is usually paid in regular installments for life after retirement, while the latter is typically paid as a fixed amount after involuntary termination of employment prior to retirement.

Exam Probability: **Medium**

3. *Answer choices:*

(see index for correct answer)

- a. Pension
- b. hierarchical perspective
- c. information systems assessment
- d. deep-level diversity

Guidance: level 1

:: Production economics ::

_________ is the creation of a whole that is greater than the simple sum of its parts. The term _________ comes from the Attic Greek word sea synergia from synergos, , meaning "working together".

Exam Probability: **High**

4. *Answer choices:*

(see index for correct answer)

- a. Economies of scale
- b. Synergy
- c. Sharing
- d. Socially optimal firm size

Guidance: level 1

:: Socialism ::

In sociology, _________ is the process of internalizing the norms and ideologies of society. _________ encompasses both learning and teaching and is thus "the means by which social and cultural continuity are attained".

Exam Probability: **Medium**

5. *Answer choices:*

(see index for correct answer)

- a. Soviet republic
- b. Lloviznando Cantos
- c. Socialist International
- d. Socialization

Guidance: level 1

:: Project management ::

A _________ is a professional in the field of project management. _________ s have the responsibility of the planning, procurement and execution of a project, in any undertaking that has a defined scope, defined start and a defined finish; regardless of industry. _________ s are first point of contact for any issues or discrepancies arising from within the heads of various departments in an organization before the problem escalates to higher authorities. Project management is the responsibility of a _________ . This individual seldom participates directly in the activities that produce the end result, but rather strives to maintain the progress, mutual interaction and tasks of various parties in such a way that reduces the risk of overall failure, maximizes benefits, and minimizes costs.

Exam Probability: **High**

6. *Answer choices:*

(see index for correct answer)

- a. Association for Project Management
- b. Project blog
- c. Project manager
- d. The Transformation Project

Guidance: level 1

:: E-commerce ::

_________ is the activity of buying or selling of products on online services or over the Internet. Electronic commerce draws on technologies such as mobile commerce, electronic funds transfer, supply chain management, Internet marketing, online transaction processing, electronic data interchange , inventory management systems, and automated data collection systems.

Exam Probability: **Low**

7. *Answer choices:*

(see index for correct answer)

- a. Extended Validation Certificate
- b. XIPWIRE
- c. WePay
- d. E-commerce

Guidance: level 1

:: Human resource management ::

_________ encompasses values and behaviors that contribute to the unique social and psychological environment of a business. The _________ influences the way people interact, the context within which knowledge is created, the resistance they will have towards certain changes, and ultimately the way they share knowledge. _________ represents the collective values, beliefs and principles of organizational members and is a product of factors such as history, product, market, technology, strategy, type of employees, management style, and national culture; culture includes the organization`s vision, values, norms, systems, symbols, language, assumptions, environment, location, beliefs and habits.

Exam Probability: **Low**

8. *Answer choices:*

(see index for correct answer)

- a. Organizational culture
- b. Chief human resources officer
- c. Competency-based management
- d. Talent management

Guidance: level 1

:: Marketing techniques ::

In industry, product lifecycle management is the process of managing the entire lifecycle of a product from inception, through engineering design and manufacture, to service and disposal of manufactured products. PLM integrates people, data, processes and business systems and provides a product information backbone for companies and their extended enterprise.

Exam Probability: **Medium**

9. *Answer choices:*

(see index for correct answer)

- a. Blackout dates
- b. Fear, uncertainty and doubt
- c. Product life cycle
- d. Enterprise engagement

Guidance: level 1

:: Behaviorism ::

In behavioral psychology, _________ is a consequence applied that will strengthen an organism`s future behavior whenever that behavior is preceded by a specific antecedent stimulus. This strengthening effect may be measured as a higher frequency of behavior , longer duration , greater magnitude , or shorter latency . There are two types of _________ , known as positive _________ and negative _________ ; positive is where by a reward is offered on expression of the wanted behaviour and negative is taking away an undesirable element in the persons environment whenever the desired behaviour is achieved.

Exam Probability: **Medium**

10. *Answer choices:*

(see index for correct answer)

- a. Reinforcement
- b. chaining
- c. Systematic desensitization
- d. social facilitation

Guidance: level 1

:: Product design ::

_________ as a verb is to create a new product to be sold by a business to its customers. A very broad coefficient and effective generation and development of ideas through a process that leads to new products. Thus, it is a major aspect of new product development.

Exam Probability: **High**

11. *Answer choices:*

(see index for correct answer)

- a. Andrea Fogli
- b. Beta Tank
- c. Production drawing
- d. Product design

Guidance: level 1

:: Electronic feedback ::

_________ occurs when outputs of a system are routed back as inputs as part of a chain of cause-and-effect that forms a circuit or loop. The system can then be said to feed back into itself. The notion of cause-and-effect has to be handled carefully when applied to _________ systems.

Exam Probability: **High**

12. *Answer choices:*

(see index for correct answer)

- a. Feedback
- b. Positive feedback

Guidance: level 1

:: ::

A _________ is monetary compensation paid by an employer to an employee in exchange for work done. Payment may be calculated as a fixed amount for each task completed , or at an hourly or daily rate , or based on an easily measured quantity of work done.

Exam Probability: **High**

13. *Answer choices:*

(see index for correct answer)

- a. Wage
- b. similarity-attraction theory
- c. hierarchical
- d. levels of analysis

Guidance: level 1

:: Summary statistics ::

_________ is the number of occurrences of a repeating event per unit of time. It is also referred to as temporal _________, which emphasizes the contrast to spatial _________ and angular _________. The period is the duration of time of one cycle in a repeating event, so the period is the reciprocal of the _________. For example: if a newborn baby's heart beats at a _________ of 120 times a minute, its period—the time interval between beats—is half a second. _________ is an important parameter used in science and engineering to specify the rate of oscillatory and vibratory phenomena, such as mechanical vibrations, audio signals , radio waves, and light.

Exam Probability: **Low**

14. *Answer choices:*

(see index for correct answer)

- a. Five-number summary
- b. Pareto index
- c. Generalized entropy index
- d. Frequency

Guidance: level 1

:: ::

_________ is the administration of an organization, whether it is a business, a not-for-profit organization, or government body. _________ includes the activities of setting the strategy of an organization and coordinating the efforts of its employees to accomplish its objectives through the application of available resources, such as financial, natural, technological, and human resources. The term " _________ " may also refer to those people who manage an organization.

Exam Probability: **High**

15. *Answer choices:*

(see index for correct answer)

- a. Management
- b. similarity-attraction theory
- c. surface-level diversity
- d. interpersonal communication

Guidance: level 1

:: Costs ::

In economics, _________ is the total economic cost of production and is made up of variable cost, which varies according to the quantity of a good produced and includes inputs such as labour and raw materials, plus fixed cost, which is independent of the quantity of a good produced and includes inputs that cannot be varied in the short term: fixed costs such as buildings and machinery, including sunk costs if any. Since cost is measured per unit of time, it is a flow variable.

Exam Probability: **High**

16. *Answer choices:*

(see index for correct answer)

- a. Opportunity cost
- b. Prospective costs
- c. Total cost
- d. Cost reduction

Guidance: level 1

:: Management occupations ::

_________ ship is the process of designing, launching and running a new business, which is often initially a small business. The people who create these businesses are called _________ s.

Exam Probability: **Low**

17. *Answer choices:*

(see index for correct answer)

- a. County administrator
- b. Entrepreneur
- c. Chief diversity officer
- d. Chief gaming officer

Guidance: level 1

:: Social psychology ::

In social psychology, _________ is the phenomenon of a person exerting less effort to achieve a goal when he or she works in a group than when working alone. This is seen as one of the main reasons groups are sometimes less productive than the combined performance of their members working as individuals, but should be distinguished from the accidental coordination problems that groups sometimes experience.

Exam Probability: **Low**

18. *Answer choices:*

(see index for correct answer)

- a. Dehumanization
- b. co-optation
- c. Cross-cultural leadership
- d. Social loafing

Guidance: level 1

:: Planning ::

_________ is a high level plan to achieve one or more goals under conditions of uncertainty. In the sense of the "art of the general," which included several subsets of skills including tactics, siegecraft, logistics etc., the term came into use in the 6th century C.E. in East Roman terminology, and was translated into Western vernacular languages only in the 18th century. From then until the 20th century, the word " _________ " came to denote "a comprehensive way to try to pursue political ends, including the threat or actual use of force, in a dialectic of wills" in a military conflict, in which both adversaries interact.

Exam Probability: **Low**

19. *Answer choices:*

(see index for correct answer)

- a. Reproductive life plan
- b. Concept driven strategy
- c. Strategy
- d. Group information management

Guidance: level 1

:: Leadership ::

_________ is a theory of leadership where a leader works with teams to identify needed change, creating a vision to guide the change through inspiration, and executing the change in tandem with committed members of a group; it is an integral part of the Full Range Leadership Model. _________ serves to enhance the motivation, morale, and job performance of followers through a variety of mechanisms; these include connecting the follower`s sense of identity and self to a project and to the collective identity of the organization; being a role model for followers in order to inspire them and to raise their interest in the project; challenging followers to take greater ownership for their work, and understanding the strengths and weaknesses of followers, allowing the leader to align followers with tasks that enhance their performance.

Exam Probability: **Medium**

20. *Answer choices:*

(see index for correct answer)

- a. Motivational Leadership
- b. Outstanding leadership theory
- c. Transformational leadership
- d. BTS Group

Guidance: level 1

:: Marketing ::

_________ , in marketing, manufacturing, call centres and management, is the use of flexible computer-aided manufacturing systems to produce custom output. Such systems combine the low unit costs of mass production processes with the flexibility of individual customization.

Exam Probability: **Medium**

21. *Answer choices:*

(see index for correct answer)

- a. Packshot
- b. Macromarketing
- c. Albuquerque Craft Beer Market
- d. Mass customization

Guidance: level 1

:: ::

_________ or accountancy is the measurement, processing, and communication of financial information about economic entities such as businesses and corporations. The modern field was established by the Italian mathematician Luca Pacioli in 1494. _________ , which has been called the "language of business", measures the results of an organization`s economic activities and conveys this information to a variety of users, including investors, creditors, management, and regulators. Practitioners of _________ are known as accountants. The terms " _________ " and "financial reporting" are often used as synonyms.

Exam Probability: **High**

22. *Answer choices:*

(see index for correct answer)

- a. Accounting
- b. surface-level diversity
- c. hierarchical perspective
- d. personal values

Guidance: level 1

:: Customs duties ::

A _________ is a tax on imports or exports between sovereign states. It is a form of regulation of foreign trade and a policy that taxes foreign products to encourage or safeguard domestic industry. _________ s are the simplest and oldest instrument of trade policy. Traditionally, states have used them as a source of income. Now, they are among the most widely used instruments of protection, along with import and export quotas.

Exam Probability: **High**

23. *Answer choices:*

(see index for correct answer)

- a. Import Surtaxes
- b. Immigration tariff
- c. Canada Corn Act

- d. Court of Exchequer

Guidance: level 1

:: Mereology ::

__________ , in the abstract, is what belongs to or with something, whether as an attribute or as a component of said thing. In the context of this article, it is one or more components , whether physical or incorporeal, of a person`s estate; or so belonging to, as in being owned by, a person or jointly a group of people or a legal entity like a corporation or even a society. Depending on the nature of the __________ , an owner of __________ has the right to consume, alter, share, redefine, rent, mortgage, pawn, sell, exchange, transfer, give away or destroy it, or to exclude others from doing these things, as well as to perhaps abandon it; whereas regardless of the nature of the __________ , the owner thereof has the right to properly use it , or at the very least exclusively keep it.

Exam Probability: **Medium**

24. *Answer choices:*

(see index for correct answer)

- a. Property
- b. Mereotopology
- c. Non-wellfounded mereology
- d. Mereological nihilism

Guidance: level 1

:: ::

__________ is the exchange of capital, goods, and services across international borders or territories.

Exam Probability: **High**

25. *Answer choices:*

(see index for correct answer)

- a. empathy
- b. International trade
- c. surface-level diversity
- d. similarity-attraction theory

Guidance: level 1

:: Systems thinking ::

In business management, a _________ is a company that facilitates the learning of its members and continuously transforms itself. The concept was coined through the work and research of Peter Senge and his colleagues.

Exam Probability: **High**

26. *Answer choices:*

(see index for correct answer)

- a. Tt30
- b. Thought leader
- c. Learning organization
- d. Club of Budapest

Guidance: level 1

:: Human resource management ::

_________ is a core function of human resource management and it is related to the specification of contents, methods and relationship of jobs in order to satisfy technological and organizational requirements as well as the social and personal requirements of the job holder or the employee. Its principles are geared towards how the nature of a person's job affects their attitudes and behavior at work, particularly relating to characteristics such as skill variety and autonomy. The aim of a _________ is to improve job satisfaction, to improve through-put, to improve quality and to reduce employee problems .

Exam Probability: **Low**

27. *Answer choices:*

(see index for correct answer)

- a. Human resources
- b. Organizational behavior and human resources
- c. Vendor management system
- d. Job design

Guidance: level 1

:: Evaluation ::

__________ is the practice of being honest and showing a consistent and uncompromising adherence to strong moral and ethical principles and values.In ethics, __________ is regarded as the honesty and truthfulness or accuracy of one`s actions. __________ can stand in opposition to hypocrisy, in that judging with the standards of __________ involves regarding internal consistency as a virtue, and suggests that parties holding within themselves apparently conflicting values should account for the discrepancy or alter their beliefs. The word __________ evolved from the Latin adjective integer, meaning whole or complete. In this context, __________ is the inner sense of "wholeness" deriving from qualities such as honesty and consistency of character. As such, one may judge that others "have __________ " to the extent that they act according to the values, beliefs and principles they claim to hold.

Exam Probability: **High**

28. *Answer choices:*

(see index for correct answer)

- a. CESG Claims Tested Mark
- b. Integrity
- c. Technology assessment
- d. American Evaluation Association

Guidance: level 1

:: Monopoly (economics) ::

A __________ is a form of intellectual property that gives its owner the legal right to exclude others from making, using, selling, and importing an invention for a limited period of years, in exchange for publishing an enabling public disclosure of the invention. In most countries __________ rights fall under civil law and the __________ holder needs to sue someone infringing the __________ in order to enforce his or her rights. In some industries __________ s are an essential form of competitive advantage; in others they are irrelevant.

Exam Probability: **Low**

29. *Answer choices:*

(see index for correct answer)

- a. Patent
- b. Practice of law
- c. Sherman Antitrust Act
- d. Herfindahl index

Guidance: level 1

:: Game theory ::

_________ is the idea that rationality is limited when individuals make decisions: by the tractability of the decision problem, the cognitive limitations of the mind, and the time available to make the decision. Decision-makers, in this view, act as satisficers, seeking a satisfactory solution rather than an optimal one.

Exam Probability: **Medium**

30. *Answer choices:*

(see index for correct answer)

- a. Focal point
- b. Simultaneous game
- c. Bounded rationality
- d. Public goods game

Guidance: level 1

:: Business models ::

A _________ , _________ company or daughter company is a company that is owned or controlled by another company, which is called the parent company, parent, or holding company. The _________ can be a company, corporation, or limited liability company. In some cases it is a government or state-owned enterprise. In some cases, particularly in the music and book publishing industries, subsidiaries are referred to as imprints.

Exam Probability: **Medium**

31. *Answer choices:*

(see index for correct answer)

- a. Premium business model
- b. Subsidiary

- c. One stop shop
- d. Praenumeration

Guidance: level 1

:: Supply chain management terms ::

In business and finance, _________ is a system of organizations, people, activities, information, and resources involved inmoving a product or service from supplier to customer. _________ activities involve the transformation of natural resources, raw materials, and components into a finished product that is delivered to the end customer. In sophisticated _________ systems, used products may re-enter the _________ at any point where residual value is recyclable. _________ s link value chains.

Exam Probability: **High**

32. *Answer choices:*

(see index for correct answer)

- a. inventory management
- b. Will call
- c. Most valuable customers
- d. Supply chain

Guidance: level 1

:: Organizational structure ::

An _________ defines how activities such as task allocation, coordination, and supervision are directed toward the achievement of organizational aims.

Exam Probability: **High**

33. *Answer choices:*

(see index for correct answer)

- a. The Starfish and the Spider
- b. Automated Bureaucracy
- c. Blessed Unrest
- d. Unorganisation

Guidance: level 1

:: Free trade agreements ::

A _________ is a wide-ranging taxes, tariff and trade treaty that often includes investment guarantees. It exists when two or more countries agree on terms that helps them trade with each other. The most common _________ s are of the preferential and free trade types are concluded in order to reduce tariffs, quotas and other trade restrictions on items traded between the signatories.

Exam Probability: **Low**

34. *Answer choices:*

(see index for correct answer)

- a. European Union Central American Association Agreement
- b. Trade agreement
- c. Regional Comprehensive Economic Partnership
- d. Trade, Development and Cooperation Agreement

Guidance: level 1

:: ::

_________ refers to the overall process of attracting, shortlisting, selecting and appointing suitable candidates for jobs within an organization. _________ can also refer to processes involved in choosing individuals for unpaid roles. Managers, human resource generalists and _________ specialists may be tasked with carrying out _________, but in some cases public-sector employment agencies, commercial _________ agencies, or specialist search consultancies are used to undertake parts of the process. Internet-based technologies which support all aspects of _________ have become widespread.

Exam Probability: **Low**

35. *Answer choices:*

(see index for correct answer)

- a. Sarbanes-Oxley act of 2002
- b. co-culture
- c. levels of analysis
- d. corporate values

Guidance: level 1

:: ::

In organizational behavior and industrial/organizational psychology, proactivity or _________ behavior by individuals refers to anticipatory, change-oriented and self-initiated behavior in situations. _________ behavior involves acting in advance of a future situation, rather than just reacting. It means taking control and making things happen rather than just adjusting to a situation or waiting for something to happen. _________ employees generally do not need to be asked to act, nor do they require detailed instructions.

Exam Probability: **Low**

36. *Answer choices:*

(see index for correct answer)

- a. Proactive
- b. hierarchical
- c. levels of analysis
- d. co-culture

Guidance: level 1

:: ::

In a supply chain, a _________, or a seller, is an enterprise that contributes goods or services. Generally, a supply chain _________ manufactures inventory/stock items and sells them to the next link in the chain. Today, these terms refer to a supplier of any good or service.

Exam Probability: **Medium**

37. *Answer choices:*

(see index for correct answer)

- a. Vendor
- b. deep-level diversity
- c. levels of analysis
- d. hierarchical

Guidance: level 1

:: Employee relations ::

_________ ownership, or employee share ownership, is an ownership interest in a company held by the company`s workforce. The ownership interest may be facilitated by the company as part of employees` remuneration or incentive compensation for work performed, or the company itself may be employee owned.

Exam Probability: **High**

38. *Answer choices:*

(see index for correct answer)

- a. Employee morale
- b. Employee engagement
- c. Fringe benefit
- d. Employee stock

Guidance: level 1

:: Human resource management ::

_________ are the people who make up the workforce of an organization, business sector, or economy. "Human capital" is sometimes used synonymously with " _________ ", although human capital typically refers to a narrower effect . Likewise, other terms sometimes used include manpower, talent, labor, personnel, or simply people.

Exam Probability: **Medium**

39. *Answer choices:*

(see index for correct answer)

- a. Cultural capital
- b. Human resources
- c. Progress, plans, problems
- d. Turnover

Guidance: level 1

:: Export and import control ::

" _________ " means the Government Service which is responsible for the administration of _________ law and the collection of duties and taxes and which also has the responsibility for the application of other laws and regulations relating to the importation, exportation, movement or storage of goods.

Exam Probability: **Low**

40. *Answer choices:*

(see index for correct answer)

- a. VNIIS Exemption Letter
- b. Customs
- c. Export parity price
- d. Wassenaar Arrangement

Guidance: level 1

:: ::

A _________ is a leader`s method of providing direction, implementing plans, and motivating people. Various authors have proposed identifying many different _________ s as exhibited by leaders in the political, business or other fields. Studies on _________ are conducted in the military field, expressing an approach that stresses a holistic view of leadership, including how a leader`s physical presence determines how others perceive that leader. The factors of physical presence in this context include military bearing, physical fitness, confidence, and resilience. The leader`s intellectual capacity helps to conceptualize solutions and to acquire knowledge to do the job. A leader`s conceptual abilities apply agility, judgment, innovation, interpersonal tact, and domain knowledge. Domain knowledge encompasses tactical and technical knowledge as well as cultural and geopolitical awareness. Daniel Goleman in his article "Leadership that Gets Results" talks about six styles of leadership.

Exam Probability: **High**

41. *Answer choices:*

(see index for correct answer)

- a. hierarchical perspective
- b. Leadership style
- c. levels of analysis

- d. personal values

Guidance: level 1

:: Types of marketing ::

In microeconomics and management, _________ is an arrangement in which the supply chain of a company is owned by that company. Usually each member of the supply chain produces a different product or service, and the products combine to satisfy a common need. It is contrasted with horizontal integration, wherein a company produces several items which are related to one another. _________ has also described management styles that bring large portions of the supply chain not only under a common ownership, but also into one corporation .

Exam Probability: **Medium**

42. *Answer choices:*

(see index for correct answer)

- a. Customerization
- b. Close Range Marketing
- c. Guerrilla marketing
- d. Relationship marketing

Guidance: level 1

:: Human resource management ::

_________ is a family of procedures to identify the content of a job in terms of activities involved and attributes or job requirements needed to perform the activities. _________ provides information of organizations which helps to determine which employees are best fit for specific jobs. Through _________ , the analyst needs to understand what the important tasks of the job are, how they are carried out, and the necessary human qualities needed to complete the job successfully.

Exam Probability: **Low**

43. *Answer choices:*

(see index for correct answer)

- a. CEO succession
- b. Job analysis
- c. Autonomous work group

- d. Disciplinary probation

Guidance: level 1

:: Majority–minority relations ::

_________, also known as reservation in India and Nepal, positive discrimination / action in the United Kingdom, and employment equity in Canada and South Africa, is the policy of promoting the education and employment of members of groups that are known to have previously suffered from discrimination. Historically and internationally, support for _________ has sought to achieve goals such as bridging inequalities in employment and pay, increasing access to education, promoting diversity, and redressing apparent past wrongs, harms, or hindrances.

Exam Probability: **High**

44. *Answer choices:*

(see index for correct answer)

- a. positive discrimination
- b. cultural Relativism
- c. cultural dissonance

Guidance: level 1

:: Management ::

The _________ is a strategy performance management tool – a semi-standard structured report, that can be used by managers to keep track of the execution of activities by the staff within their control and to monitor the consequences arising from these actions.

Exam Probability: **Medium**

45. *Answer choices:*

(see index for correct answer)

- a. Success trap
- b. Value migration
- c. Professional performances
- d. Balanced scorecard

Guidance: level 1

:: Market research ::

__________ is an organized effort to gather information about target markets or customers. It is a very important component of business strategy. The term is commonly interchanged with marketing research; however, expert practitioners may wish to draw a distinction, in that marketing research is concerned specifically about marketing processes, while __________ is concerned specifically with markets.

Exam Probability: **Low**

46. *Answer choices:*

(see index for correct answer)

- a. Market research
- b. Friday night death slot
- c. CoolBrands
- d. Eddie Chung

Guidance: level 1

:: Marketing ::

__________ or stock is the goods and materials that a business holds for the ultimate goal of resale .

Exam Probability: **High**

47. *Answer choices:*

(see index for correct answer)

- a. Customer acquisition management
- b. Inventory
- c. Branded asset management
- d. Movement marketing

Guidance: level 1

:: ::

A _________ is a type of job aid used to reduce failure by compensating for potential limits of human memory and attention. It helps to ensure consistency and completeness in carrying out a task. A basic example is the "to do list". A more advanced _________ would be a schedule, which lays out tasks to be done according to time of day or other factors. A primary task in _________ is documentation of the task and auditing against the documentation.

Exam Probability: **Low**

48. *Answer choices:*

(see index for correct answer)

- a. deep-level diversity
- b. surface-level diversity
- c. Checklist
- d. hierarchical perspective

Guidance: level 1

:: Marketing ::

A _________ is an overall experience of a customer that distinguishes an organization or product from its rivals in the eyes of the customer. _________ s are used in business, marketing, and advertising. Name _________ s are sometimes distinguished from generic or store _________ s.

Exam Probability: **Medium**

49. *Answer choices:*

(see index for correct answer)

- a. Brand
- b. Business-to-government
- c. Marketing activation
- d. Green marketing

Guidance: level 1

:: Employment compensation ::

_________ refers to various incentive plans introduced by businesses that provide direct or indirect payments to employees that depend on company`s profitability in addition to employees` regular salary and bonuses. In publicly traded companies these plans typically amount to allocation of shares to employees. One of the earliest pioneers of _________ was Englishman Theodore Cooke Taylor, who is known to have introduced the practice in his woollen mills during the late 1800s .

Exam Probability: **Medium**

50. *Answer choices:*

(see index for correct answer)

- a. Profit sharing
- b. Labour code
- c. Dearness allowance
- d. Fiduciary management

Guidance: level 1

:: Management ::

A _________ is a method or technique that has been generally accepted as superior to any alternatives because it produces results that are superior to those achieved by other means or because it has become a standard way of doing things, e.g., a standard way of complying with legal or ethical requirements.

Exam Probability: **Low**

51. *Answer choices:*

(see index for correct answer)

- a. Best practice
- b. Logistics management
- c. Director
- d. Automated decision support

Guidance: level 1

:: Training ::

_________ is teaching, or developing in oneself or others, any skills and knowledge that relate to specific useful competencies. _________ has specific goals of improving one`s capability, capacity, productivity and performance. It forms the core of apprenticeships and provides the backbone of content at institutes of technology . In addition to the basic _________ required for a trade, occupation or profession, observers of the labor-market recognize as of 2008 the need to continue _________ beyond initial qualifications: to maintain, upgrade and update skills throughout working life. People within many professions and occupations may refer to this sort of _________ as professional development.

Exam Probability: **High**

52. *Answer choices:*
(see index for correct answer)

- a. Training
- b. Training workshop
- c. Arts-based training
- d. American Council on Exercise

Guidance: level 1

:: Project management ::

A _________ is a type of bar chart that illustrates a project schedule, named after its inventor, Henry Gantt , who designed such a chart around the years 1910–1915. Modern _________ s also show the dependency relationships between activities and current schedule status.

Exam Probability: **High**

53. *Answer choices:*
(see index for correct answer)

- a. Schedule
- b. Disciplined Agile Delivery
- c. Task
- d. Gantt chart

Guidance: level 1

:: Social networks ::

_________ broadly refers to those factors of effectively functioning social groups that include such things as interpersonal relationships, a shared sense of identity, a shared understanding, shared norms, shared values, trust, cooperation, and reciprocity. However, the many views of this complex subject make a single definition difficult.

Exam Probability: **High**

54. *Answer choices:*

(see index for correct answer)

- a. First Tuesday
- b. Alpha centrality
- c. Social network automation
- d. Structural endogamy

Guidance: level 1

:: Organizational theory ::

Decentralisation is the process by which the activities of an organization, particularly those regarding planning and decision making, are distributed or delegated away from a central, authoritative location or group. Concepts of _________ have been applied to group dynamics and management science in private businesses and organizations, political science, law and public administration, economics, money and technology.

Exam Probability: **High**

55. *Answer choices:*

(see index for correct answer)

- a. Contingency theory
- b. Organizational change fatigue
- c. Decentralization
- d. Cooperation

Guidance: level 1

:: Project management ::

A _________ is a team whose members usually belong to different groups, functions and are assigned to activities for the same project. A team can be divided into sub-teams according to need. Usually _________ s are only used for a defined period of time. They are disbanded after the project is deemed complete. Due to the nature of the specific formation and disbandment, _________ s are usually in organizations.

Exam Probability: **Low**

56. *Answer choices:*

(see index for correct answer)

- a. Product description
- b. TELOS
- c. Project team
- d. Risk register

Guidance: level 1

:: ::

A _________ or sample _________ is a single measure of some attribute of a sample . It is calculated by applying a function to the values of the items of the sample, which are known together as a set of data.

Exam Probability: **High**

57. *Answer choices:*

(see index for correct answer)

- a. Sarbanes-Oxley act of 2002
- b. Statistic
- c. similarity-attraction theory
- d. levels of analysis

Guidance: level 1

:: ::

The _________ or just chief executive , is the most senior corporate, executive, or administrative officer in charge of managing an organization especially an independent legal entity such as a company or nonprofit institution. CEOs lead a range of organizations, including public and private corporations, non-profit organizations and even some government organizations . The CEO of a corporation or company typically reports to the board of directors and is charged with maximizing the value of the entity, which may include maximizing the share price, market share, revenues or another element. In the non-profit and government sector, CEOs typically aim at achieving outcomes related to the organization`s mission, such as reducing poverty, increasing literacy, etc.

Exam Probability: **High**

58. *Answer choices:*

(see index for correct answer)

- a. Chief executive officer
- b. cultural
- c. similarity-attraction theory
- d. information systems assessment

Guidance: level 1

:: Elementary mathematics ::

_________ is a numerical measurement of how far apart objects are. In physics or everyday usage, _________ may refer to a physical length or an estimation based on other criteria . In most cases, " _________ from A to B" is interchangeable with " _________ from B to A". In mathematics, a _________ function or metric is a generalization of the concept of physical _________ . A metric is a function that behaves according to a specific set of rules, and is a way of describing what it means for elements of some space to be "close to" or "far away from" each other.

Exam Probability: **Medium**

59. *Answer choices:*

(see index for correct answer)

- a. Distance
- b. Order of magnitude
- c. Distinct

- d. Subsequence

Guidance: level 1

Business law

Corporate law (also known as business law) is the body of law governing the rights, relations, and conduct of persons, companies, organizations and businesses. It refers to the legal practice relating to, or the theory of corporations. Corporate law often describes the law relating to matters which derive directly from the life-cycle of a corporation. It thus encompasses the formation, funding, governance, and death of a corporation.

:: ::

A _________ is a person or firm who arranges transactions between a buyer and a seller for a commission when the deal is executed. A _________ who also acts as a seller or as a buyer becomes a principal party to the deal. Neither role should be confused with that of an agent—one who acts on behalf of a principal party in a deal.

Exam Probability: **High**

1. *Answer choices:*

(see index for correct answer)

- a. information systems assessment
- b. levels of analysis
- c. Broker
- d. open system

Guidance: level 1

:: Insurance law ::

_________ exists when an insured person derives a financial or other kind of benefit from the continuous existence, without repairment or damage, of the insured object . A person has an _________ in something when loss of or damage to that thing would cause the person to suffer a financial or other kind of loss.Normally, _________ is established by ownership, possession, or direct relationship. For example, people have _________ s in their own homes and vehicles, but not in their neighbors` homes and vehicles, and almost certainly not those of strangers.

Exam Probability: **High**

2. *Answer choices:*

(see index for correct answer)

- a. Bermuda Form
- b. QC clause
- c. Hangarter v. Provident
- d. Insurable interest

Guidance: level 1

:: Fair use ::

_________ is a doctrine in the law of the United States that permits limited use of copyrighted material without having to first acquire permission from the copyright holder. _________ is one of the limitations to copyright intended to balance the interests of copyright holders with the public interest in the wider distribution and use of creative works by allowing as a defense to copyright infringement claims certain limited uses that might otherwise be considered infringement.

Exam Probability: **Medium**

3. *Answer choices:*

(see index for correct answer)

- a. Fair use
- b. Transformation
- c. Nominative use
- d. Derivative work

Guidance: level 1

:: Monopoly (economics) ::

__________ is a category of property that includes intangible creations of the human intellect. __________ encompasses two types of rights: industrial property rights and copyright. It was not until the 19th century that the term " __________ " began to be used, and not until the late 20th century that it became commonplace in the majority of the world.

Exam Probability: **High**

4. *Answer choices:*

(see index for correct answer)

- a. Ramsey problem
- b. Legal monopoly
- c. De facto monopoly
- d. Intellectual property

Guidance: level 1

:: Majority–minority relations ::

__________ , also known as reservation in India and Nepal, positive discrimination / action in the United Kingdom, and employment equity in Canada and South Africa, is the policy of promoting the education and employment of members of groups that are known to have previously suffered from discrimination. Historically and internationally, support for __________ has sought to achieve goals such as bridging inequalities in employment and pay, increasing access to education, promoting diversity, and redressing apparent past wrongs, harms, or hindrances.

Exam Probability: **Low**

5. *Answer choices:*

(see index for correct answer)

- a. Affirmative action
- b. cultural Relativism
- c. positive discrimination

Guidance: level 1

:: Business law ::

A _________ is a form of security interest granted over an item of property to secure the payment of a debt or performance of some other obligation. The owner of the property, who grants the _________, is referred to as the _________ ee and the person who has the benefit of the _________ is referred to as the _________ or or _________ holder.

Exam Probability: **Low**

6. *Answer choices:*

(see index for correct answer)

- a. Bulk sale
- b. Consularization
- c. Personal Property Security Act
- d. Lien

Guidance: level 1

:: Decision theory ::

A _________ is a deliberate system of principles to guide decisions and achieve rational outcomes. A _________ is a statement of intent, and is implemented as a procedure or protocol. Policies are generally adopted by a governance body within an organization. Policies can assist in both subjective and objective decision making. Policies to assist in subjective decision making usually assist senior management with decisions that must be based on the relative merits of a number of factors, and as a result are often hard to test objectively, e.g. work-life balance _________. In contrast policies to assist in objective decision making are usually operational in nature and can be objectively tested, e.g. password _________.

Exam Probability: **Medium**

7. *Answer choices:*

(see index for correct answer)

- a. Decision field theory
- b. Model-based reasoning
- c. Policy
- d. Cognitive bias

Guidance: level 1

:: Utilitarianism ::

_________ is a family of consequentialist ethical theories that promotes actions that maximize happiness and well-being for the majority of a population. Although different varieties of _________ admit different characterizations, the basic idea behind all of them is to in some sense maximize utility, which is often defined in terms of well-being or related concepts. For instance, Jeremy Bentham, the founder of _________, described utility as

Exam Probability: **Low**

8. *Answer choices:*

(see index for correct answer)

- a. Utilitarianism
- b. Utility monster
- c. Mohism
- d. Equal consideration of interests

Guidance: level 1

:: Commercial crimes ::

In law, _________ is the unauthorized use of another`s name, likeness, or identity without that person`s permission, resulting in harm to that person.

Exam Probability: **High**

9. *Answer choices:*

(see index for correct answer)

- a. Misappropriation
- b. Sweethearting
- c. Global Forum on Transparency and Exchange of Information for Tax Purposes
- d. pilferage

Guidance: level 1

:: Legal doctrines and principles ::

In some common law jurisdictions, _________ is a defense to a tort claim based on negligence. If it is available, the defense completely bars plaintiffs from any recovery if they contribute to their own injury through their own negligence.

Exam Probability: **Low**

10. *Answer choices:*

(see index for correct answer)

- a. Attractive nuisance
- b. Eminent domain
- c. Caveat emptor
- d. Respondeat superior

Guidance: level 1

:: ::

_________ is the principled guide to action taken by the administrative executive branches of the state with regard to a class of issues, in a manner consistent with law and institutional customs.

Exam Probability: **Low**

11. *Answer choices:*

(see index for correct answer)

- a. hierarchical perspective
- b. open system
- c. deep-level diversity
- d. corporate values

Guidance: level 1

:: Legal doctrines and principles ::

The _________ rule is a rule in the Anglo-American common law that governs what kinds of evidence parties to a contract dispute can introduce when trying to determine the specific terms of a contract. The rule also prevents parties who have reduced their agreement to a final written document from later introducing other evidence, such as the content of oral discussions from earlier in the negotiation process, as evidence of a different intent as to the terms of the contract. The rule provides that "extrinsic evidence is inadmissible to vary a written contract". The term "parol" derives from the Anglo-Norman French parol or parole, meaning "word of mouth" or "verbal", and in medieval times referred to oral pleadings in a court case.

Exam Probability: **Medium**

12. *Answer choices:*

(see index for correct answer)

- a. Abstention doctrine
- b. Parol evidence
- c. Res ipsa
- d. Act of state

Guidance: level 1

:: American legal terms ::

The phrase "by _________ " is a legal term that indicates that a right or liability has been created for a party, irrespective of the intent of that party, because it is dictated by existing legal principles. For example, if a person dies without a will, his or her heirs are determined by _________ . Similarly, if a person marries or has a child after his or her will has been executed, the law writes this pretermitted spouse or pretermitted heir into the will if no provision for this situation was specifically included. Adverse possession, in which title to land passes because non-owners have occupied it for a certain period of time, is another important right that vests by _________ .

Exam Probability: **Medium**

13. *Answer choices:*

(see index for correct answer)

- a. Operation of law
- b. Chilling effect

Guidance: level 1

:: Contract law ::

__________ , also called an anticipatory breach, is a term in the law of contracts that describes a declaration by the promising party to a contract that he or she does not intend to live up to his or her obligations under the contract.

Exam Probability: **Medium**

14. *Answer choices:*

(see index for correct answer)

- a. Undue influence
- b. Liquidated damages
- c. Anticipatory repudiation
- d. Performance Based Contracting

Guidance: level 1

:: Progressive Era in the United States ::

The Clayton Antitrust Act of 1914 , was a part of United States antitrust law with the goal of adding further substance to the U.S. antitrust law regime; the __________ sought to prevent anticompetitive practices in their incipiency. That regime started with the Sherman Antitrust Act of 1890, the first Federal law outlawing practices considered harmful to consumers . The __________ specified particular prohibited conduct, the three-level enforcement scheme, the exemptions, and the remedial measures.

Exam Probability: **Medium**

15. *Answer choices:*

(see index for correct answer)

- a. Clayton Antitrust Act
- b. pragmatism
- c. Clayton Act

Guidance: level 1

:: Commercial item transport and distribution ::

A _________ is a commitment or expectation to perform some action in general or if certain circumstances arise. A _________ may arise from a system of ethics or morality, especially in an honor culture. Many duties are created by law, sometimes including a codified punishment or liability for non-performance. Performing one`s _________ may require some sacrifice of self-interest.

Exam Probability: **Medium**

16. *Answer choices:*

(see index for correct answer)

- a. Bulkhaul Limited
- b. Tractor unit
- c. Humanitarian Logistics
- d. Refrigerator truck

Guidance: level 1

:: Legal procedure ::

_________, adjective law, or rules of court comprises the rules by which a court hears and determines what happens in civil, lawsuit, criminal or administrative proceedings. The rules are designed to ensure a fair and consistent application of due process or fundamental justice to all cases that come before a court.

Exam Probability: **High**

17. *Answer choices:*

(see index for correct answer)

- a. civil procedure
- b. Opening statement
- c. Closing argument
- d. Procedural law

Guidance: level 1

:: Business ethics ::

_________ is a type of harassment technique that relates to a sexual nature and the unwelcome or inappropriate promise of rewards in exchange for sexual favors. _________ includes a range of actions from mild transgressions to sexual abuse or assault. Harassment can occur in many different social settings such as the workplace, the home, school, churches, etc. Harassers or victims may be of any gender.

Exam Probability: **Low**

18. *Answer choices:*

(see index for correct answer)

- a. Symantec
- b. Being Globally Responsible Conference
- c. Sexual harassment
- d. Conspiracy of Fools

Guidance: level 1

:: Contract law ::

An _________ is a contract that has not yet been fully performed or fully executed. It is a contract in which both sides still have important performance remaining. However, an obligation to pay money, even if such obligation is material, does not usually make a contract executory. An obligation is material if a breach of contract would result from the failure to satisfy the obligation. A contract that has been fully performed by one party but not by the other party is not an _________ .

Exam Probability: **Low**

19. *Answer choices:*

(see index for correct answer)

- a. Implied warranty
- b. Expectation damages
- c. Contract
- d. Contract price

Guidance: level 1

:: Real estate ::

_________ , real estate, realty, or immovable property In English common law refers to landed properties belonging to some person. It include all structures, crops, buildings, machinery, wells, dams, ponds, mines, canals, and roads, among other things. The term is historic, arising from the now-discontinued form of action, which distinguish between _________ disputes and personal property disputes. Personal property was, and continues to refer to all properties that are not real properties.

Exam Probability: **Medium**

20. *Answer choices:*

(see index for correct answer)

- a. Pad site
- b. Decorative Allowance
- c. Real property
- d. Home inspection

Guidance: level 1

:: Writs ::

In common law, a _________ is a formal _________ ten order issued by a body with administrative or judicial jurisdiction; in modern usage, this body is generally a court. Warrants, prerogative _________ s, and subpoenas are common types of _________ , but many forms exist and have existed.

Exam Probability: **High**

21. *Answer choices:*

(see index for correct answer)

- a. Writ
- b. Qui tam
- c. Writ of assistance

Guidance: level 1

:: Insolvency ::

__________ is the state of being unable to pay the money owed, by a person or company, on time; those in a state of __________ are said to be insolvent. There are two forms: cash-flow __________ and balance-sheet __________.

Exam Probability: **Medium**

22. *Answer choices:*

(see index for correct answer)

- a. Insolvency
- b. Liquidation
- c. George Samuel Ford
- d. Financial distress

Guidance: level 1

:: Contract law ::

An __________, or simply option, is defined as "a promise which meets the requirements for the formation of a contract and limits the promisor`s power to revoke an offer."

Exam Probability: **High**

23. *Answer choices:*

(see index for correct answer)

- a. Invitation to treat
- b. Option contract
- c. Illusory promise
- d. Unenforceable

Guidance: level 1

:: ::

An __________ is an area of the production, distribution, or trade, and consumption of goods and services by different agents. Understood in its broadest sense, `The __________ is defined as a social domain that emphasize the practices, discourses, and material expressions associated with the production, use, and management of resources`. Economic agents can be individuals, businesses, organizations, or governments. Economic transactions occur when two parties agree to the value or price of the transacted good or service, commonly expressed in a certain currency. However, monetary transactions only account for a small part of the economic domain.

Exam Probability: **High**

24. *Answer choices:*

(see index for correct answer)

- a. hierarchical perspective
- b. Sarbanes-Oxley act of 2002
- c. Economy
- d. deep-level diversity

Guidance: level 1

:: ::

__________ is the practical authority granted to a legal body to administer justice within a defined field of responsibility, e.g., Michigan tax law. In federations like the United States, areas of __________ apply to local, state, and federal levels; e.g. the court has __________ to apply federal law.

Exam Probability: **Low**

25. *Answer choices:*

(see index for correct answer)

- a. imperative
- b. functional perspective
- c. personal values
- d. Jurisdiction

Guidance: level 1

:: ::

In common law legal systems, _________ is a principle or rule established in a previous legal case that is either binding on or persuasive for a court or other tribunal when deciding subsequent cases with similar issues or facts. Common-law legal systems place great value on deciding cases according to consistent principled rules, so that similar facts will yield similar and predictable outcomes, and observance of _________ is the mechanism by which that goal is attained. The principle by which judges are bound to _________ s is known as stare decisis. Common-law _________ is a third kind of law, on equal footing with statutory law and delegated legislation or regulatory law

.

Exam Probability: **Low**

26. *Answer choices:*

(see index for correct answer)

- a. co-culture
- b. functional perspective
- c. cultural
- d. Precedent

Guidance: level 1

:: ::

Credit is the trust which allows one party to provide money or resources to another party wherein the second party does not reimburse the first party immediately , but promises either to repay or return those resources at a later date. In other words, credit is a method of making reciprocity formal, legally enforceable, and extensible to a large group of unrelated people.

Exam Probability: **High**

27. *Answer choices:*

(see index for correct answer)

- a. cultural
- b. imperative
- c. Consumer credit
- d. functional perspective

Guidance: level 1

:: Contract law ::

Generally, a _________ is a loan or a credit transaction in which the lender acquires a security interest in collateral owned by the borrower and is entitled to foreclose on or repossess the collateral in the event of the borrower`s default. The terms of the relationship are governed by a contract, or security agreement. A common example would be a consumer who purchases a car on credit. If the consumer fails to make the payments on time, the lender will take the car and resell it, applying the proceeds of the sale toward the loan. Mortgages and deeds of trust are another example. In the United States, _________ s in personal property are governed by Article 9 of the Uniform Commercial Code .

Exam Probability: **High**

28. *Answer choices:*

(see index for correct answer)

- a. Condition subsequent
- b. Transmutation agreement
- c. Verbal contract
- d. Material transfer agreement

Guidance: level 1

:: ::

_________ , in law, is a transaction or action that is valid but may be annulled by one of the parties to the transaction. _________ is usually used in distinction to void ab initio and unenforceable.

Exam Probability: **Medium**

29. *Answer choices:*

(see index for correct answer)

- a. corporate values
- b. personal values
- c. Voidable
- d. surface-level diversity

Guidance: level 1

:: Contract law ::

A _________ is an event or state of affairs that is required before something else will occur. In contract law, a _________ is an event which must occur, unless its non-occurrence is excused, before performance under a contract becomes due, i.e., before any contractual duty exists.

Exam Probability: **Medium**

30. *Answer choices:*

(see index for correct answer)

- a. Liquidated damages
- b. Condition precedent
- c. Scots contract law
- d. Transaction document

Guidance: level 1

:: Advertising ::

In law, _________ is speech or writing on behalf of a business with the intent of earning revenue or a profit. It is economic in nature and usually attempts to persuade consumers to purchase the business`s product or service. The Supreme Court of the United States defines _________ as speech that "proposes a commercial transaction".

Exam Probability: **Low**

31. *Answer choices:*

(see index for correct answer)

- a. Under the Anheuser Bush
- b. Student-run advertising agency
- c. Advertising Producers Association
- d. Video advertising

Guidance: level 1

:: Business law ::

A _________ is a form of partnership similar to a general partnership except that while a general partnership must have at least two general partners , a _________ must have at least one GP and at least one limited partner.

Exam Probability: **Low**

32. *Answer choices:*

(see index for correct answer)

- a. Limited partnership
- b. Negotiable instrument
- c. Independent contractor
- d. Companies law

Guidance: level 1

:: Real estate valuation ::

_________ or OMV is the price at which an asset would trade in a competitive auction setting. _________ is often used interchangeably with open _________ , fair value or fair _________ , although these terms have distinct definitions in different standards, and may or may not differ in some circumstances.

Exam Probability: **Medium**

33. *Answer choices:*

(see index for correct answer)

- a. International Right of Way Association
- b. Chartered Surveyor
- c. Broker%27s Price Opinion
- d. Market value

Guidance: level 1

:: ::

The words " _________ " and "testify" both derive from the Latin word testis, referring to the notion of a disinterested third-party witness.

Exam Probability: **Low**

34. *Answer choices:*

(see index for correct answer)

- a. levels of analysis
- b. information systems assessment
- c. Testimony
- d. open system

Guidance: level 1

:: Industrial agreements ::

__________ is a process of negotiation between employers and a group of employees aimed at agreements to regulate working salaries, working conditions, benefits, and other aspects of workers` compensation and rights for workers. The interests of the employees are commonly presented by representatives of a trade union to which the employees belong. The collective agreements reached by these negotiations usually set out wage scales, working hours, training, health and safety, overtime, grievance mechanisms, and rights to participate in workplace or company affairs.

Exam Probability: **Low**

35. *Answer choices:*

(see index for correct answer)

- a. Compromise agreement
- b. Collective bargaining
- c. Industrial arbitration
- d. Mutual gains bargaining

Guidance: level 1

:: International trade ::

__________ involves the transfer of goods or services from one person or entity to another, often in exchange for money. A system or network that allows __________ is called a market.

Exam Probability: **Low**

36. *Answer choices:*

(see index for correct answer)

- a. Trade in Services Agreement
- b. Reimportation
- c. Uppsala model
- d. Trade

Guidance: level 1

:: ::

The _________ is an intergovernmental organization that is concerned with the regulation of international trade between nations. The WTO officially commenced on 1 January 1995 under the Marrakesh Agreement, signed by 124 nations on 15 April 1994, replacing the General Agreement on Tariffs and Trade , which commenced in 1948. It is the largest international economic organization in the world.

Exam Probability: **Low**

37. *Answer choices:*

(see index for correct answer)

- a. cultural
- b. hierarchical
- c. functional perspective
- d. World Trade Organization

Guidance: level 1

:: Business law ::

A _________ is a document guaranteeing the payment of a specific amount of money, either on demand, or at a set time, with the payer usually named on the document. More specifically, it is a document contemplated by or consisting of a contract, which promises the payment of money without condition, which may be paid either on demand or at a future date. The term can have different meanings, depending on what law is being applied and what country and context it is used in.

Exam Probability: **High**

38. *Answer choices:*

(see index for correct answer)

- a. Statutory authority
- b. Negotiable instrument
- c. Participation
- d. Single business enterprise

Guidance: level 1

:: Contract law ::

A __________ is a contract in which one party agrees to supply as much of a good or service as is required by the other party, and in exchange the other party expressly or implicitly promises that it will obtain its goods or services exclusively from the first party. For example, a grocery store might enter into a contract with the farmer who grows oranges under which the farmer would supply the grocery store with as many oranges as the store could sell. The farmer could sue for breach of contract if the store were thereafter to purchase oranges for this purpose from any other party. The converse of this situation is an output contract, in which one buyer agrees to purchase however much of a good or service the seller is able to produce.

Exam Probability: **High**

39. *Answer choices:*

(see index for correct answer)

- a. Beneficial interest
- b. Requirements contract
- c. first refusal
- d. Undue influence

Guidance: level 1

:: Contract law ::

__________ is a legal cause of action and a type of civil wrong, in which a binding agreement or bargained-for exchange is not honored by one or more of the parties to the contract by non-performance or interference with the other party`s performance. Breach occurs when a party to a contract fails to fulfill its obligation as described in the contract, or communicates an intent to fail the obligation or otherwise appears not to be able to perform its obligation under the contract. Where there is __________, the resulting damages will have to be paid by the party breaching the contract to the aggrieved party.

Exam Probability: **Low**

40. *Answer choices:*

(see index for correct answer)

- a. Exceptio non adimpleti contractus
- b. Subcontractor
- c. Breach of contract
- d. Quasi-contract

Guidance: level 1

:: ::

_________ is the assignment of any responsibility or authority to another person to carry out specific activities. It is one of the core concepts of management leadership. However, the person who delegated the work remains accountable for the outcome of the delegated work. _________ empowers a subordinate to make decisions, i.e. it is a shifting of decision-making authority from one organizational level to a lower one. _________ , if properly done, is not fabrication. The opposite of effective _________ is micromanagement, where a manager provides too much input, direction, and review of delegated work. In general, _________ is good and can save money and time, help in building skills, and motivate people. On the other hand, poor _________ might cause frustration and confusion to all the involved parties. Some agents, however, do not favour a _________ and consider the power of making a decision rather burdensome.

Exam Probability: **High**

41. *Answer choices:*

(see index for correct answer)

- a. empathy
- b. information systems assessment
- c. imperative
- d. Delegation

Guidance: level 1

:: Business law ::

An _________ is a natural person, business, or corporation that provides goods or services to another entity under terms specified in a contract or within a verbal agreement. Unlike an employee, an _________ does not work regularly for an employer but works as and when required, during which time they may be subject to law of agency. _________ s are usually paid on a freelance basis. Contractors often work through a limited company or franchise, which they themselves own, or may work through an umbrella company.

Exam Probability: **Low**

42. *Answer choices:*

(see index for correct answer)

- a. Independent contractor
- b. Subordination
- c. Unfair Commercial Practices Directive
- d. Lease

Guidance: level 1

:: Stock market ::

The _________ of a corporation is all of the shares into which ownership of the corporation is divided. In American English, the shares are commonly known as " _________ s". A single share of the _________ represents fractional ownership of the corporation in proportion to the total number of shares. This typically entitles the _________ holder to that fraction of the company's earnings, proceeds from liquidation of assets , or voting power, often dividing these up in proportion to the amount of money each _________ holder has invested. Not all _________ is necessarily equal, as certain classes of _________ may be issued for example without voting rights, with enhanced voting rights, or with a certain priority to receive profits or liquidation proceeds before or after other classes of shareholders.

Exam Probability: **Medium**

43. *Answer choices:*

(see index for correct answer)

- a. Penny stock
- b. Whisper number
- c. Stock
- d. Erie War

Guidance: level 1

:: Corporate finance ::

__________ is a contract law concept about the purchase of the release from a debt obligation. It is one of the methods by which parties to a contract may terminate their agreement. The release is completed by the transfer of valuable consideration that must not be the actual performance of the obligation itself. The accord is the agreement to discharge the obligation and the satisfaction is the legal "consideration" which binds the parties to the agreement. A valid accord does not discharge the prior contract; instead it suspends the right to enforce it in accordance with the terms of the accord contract, in which satisfaction, or performance of the contract will discharge both contracts . If the creditor breaches the accord, then the debtor will be able to bring up the existence of the accord in order to enjoin any action against him.

Exam Probability: **High**

44. *Answer choices:*

(see index for correct answer)

- a. Bankmail
- b. Accord and satisfaction
- c. Demutualization
- d. Master limited partnership

Guidance: level 1

:: ::

__________ Corporation was an American energy, commodities, and services company based in Houston, Texas. It was founded in 1985 as a merger between Houston Natural Gas and InterNorth, both relatively small regional companies. Before its bankruptcy on December 3, 2001, __________ employed approximately 29,000 staff and was a major electricity, natural gas, communications and pulp and paper company, with claimed revenues of nearly $101 billion during 2000. Fortune named __________ "America's Most Innovative Company" for six consecutive years.

Exam Probability: **High**

45. *Answer choices:*

(see index for correct answer)

- a. Enron
- b. cultural
- c. similarity-attraction theory

- d. open system

Guidance: level 1

:: ::

_________ is the collection of techniques, skills, methods, and processes used in the production of goods or services or in the accomplishment of objectives, such as scientific investigation. _________ can be the knowledge of techniques, processes, and the like, or it can be embedded in machines to allow for operation without detailed knowledge of their workings. Systems applying _________ by taking an input, changing it according to the system`s use, and then producing an outcome are referred to as _________ systems or technological systems.

Exam Probability: **High**

46. *Answer choices:*

(see index for correct answer)

- a. imperative
- b. co-culture
- c. similarity-attraction theory
- d. hierarchical perspective

Guidance: level 1

:: ::

_________ is a process whereby a person assumes the parenting of another, usually a child, from that person`s biological or legal parent or parents. Legal _________ s permanently transfers all rights and responsibilities, along with filiation, from the biological parent or parents.

Exam Probability: **High**

47. *Answer choices:*

(see index for correct answer)

- a. Adoption
- b. Character
- c. cultural
- d. process perspective

Guidance: level 1

:: ::

A _________ is an individual or institution that legally owns one or more shares of stock in a public or private corporation. _________ s may be referred to as members of a corporation. Legally, a person is not a _________ in a corporation until their name and other details are entered in the corporation`s register of _________ s or members.

Exam Probability: **Medium**

48. *Answer choices:*

(see index for correct answer)

- a. co-culture
- b. Shareholder
- c. cultural
- d. Character

Guidance: level 1

:: ::

_________ is property that is movable. In common law systems, _________ may also be called chattels or personalty. In civil law systems, _________ is often called movable property or movables – any property that can be moved from one location to another.

Exam Probability: **Medium**

49. *Answer choices:*

(see index for correct answer)

- a. hierarchical perspective
- b. Personal property
- c. interpersonal communication
- d. process perspective

Guidance: level 1

:: ::

The ________ to the United States Constitution prevents the government from making laws which respect an establishment of religion, prohibit the free exercise of religion, or abridge the freedom of speech, the freedom of the press, the right to peaceably assemble, or the right to petition the government for redress of grievances. It was adopted on December 15, 1791, as one of the ten amendments that constitute the Bill of Rights.

Exam Probability: **Medium**

50. *Answer choices:*

(see index for correct answer)

- a. interpersonal communication
- b. co-culture
- c. functional perspective
- d. First Amendment

Guidance: level 1

:: Marketing ::

A ________ is an overall experience of a customer that distinguishes an organization or product from its rivals in the eyes of the customer. ________ s are used in business, marketing, and advertising. Name ________ s are sometimes distinguished from generic or store ________ s.

Exam Probability: **Low**

51. *Answer choices:*

(see index for correct answer)

- a. Interactive marketing
- b. Local store marketing
- c. Kano model
- d. Online lead generation

Guidance: level 1

:: ::

A contract is a legally-binding agreement which recognises and governs the rights and duties of the parties to the agreement. A contract is legally enforceable because it meets the requirements and approval of the law. An agreement typically involves the exchange of goods, services, money, or promises of any of those. In the event of breach of contract, the law awards the injured party access to legal remedies such as damages and cancellation.

Exam Probability: **High**

52. *Answer choices:*

(see index for correct answer)

- a. Contract law
- b. deep-level diversity
- c. hierarchical
- d. imperative

Guidance: level 1

:: Real property law ::

A __________ is the grant of authority or rights, stating that the granter formally recognizes the prerogative of the recipient to exercise the rights specified. It is implicit that the granter retains superiority , and that the recipient admits a limited status within the relationship, and it is within that sense that __________ s were historically granted, and that sense is retained in modern usage of the term.

Exam Probability: **High**

53. *Answer choices:*

(see index for correct answer)

- a. Charter
- b. Lesion beyond moiety
- c. Right of entry
- d. Retaliatory eviction

Guidance: level 1

:: Commerce ::

_________ relates to "the exchange of goods and services, especially on a large scale". It includes legal, economic, political, social, cultural and technological systems that operate in a country or in international trade.

Exam Probability: **High**

54. *Answer choices:*

(see index for correct answer)

- a. Statutory holdback
- b. Hong Kong Mercantile Exchange
- c. Customs broking
- d. Commerce

Guidance: level 1

:: Decision theory ::

Within economics the concept of _________ is used to model worth or value, but its usage has evolved significantly over time. The term was introduced initially as a measure of pleasure or satisfaction within the theory of utilitarianism by moral philosophers such as Jeremy Bentham and John Stuart Mill. But the term has been adapted and reapplied within neoclassical economics, which dominates modern economic theory, as a _________ function that represents a consumer`s preference ordering over a choice set. As such, it is devoid of its original interpretation as a measurement of the pleasure or satisfaction obtained by the consumer from that choice.

Exam Probability: **High**

55. *Answer choices:*

(see index for correct answer)

- a. Minimax
- b. Utility
- c. Action axiom
- d. Rete algorithm

Guidance: level 1

:: ::

The __________ is one of the several United States Uniform Acts proposed by the National Conference of Commissioners on Uniform State Laws . Forty-seven states, the District of Columbia, and the U.S. Virgin Islands have adopted the UETA. Its purpose is to harmonize state laws concerning retention of paper records and the validity of electronic signatures.

Exam Probability: **Low**

56. *Answer choices:*

(see index for correct answer)

- a. levels of analysis
- b. functional perspective
- c. hierarchical perspective
- d. Uniform Electronic Transactions Act

Guidance: level 1

:: Information technology audit ::

__________ is the act of using a computer to take or alter electronic data, or to gain unlawful use of a computer or system. In the United States, __________ is specifically proscribed by the __________ and Abuse Act, which criminalizes computer-related acts under federal jurisdiction. Types of __________ include.

Exam Probability: **High**

57. *Answer choices:*

(see index for correct answer)

- a. Information technology audit
- b. Computer forensics
- c. Information security audit
- d. National Information Infrastructure Protection Act

Guidance: level 1

:: Auctioneering ::

An _________ is a process of buying and selling goods or services by offering them up for bid, taking bids, and then selling the item to the highest bidder. The open ascending price _________ is arguably the most common form of _________ in use today. Participants bid openly against one another, with each subsequent bid required to be higher than the previous bid. An _________ eer may announce prices, bidders may call out their bids themselves , or bids may be submitted electronically with the highest current bid publicly displayed. In a Dutch _________ , the _________ eer begins with a high asking price for some quantity of like items; the price is lowered until a participant is willing to accept the _________ eer`s price for some quantity of the goods in the lot or until the seller`s reserve price is met. While _________ s are most associated in the public imagination with the sale of antiques, paintings, rare collectibles and expensive wines, _________ s are also used for commodities, livestock, radio spectrum and used cars. In economic theory, an _________ may refer to any mechanism or set of trading rules for exchange.

Exam Probability: **Medium**

58. *Answer choices:*

(see index for correct answer)

- a. Public auction
- b. Name Your Own Price
- c. Pie supper
- d. Auction

Guidance: level 1

:: Manufactured goods ::

A _________ or final good is any commodity that is produced or consumed by the consumer to satisfy current wants or needs. _________ s are ultimately consumed, rather than used in the production of another good. For example, a microwave oven or a bicycle that is sold to a consumer is a final good or _________ , but the components that are sold to be used in those goods are intermediate goods. For example, textiles or transistors can be used to make some further goods.

Exam Probability: **High**

59. *Answer choices:*

(see index for correct answer)

- a. Bespoke
- b. Consumer Good
- c. Household goods
- d. Tarpaulin

Guidance: level 1

Finance

Finance is a field that is concerned with the allocation (investment) of assets and liabilities over space and time, often under conditions of risk or uncertainty. Finance can also be defined as the science of money management. Participants in the market aim to price assets based on their risk level, fundamental value, and their expected rate of return. Finance can be split into three sub-categories: public finance, corporate finance and personal finance.

:: International taxation ::

_________ is the levying of tax by two or more jurisdictions on the same declared income , asset , or financial transaction . Double liability is mitigated in a number of ways, for example.

Exam Probability: **High**

1. *Answer choices:*

(see index for correct answer)

- a. Spahn tax
- b. Double taxation
- c. Euromod
- d. Exchange of information

Guidance: level 1

:: Accounting systems ::

In bookkeeping, a _________ statement is a process that explains the difference on a specified date between the bank balance shown in an organization`s bank statement, as supplied by the bank and the corresponding amount shown in the organization`s own accounting records.

Exam Probability: **Low**

2. *Answer choices:*

(see index for correct answer)

- a. Entity concept
- b. Invoice processing
- c. Accounting practice
- d. Unified ledger accounting

Guidance: level 1

:: Financial ratios ::

The _________ is a liquidity ratio that measures whether a firm has enough resources to meet its short-term obligations. It compares a firm's current assets to its current liabilities, and is expressed as follows.

Exam Probability: **Low**

3. *Answer choices:*

(see index for correct answer)

- a. Current ratio
- b. EV/GCI
- c. Jaws ratio
- d. Total expense ratio

Guidance: level 1

:: Financial accounting ::

_________ refers to any one of several methods by which a company, for 'financial accounting' or tax purposes, depreciates a fixed asset in such a way that the amount of depreciation taken each year is higher during the earlier years of an asset's life. For financial accounting purposes, _________ is expected to be much more productive during its early years, so that depreciation expense will more accurately represent how much of an asset's usefulness is being used up each year. For tax purposes, _________ provides a way of deferring corporate income taxes by reducing taxable income in current years, in exchange for increased taxable income in future years. This is a valuable tax incentive that encourages businesses to purchase new assets.

Exam Probability: **High**

4. *Answer choices:*

(see index for correct answer)

- a. Accelerated depreciation
- b. Capital account
- c. Asset recovery
- d. Money measurement concept

Guidance: level 1

:: Accounting journals and ledgers ::

_________ is a daybook or journal which is used to record transactions relating to adjustment entries, opening stock, accounting errors etc. The source documents of this prime entry book are journal voucher, copy of management reports and invoices.

Exam Probability: **High**

5. *Answer choices:*

(see index for correct answer)

- a. Journal entry
- b. General journal
- c. Cash receipts journal
- d. Subsidiary ledger

Guidance: level 1

:: Generally Accepted Accounting Principles ::

In accounting, an economic item`s _________ is the original nominal monetary value of that item. _________ accounting involves reporting assets and liabilities at their _________ s, which are not updated for changes in the items` values. Consequently, the amounts reported for these balance sheet items often differ from their current economic or market values.

Exam Probability: **Low**

6. *Answer choices:*

(see index for correct answer)

- a. Completed-contract method
- b. Deferral
- c. Engagement letter
- d. Cost pool

Guidance: level 1

:: Shareholders ::

A _________ is a payment made by a corporation to its shareholders, usually as a distribution of profits. When a corporation earns a profit or surplus, the corporation is able to re-invest the profit in the business and pay a proportion of the profit as a _________ to shareholders. Distribution to shareholders may be in cash or, if the corporation has a _________ reinvestment plan, the amount can be paid by the issue of further shares or share repurchase. When _________ s are paid, shareholders typically must pay income taxes, and the corporation does not receive a corporate income tax deduction for the _________ payments.

Exam Probability: **High**

7. *Answer choices:*

(see index for correct answer)

- a. Friedman doctrine
- b. Shareholder ownership value
- c. Shareholders in the United Kingdom
- d. Shareholder oppression

Guidance: level 1

:: Generally Accepted Accounting Principles ::

_________ is the accounting classification of an account. It is part of double-entry book-keeping technique.

Exam Probability: **High**

8. *Answer choices:*

(see index for correct answer)

- a. Vendor-specific objective evidence
- b. Chinese accounting standards
- c. Paid in capital
- d. Normal balance

Guidance: level 1

:: Social security ::

_________ is "any government system that provides monetary assistance to people with an inadequate or no income." In the United States, this is usually called welfare or a social safety net, especially when talking about Canada and European countries.

Exam Probability: **Low**

9. *Answer choices:*
(see index for correct answer)

- a. Social security in Sweden
- b. Social security
- c. Government Service Insurance System
- d. Child benefit

Guidance: level 1

:: Asset ::

In accounting, a _________ is any asset which can reasonably be expected to be sold, consumed, or exhausted through the normal operations of a business within the current fiscal year or operating cycle . Typical _________ s include cash, cash equivalents, short-term investments , accounts receivable, stock inventory, supplies, and the portion of prepaid liabilities which will be paid within a year.In simple words, assets which are held for a short period are known as _________ s. Such assets are expected to be realised in cash or consumed during the normal operating cycle of the business.

Exam Probability: **Medium**

10. *Answer choices:*
(see index for correct answer)

- a. Current asset
- b. Fixed asset

Guidance: level 1

:: Notes (finance) ::

A __________, sometimes referred to as a note payable, is a legal instrument , in which one party promises in writing to pay a determinate sum of money to the other , either at a fixed or determinable future time or on demand of the payee, under specific terms.

Exam Probability: **High**

11. *Answer choices:*

(see index for correct answer)

- a. A notes
- b. Promissory note
- c. Interest Bearing Note
- d. Capital note

Guidance: level 1

:: Stock market ::

A __________, securities exchange or bourse, is a facility where stock brokers and traders can buy and sell securities, such as shares of stock and bonds and other financial instruments. __________s may also provide for facilities the issue and redemption of such securities and instruments and capital events including the payment of income and dividends. Securities traded on a __________ include stock issued by listed companies, unit trusts, derivatives, pooled investment products and bonds. __________s often function as "continuous auction" markets with buyers and sellers consummating transactions via open outcry at a central location such as the floor of the exchange or by using an electronic trading platform.

Exam Probability: **Low**

12. *Answer choices:*

(see index for correct answer)

- a. Clientele effect
- b. Stock exchange
- c. SPI 200 futures contract
- d. Trading curb

Guidance: level 1

:: Generally Accepted Accounting Principles ::

__________ , also referred to as the bottom line, net income, or net earnings is a measure of the profitability of a venture after accounting for all costs and taxes. It is the actual profit, and includes the operating expenses that are excluded from gross profit.

Exam Probability: **Low**

13. *Answer choices:*

(see index for correct answer)

- a. Normal balance
- b. Net profit
- c. Standard Business Reporting
- d. Paid in capital

Guidance: level 1

:: Insolvency ::

__________ is the process in accounting by which a company is brought to an end in the United Kingdom, Republic of Ireland and United States. The assets and property of the company are redistributed. __________ is also sometimes referred to as winding-up or dissolution, although dissolution technically refers to the last stage of __________ . The process of __________ also arises when customs, an authority or agency in a country responsible for collecting and safeguarding customs duties, determines the final computation or ascertainment of the duties or drawback accruing on an entry.

Exam Probability: **Low**

14. *Answer choices:*

(see index for correct answer)

- a. George Samuel Ford
- b. Insolvency law of Russia
- c. Liquidation
- d. Bankruptcy

Guidance: level 1

:: Income ::

__________ is a ratio between the net profit and cost of investment resulting from an investment of some resources. A high ROI means the investment`s gains favorably to its cost. As a performance measure, ROI is used to evaluate the efficiency of an investment or to compare the efficiencies of several different investments. In purely economic terms, it is one way of relating profits to capital invested. __________ is a performance measure used by businesses to identify the efficiency of an investment or number of different investments.

Exam Probability: **Medium**

15. *Answer choices:*

(see index for correct answer)

- a. Stipend
- b. Return of investment
- c. Giganomics
- d. Return on investment

Guidance: level 1

:: ::

A __________ is any person who contracts to acquire an asset in return for some form of consideration.

Exam Probability: **High**

16. *Answer choices:*

(see index for correct answer)

- a. co-culture
- b. functional perspective
- c. personal values
- d. cultural

Guidance: level 1

:: ::

In the field of analysis of algorithms in computer science, the _________ is a method of amortized analysis based on accounting. The _________ often gives a more intuitive account of the amortized cost of an operation than either aggregate analysis or the potential method. Note, however, that this does not guarantee such analysis will be immediately obvious; often, choosing the correct parameters for the _________ requires as much knowledge of the problem and the complexity bounds one is attempting to prove as the other two methods.

Exam Probability: **Medium**

17. *Answer choices:*

(see index for correct answer)

- a. imperative
- b. co-culture
- c. surface-level diversity
- d. Accounting method

Guidance: level 1

:: ::

_________ is a costing method that identifies activities in an organization and assigns the cost of each activity to all products and services according to the actual consumption by each. This model assigns more indirect costs into direct costs compared to conventional costing.

Exam Probability: **Medium**

18. *Answer choices:*

(see index for correct answer)

- a. hierarchical perspective
- b. cultural
- c. information systems assessment
- d. Activity-based costing

Guidance: level 1

:: Accounting ::

It is the period for which books are balanced and the financial statements are prepared. Generally, the _________ consists of 12 months. However the beginning of the _________ differs according to the jurisdiction. For example, one entity may follow the regular calendar year, i.e. January to December as the accounting year, while another entity may follow April to March as the _________.

Exam Probability: **Low**

19. *Answer choices:*

(see index for correct answer)

- a. AICPA Code of Professional Conduct
- b. Accounting period
- c. FreeAgent
- d. Professional services networks

Guidance: level 1

:: Management ::

The _________ is a strategy performance management tool – a semi-standard structured report, that can be used by managers to keep track of the execution of activities by the staff within their control and to monitor the consequences arising from these actions.

Exam Probability: **High**

20. *Answer choices:*

(see index for correct answer)

- a. Balanced scorecard
- b. Risk appetite
- c. Value migration
- d. Overtime rate

Guidance: level 1

:: Stock market ::

The _________ of a corporation is all of the shares into which ownership of the corporation is divided. In American English, the shares are commonly known as " _________ s". A single share of the _________ represents fractional ownership of the corporation in proportion to the total number of shares. This typically entitles the _________ holder to that fraction of the company`s earnings, proceeds from liquidation of assets , or voting power, often dividing these up in proportion to the amount of money each _________ holder has invested. Not all _________ is necessarily equal, as certain classes of _________ may be issued for example without voting rights, with enhanced voting rights, or with a certain priority to receive profits or liquidation proceeds before or after other classes of shareholders.

Exam Probability: **Low**

21. *Answer choices:*

(see index for correct answer)

- a. Tech Buzz
- b. Automated trading system
- c. London Stock Exchange Group
- d. Erie War

Guidance: level 1

:: ::

A _________ , in the word`s original meaning, is a sheet of paper on which one performs work. They come in many forms, most commonly associated with children`s school work assignments, tax forms, and accounting or other business environments. Software is increasingly taking over the paper-based _________ .

Exam Probability: **High**

22. *Answer choices:*

(see index for correct answer)

- a. corporate values
- b. deep-level diversity
- c. cultural
- d. levels of analysis

Guidance: level 1

:: Inventory ::

__________ is a system of inventory in which updates are made on a periodic basis. This differs from perpetual inventory systems, where updates are made as seen fit.

Exam Probability: **Low**

23. *Answer choices:*

(see index for correct answer)

- a. Lower of cost or market
- b. Inventory control problem
- c. Consignment stock
- d. Safety stock

Guidance: level 1

:: Bonds (finance) ::

In finance, a __________ or convertible note or convertible debt is a type of bond that the holder can convert into a specified number of shares of common stock in the issuing company or cash of equal value. It is a hybrid security with debt- and equity-like features. It originated in the mid-19th century, and was used by early speculators such as Jacob Little and Daniel Drew to counter market cornering.

Exam Probability: **High**

24. *Answer choices:*

(see index for correct answer)

- a. Bullet strategy
- b. Luxembourg Depositary Receipt
- c. Convertible bond
- d. Non-corporate credit

Guidance: level 1

:: Marketing terminology ::

_________ in capital budgeting refers to the period of time required to recoup the funds expended in an investment, or to reach the break-even point. For example, a $1000 investment made at the start of year 1 which returned $500 at the end of year 1 and year 2 respectively would have a two-year _________ . _________ is usually expressed in years. Starting from investment year by calculating Net Cash Flow for each year: Net Cash Flow Year 1 = Cash Inflow Year 1 - Cash Outflow Year 1. Then Cumulative Cash Flow = Accumulate by year until Cumulative Cash Flow is a positive number: that year is the payback year.

Exam Probability: **Low**

25. *Answer choices:*

(see index for correct answer)

- a. Target rating point
- b. Marketing exposure
- c. Arrow information paradox
- d. Customer value maximization

Guidance: level 1

:: Capital (economics) ::

In Economics and Accounting, the _________ is the cost of a company`s funds , or, from an investor`s point of view "the required rate of return on a portfolio company`s existing securities". It is used to evaluate new projects of a company. It is the minimum return that investors expect for providing capital to the company, thus setting a benchmark that a new project has to meet.

Exam Probability: **Medium**

26. *Answer choices:*

(see index for correct answer)

- a. patient capital
- b. required rate of return
- c. financial capital
- d. operating capital

Guidance: level 1

:: Human resource management ::

_________ is the corporate management term for the act of reorganizing the legal, ownership, operational, or other structures of a company for the purpose of making it more profitable, or better organized for its present needs. Other reasons for _________ include a change of ownership or ownership structure, demerger, or a response to a crisis or major change in the business such as bankruptcy, repositioning, or buyout. _________ may also be described as corporate _________ , debt _________ and financial _________ .

Exam Probability: **Medium**

27. *Answer choices:*

(see index for correct answer)

- a. Personal development planning
- b. Corporate Equality Index
- c. Human resources
- d. Restructuring

Guidance: level 1

:: ::

_________ is the consumption and saving opportunity gained by an entity within a specified timeframe, which is generally expressed in monetary terms. For households and individuals, " _________ is the sum of all the wages, salaries, profits, interest payments, rents, and other forms of earnings received in a given period of time."

Exam Probability: **Low**

28. *Answer choices:*

(see index for correct answer)

- a. levels of analysis
- b. open system
- c. hierarchical
- d. Income

Guidance: level 1

:: Investment ::

_________, and investment appraisal, is the planning process used to determine whether an organization`s long term investments such as new machinery, replacement of machinery, new plants, new products, and research development projects are worth the funding of cash through the firm`s capitalization structure . It is the process of allocating resources for major capital, or investment, expenditures. One of the primary goals of _________ investments is to increase the value of the firm to the shareholders.

Exam Probability: **High**

29. *Answer choices:*

(see index for correct answer)

- a. Special settlement
- b. Personal pension scheme
- c. Media for equity
- d. Lehman scale

Guidance: level 1

:: Financial accounting ::

_________ is a financial metric which represents operating liquidity available to a business, organisation or other entity, including governmental entities. Along with fixed assets such as plant and equipment, _________ is considered a part of operating capital. Gross _________ is equal to current assets. _________ is calculated as current assets minus current liabilities. If current assets are less than current liabilities, an entity has a _________ deficiency, also called a _________ deficit.

Exam Probability: **Low**

30. *Answer choices:*

(see index for correct answer)

- a. Money measurement concept
- b. Advance payment
- c. Working capital
- d. Hidden asset

Guidance: level 1

:: Financial markets ::

The _________ is the part of the capital market that deals with the issuance and sale of equity-backed securities to investors directly by the issuer. Investor buy securities that were never traded before. _________ s create long term instruments through which corporate entities raise funds from the capital market. It is also known as the New Issue Market .

Exam Probability: **High**

31. *Answer choices:*

(see index for correct answer)

- a. Forex signal
- b. Marketcetera
- c. Primary market
- d. Third market

Guidance: level 1

:: Commerce ::

A _________ , is a document acknowledging that a person has received money or property in payment following a sale or other transfer of goods or provision of a service. All _________ s must have the date of purchase on them. If the recipient of the payment is legally required to collect sales tax or VAT from the customer, the amount would be added to the _________ and the collection would be deemed to have been on behalf of the relevant tax authority. In many countries, a retailer is required to include the sales tax or VAT in the displayed price of goods sold, from which the tax amount would be calculated at point of sale and remitted to the tax authorities in due course. Similarly, amounts may be deducted from amounts payable, as in the case of wage withholding taxes. On the other hand, tips or other gratuities given by a customer, for example in a restaurant, would not form part of the payment amount or appear on the _________ .

Exam Probability: **Low**

32. *Answer choices:*

(see index for correct answer)

- a. Receipt
- b. Emerging Markets Index
- c. Economic entity
- d. DataCash

Guidance: level 1

:: Business law ::

_________ is where a person`s financial liability is limited to a fixed sum, most commonly the value of a person`s investment in a company or partnership. If a company with _________ is sued, then the claimants are suing the company, not its owners or investors. A shareholder in a limited company is not personally liable for any of the debts of the company, other than for the amount already invested in the company and for any unpaid amount on the shares in the company, if any. The same is true for the members of a _________ partnership and the limited partners in a limited partnership. By contrast, sole proprietors and partners in general partnerships are each liable for all the debts of the business .

Exam Probability: **High**

33. *Answer choices:*

(see index for correct answer)

- a. Secret rebate
- b. Limited liability
- c. Negotiable instrument
- d. European Patent Convention

Guidance: level 1

:: Management accounting ::

_________ s are costs that change as the quantity of the good or service that a business produces changes. _________ s are the sum of marginal costs over all units produced. They can also be considered normal costs. Fixed costs and _________ s make up the two components of total cost. Direct costs are costs that can easily be associated with a particular cost object. However, not all _________ s are direct costs. For example, variable manufacturing overhead costs are _________ s that are indirect costs, not direct costs. _________ s are sometimes called unit-level costs as they vary with the number of units produced.

Exam Probability: **Medium**

34. *Answer choices:*

(see index for correct answer)

- a. Direct material usage variance
- b. Variable cost
- c. Institute of Management Accountants
- d. Certified Management Accountant

Guidance: level 1

:: Fixed income market ::

The _________ is a financial market where participants can issue new debt, known as the primary market, or buy and sell debt securities, known as the secondary market. This is usually in the form of bonds, but it may include notes, bills, and so on.

Exam Probability: **High**

35. *Answer choices:*

(see index for correct answer)

- a. Pool factor
- b. Fixed income
- c. credit market
- d. Bond Exchange of South Africa

Guidance: level 1

:: Accounting in the United States ::

_________ is the title of qualified accountants in numerous countries in the English-speaking world. In the United States, the CPA is a license to provide accounting services to the public. It is awarded by each of the 50 states for practice in that state. Additionally, almost every state has passed mobility laws to allow CPAs from other states to practice in their state. State licensing requirements vary, but the minimum standard requirements include passing the Uniform _________ Examination, 150 semester units of college education, and one year of accounting related experience.

Exam Probability: **High**

36. *Answer choices:*

(see index for correct answer)

- a. Financial Accounting Foundation

- b. Governmental Accounting Standards Board
- c. Certified Public Accountant
- d. National Association of State Boards of Accountancy

Guidance: level 1

:: ::

In sales, commerce and economics, a _________ is the recipient of a good, service, product or an idea - obtained from a seller, vendor, or supplier via a financial transaction or exchange for money or some other valuable consideration.

Exam Probability: **Medium**

37. *Answer choices:*

(see index for correct answer)

- a. open system
- b. deep-level diversity
- c. surface-level diversity
- d. similarity-attraction theory

Guidance: level 1

:: Planning ::

_________ is a high level plan to achieve one or more goals under conditions of uncertainty. In the sense of the "art of the general," which included several subsets of skills including tactics, siegecraft, logistics etc., the term came into use in the 6th century C.E. in East Roman terminology, and was translated into Western vernacular languages only in the 18th century. From then until the 20th century, the word " _________ " came to denote "a comprehensive way to try to pursue political ends, including the threat or actual use of force, in a dialectic of wills" in a military conflict, in which both adversaries interact.

Exam Probability: **Medium**

38. *Answer choices:*

(see index for correct answer)

- a. School timetable
- b. Strategy

- c. Concept driven strategy
- d. Counterplan

Guidance: level 1

:: Retirement ::

An __________ is a series of payments made at equal intervals. Examples of annuities are regular deposits to a savings account, monthly home mortgage payments, monthly insurance payments and pension payments. Annuities can be classified by the frequency of payment dates. The payments may be made weekly, monthly, quarterly, yearly, or at any other regular interval of time.

Exam Probability: **Low**

39. *Answer choices:*

(see index for correct answer)

- a. Third-party administrator
- b. Corrodian
- c. Retirement Estimator
- d. Aging in place

Guidance: level 1

:: Funds ::

__________ value is the value of an entity's assets minus the value of its liabilities, often in relation to open-end or mutual funds, since shares of such funds registered with the U.S. Securities and Exchange Commission are redeemed at their __________ value. It is also a key figure with regard to hedge funds and venture capital funds when calculating the value of the underlying investments in these funds by investors. This may also be the same as the book value or the equity value of a business. __________ value may represent the value of the total equity, or it may be divided by the number of shares outstanding held by investors, thereby representing the __________ value per share.

Exam Probability: **Medium**

40. *Answer choices:*

(see index for correct answer)

- a. Income fund

- b. Netherlands Film Fund
- c. Theorica
- d. Net asset

Guidance: level 1

:: Interest ::

In finance, _________ is the interest on a bond or loan that has accumulated since the principal investment, or since the previous coupon payment if there has been one already.

Exam Probability: **Low**

41. *Answer choices:*

(see index for correct answer)

- a. Accrued interest
- b. Deposit interest retention tax
- c. Penal interest
- d. Discretionary deposit

Guidance: level 1

:: Stock market ::

_________ is a form of stock which may have any combination of features not possessed by common stock including properties of both an equity and a debt instrument, and is generally considered a hybrid instrument. _________s are senior to common stock, but subordinate to bonds in terms of claim and may have priority over common stock in the payment of dividends and upon liquidation. Terms of the _________ are described in the issuing company`s articles of association or articles of incorporation.

Exam Probability: **Medium**

42. *Answer choices:*

(see index for correct answer)

- a. Stock market data systems
- b. Fill or kill
- c. Thinkorswim
- d. Preferred stock

Guidance: level 1

:: Inventory ::

In business and accounting/accountancy, _________ or continuous inventory describes systems of inventory where information on inventory quantity and availability is updated on a continuous basis as a function of doing business. Generally this is accomplished by connecting the inventory system with order entry and in retail the point of sale system. In this case, book inventory would be exactly the same as, or almost the same, as the real inventory.

Exam Probability: **Low**

43. *Answer choices:*

(see index for correct answer)

- a. Inventory control problem
- b. Stock-taking
- c. Specific identification
- d. Perpetual inventory

Guidance: level 1

:: Generally Accepted Accounting Principles ::

The _________ principle is a cornerstone of accrual accounting together with the matching principle. They both determine the accounting period in which revenues and expenses are recognized. According to the principle, revenues are recognized when they are realized or realizable, and are earned , no matter when cash is received. In cash accounting – in contrast – revenues are recognized when cash is received no matter when goods or services are sold.

Exam Probability: **Low**

44. *Answer choices:*

(see index for correct answer)

- a. Net income
- b. Net profit
- c. Revenue recognition
- d. Gross profit

Guidance: level 1

:: ::

An _________ is a contingent motivator. Traditional _________ s are extrinsic motivators which reward actions to yield a desired outcome. The effectiveness of traditional _________ s has changed as the needs of Western society have evolved. While the traditional _________ model is effective when there is a defined procedure and goal for a task, Western society started to require a higher volume of critical thinkers, so the traditional model became less effective. Institutions are now following a trend in implementing strategies that rely on intrinsic motivations rather than the extrinsic motivations that the traditional _________ s foster.

Exam Probability: **Low**

45. *Answer choices:*

(see index for correct answer)

- a. Character
- b. hierarchical perspective
- c. imperative
- d. levels of analysis

Guidance: level 1

:: Public finance ::

_________ is the process by which the monetary authority of a country, typically the central bank or currency board, controls either the cost of very short-term borrowing or the money supply, often targeting inflation rate or interest rate to ensure price stability and general trust in the currency.

Exam Probability: **Low**

46. *Answer choices:*

(see index for correct answer)

- a. Forced rider
- b. Monetary policy
- c. Government budget balance
- d. Budget Code of Russia

Guidance: level 1

:: ::

__________ is a political and social philosophy promoting traditional social institutions in the context of culture and civilization. The central tenets of __________ include tradition, human imperfection, organic society, hierarchy, authority, and property rights. Conservatives seek to preserve a range of institutions such as religion, parliamentary government, and property rights, with the aim of emphasizing social stability and continuity. The more traditional elements—reactionaries—oppose modernism and seek a return to "the way things were".

Exam Probability: **Low**

47. *Answer choices:*

(see index for correct answer)

- a. imperative
- b. Conservatism
- c. Character
- d. surface-level diversity

Guidance: level 1

:: Scheduling (computing) ::

Ageing or __________ is the process of becoming older. The term refers especially to human beings, many animals, and fungi, whereas for example bacteria, perennial plants and some simple animals are potentially biologically immortal. In the broader sense, ageing can refer to single cells within an organism which have ceased dividing or to the population of a species .

Exam Probability: **Medium**

48. *Answer choices:*

(see index for correct answer)

- a. Notation for theoretic scheduling problems
- b. Multikernel
- c. Adaptive partition scheduler
- d. Server hog

Guidance: level 1

:: Budgets ::

A _________ is a financial plan for a defined period, often one year. It may also include planned sales volumes and revenues, resource quantities, costs and expenses, assets, liabilities and cash flows. Companies, governments, families and other organizations use it to express strategic plans of activities or events in measurable terms.

Exam Probability: **Medium**

49. *Answer choices:*

(see index for correct answer)

- a. Budget constraint
- b. Participatory budgeting
- c. Black budget
- d. Budget

Guidance: level 1

:: Financial ratios ::

_________ or asset turns is a financial ratio that measures the efficiency of a company`s use of its assets in generating sales revenue or sales income to the company.

Exam Probability: **High**

50. *Answer choices:*

(see index for correct answer)

- a. Asset turnover
- b. Information ratio
- c. Import ratio
- d. Capital recovery factor

Guidance: level 1

:: Accounting source documents ::

A _________ or account statement is a summary of financial transactions which have occurred over a given period on a bank account held by a person or business with a financial institution.

Exam Probability: **Low**

51. *Answer choices:*

(see index for correct answer)

- a. Banknote
- b. Bank statement
- c. Purchase order
- d. Parcel audit

Guidance: level 1

:: Money market instruments ::

_________ , in the global financial market, is an unsecured promissory note with a fixed maturity of not more than 270 days.

Exam Probability: **Low**

52. *Answer choices:*

(see index for correct answer)

- a. Commercial paper in India
- b. Commercial paper

Guidance: level 1

:: Corporate finance ::

_________ in corporate finance is the way a corporation finances its assets through some combination of equity, debt, or hybrid securities.

Exam Probability: **High**

53. *Answer choices:*

(see index for correct answer)

- a. Corporate spin-off
- b. Hedge relationship
- c. Management buy-in
- d. Capital structure

Guidance: level 1

:: Competition (economics) ::

__________ arises whenever at least two parties strive for a goal which cannot be shared: where one`s gain is the other`s loss .

Exam Probability: **Medium**

54. *Answer choices:*

(see index for correct answer)

- a. School choice
- b. Currency competition
- c. Leapfrogging
- d. Competition

Guidance: level 1

:: Pharmaceutical industry ::

A __________ is a document in which data collected for a clinical trial is first recorded. This data is usually later entered in the case report form. The International Conference on Harmonisation of Technical Requirements for Registration of Pharmaceuticals for Human Use guidelines define __________ s as "original documents, data, and records." __________ s contain source data, which is defined as "all information in original records and certified copies of original records of clinical findings, observations, or other activities in a clinical trial necessary for the reconstruction and evaluation of the trial."

Exam Probability: **High**

55. *Answer choices:*

(see index for correct answer)

- a. Source document
- b. NIPTE
- c. Cytel
- d. Drug repositioning

Guidance: level 1

:: Financial risk ::

_________ is the risk that arises for bond owners from fluctuating interest rates. How much _________ a bond has depends on how sensitive its price is to interest rate changes in the market. The sensitivity depends on two things, the bond`s time to maturity, and the coupon rate of the bond.

Exam Probability: **Medium**

56. *Answer choices:*

(see index for correct answer)

- a. Concentration risk
- b. Risk modeling
- c. Interest rate risk
- d. Reputational risk

Guidance: level 1

:: Business law ::

A _________ is an arrangement where parties, known as partners, agree to cooperate to advance their mutual interests. The partners in a _________ may be individuals, businesses, interest-based organizations, schools, governments or combinations. Organizations may partner to increase the likelihood of each achieving their mission and to amplify their reach. A _________ may result in issuing and holding equity or may be only governed by a contract.

Exam Probability: **Low**

57. *Answer choices:*

(see index for correct answer)

- a. Relational contract
- b. Interest of the company
- c. Power harassment
- d. Secret rebate

Guidance: level 1

:: ::

__________ is a marketing communication that employs an openly sponsored, non-personal message to promote or sell a product, service or idea. Sponsors of __________ are typically businesses wishing to promote their products or services. __________ is differentiated from public relations in that an advertiser pays for and has control over the message. It differs from personal selling in that the message is non-personal, i.e., not directed to a particular individual. __________ is communicated through various mass media, including traditional media such as newspapers, magazines, television, radio, outdoor __________ or direct mail; and new media such as search results, blogs, social media, websites or text messages. The actual presentation of the message in a medium is referred to as an advertisement, or "ad" or advert for short.

Exam Probability: **Medium**

58. *Answer choices:*

(see index for correct answer)

- a. co-culture
- b. hierarchical perspective
- c. Advertising
- d. similarity-attraction theory

Guidance: level 1

:: Real estate ::

Amortisation is paying off an amount owed over time by making planned, incremental payments of principal and interest. To amortise a loan means "to kill it off". In accounting, amortisation refers to charging or writing off an intangible asset`s cost as an operational expense over its estimated useful life to reduce a company`s taxable income.

Exam Probability: **Medium**

59. *Answer choices:*

(see index for correct answer)

- a. Amortization
- b. Perch
- c. Premises liability
- d. Property Information Questionnaire

Guidance: level 1

Human resource management

Human resource (HR) management is the strategic approach to the effective management of organization workers so that they help the business gain a competitive advantage. It is designed to maximize employee performance in service of an employer's strategic objectives. HR is primarily concerned with the management of people within organizations, focusing on policies and on systems. HR departments are responsible for overseeing employee-benefits design, employee recruitment, training and development, performance appraisal, and rewarding (e.g., managing pay and benefit systems). HR also concerns itself with organizational change and industrial relations, that is, the balancing of organizational practices with requirements arising from collective bargaining and from governmental laws.

:: Self ::

_________ is a term that has been used in various psychology theories, often in different ways. The term was originally introduced by the organismic theorist Kurt Goldstein for the motive to realize one`s full potential. In Goldstein`s view, it is the organism`s master motive, the only real motive: "the tendency to actualize itself as fully as possible is the basic drive ... the drive of _________ ." Carl Rogers similarly wrote of "the curative force in psychotherapy man`s tendency to actualize himself, to become his potentialities ... to express and activate all the capacities of the organism." The concept was brought most fully to prominence in Abraham Maslow`s hierarchy of needs theory as the final level of psychological development that can be achieved when all basic and mental needs are essentially fulfilled and the "actualization" of the full personal potential takes place, although he adapted this viewpoint later on in life to be more flexible.

Exam Probability: **Medium**

1. *Answer choices:*

(see index for correct answer)

- a. Self-actualization
- b. Narcissism

- c. Self-presentation
- d. impression management

Guidance: level 1

:: Employment ::

__________ is measuring the output of a particular business process or procedure, then modifying the process or procedure to increase the output, increase efficiency, or increase the effectiveness of the process or procedure. __________ can be applied to either individual performance such as an athlete or organizational performance such as a racing team or a commercial business.

Exam Probability: **Low**

2. *Answer choices:*

(see index for correct answer)

- a. Performance improvement
- b. Active ageing
- c. Paradox of toil
- d. Shift work sleep disorder

Guidance: level 1

:: Design of experiments ::

In the design of experiments, treatments are applied to experimental units in the treatment group. In comparative experiments, members of the complementary group, the __________, receive either no treatment or a standard treatment.

Exam Probability: **Medium**

3. *Answer choices:*

(see index for correct answer)

- a. Field experiment
- b. Spherical design
- c. Control group
- d. Null hypothesis

Guidance: level 1

:: United States employment discrimination case law ::

_________ , 557 U.S. 557 , is a US labor law case of the United States Supreme Court on unlawful discrimination through disparate impact under the Civil Rights Act of 1964.

Exam Probability: **High**

4. *Answer choices:*

(see index for correct answer)

- a. Gross v. FBL Financial Services, Inc.
- b. Ricci v. DeStefano
- c. Executive Order 11375
- d. Griggs v. Duke Power Co.

Guidance: level 1

:: ::

A _________ , covering letter, motivation letter, motivational letter or a letter of motivation is a letter of introduction attached to, or accompanying another document such as a résumé or curriculum vitae.

Exam Probability: **High**

5. *Answer choices:*

(see index for correct answer)

- a. functional perspective
- b. open system
- c. information systems assessment
- d. Cover letter

Guidance: level 1

:: Trade unions ::

An _________ is a form of union security agreement where the employer may hire union or non-union workers, and employees need not join the union in order to remain employed. However, the non-union worker must pay a fee to cover collective bargaining costs. The fee paid by non-union members under the _________ is known as the "agency fee".

Exam Probability: **High**

6. *Answer choices:*
(see index for correct answer)

- a. Company union
- b. Vigilance committee
- c. Agency shop
- d. Strike pay

Guidance: level 1

:: Labour relations ::

An _________ is a place of employment at which one is not required to join or financially support a union as a condition of hiring or continued employment. _________ is also known as a merit shop.

Exam Probability: **Low**

7. *Answer choices:*
(see index for correct answer)

- a. Open shop
- b. Merit shop
- c. Union Wallonne des Entreprises
- d. Lockout

Guidance: level 1

:: Employment compensation ::

A _________ is the minimum income necessary for a worker to meet their basic needs. Needs are defined to include food, housing, and other essential needs such as clothing. The goal of a _________ is to allow a worker to afford a basic but decent standard of living. Due to the flexible nature of the term "needs", there is not one universally accepted measure of what a _________ is and as such it varies by location and household type.

Exam Probability: **Low**

8. *Answer choices:*
(see index for correct answer)

- a. Pay-for-Performance
- b. Agency Workers Regulations 2010

- c. Profit sharing
- d. Golden parachute

Guidance: level 1

:: Business models ::

A __________ is a diagram that is used to document the primary strategic goals being pursued by an organization or management team. It is an element of the documentation associated with the Balanced Scorecard, and in particular is characteristic of the second generation of Balanced Scorecard designs that first appeared during the mid-1990s. The first diagrams of this type appeared in the early 1990s, and the idea of using this type of diagram to help document Balanced Scorecard was discussed in a paper by Drs. Robert S. Kaplan and David P. Norton in 1996.

Exam Probability: **Low**

9. *Answer choices:*

(see index for correct answer)

- a. Lemonade stand
- b. Dependent growth business model
- c. Strategy map
- d. Fractional ownership

Guidance: level 1

:: Free market ::

Piece work is any type of employment in which a worker is paid a fixed __________ for each unit produced or action performed regardless of time.

Exam Probability: **High**

10. *Answer choices:*

(see index for correct answer)

- a. Piece rate
- b. Free market

Guidance: level 1

:: Project management ::

_________ is a name for various theories of human motivation built on Douglas McGregor`s Theory X and Theory Y. Theories X, Y and various versions of Z have been used in human resource management, organizational behavior, organizational communication and organizational development.

Exam Probability: **Medium**

11. *Answer choices:*

(see index for correct answer)

- a. Theory Z
- b. Project plan
- c. Project charter
- d. Test and evaluation master plan

Guidance: level 1

:: Labour relations ::

A _________ , also known as a post-entry closed shop, is a form of a union security clause. Under this, the employer agrees to either only hire labor union members or to require that any new employees who are not already union members become members within a certain amount of time. Use of the _________ varies widely from nation to nation, depending on the level of protection given trade unions in general.

Exam Probability: **High**

12. *Answer choices:*

(see index for correct answer)

- a. Union shop
- b. Scranton Declaration
- c. Jesse Simons
- d. Whipsaw strike

Guidance: level 1

:: Training ::

_________ is teaching, or developing in oneself or others, any skills and knowledge that relate to specific useful competencies. _________ has specific goals of improving one`s capability, capacity, productivity and performance. It forms the core of apprenticeships and provides the backbone of content at institutes of technology . In addition to the basic _________ required for a trade, occupation or profession, observers of the labor-market recognize as of 2008 the need to continue _________ beyond initial qualifications: to maintain, upgrade and update skills throughout working life. People within many professions and occupations may refer to this sort of _________ as professional development.

Exam Probability: **Low**

13. *Answer choices:*

(see index for correct answer)

- a. Officer training
- b. Training
- c. Overlearning
- d. Youth Training Scheme

Guidance: level 1

:: ::

A _________ seeks to further a particular profession, the interests of individuals engaged in that profession and the public interest. In the United States, such an association is typically a nonprofit organization for tax purposes.

Exam Probability: **Low**

14. *Answer choices:*

(see index for correct answer)

- a. Professional association
- b. open system
- c. cultural
- d. empathy

Guidance: level 1

:: Management education ::

__________ is the implementation of government policy and also an academic discipline that studies this implementation and prepares civil servants for working in the public service. As a "field of inquiry with a diverse scope" whose fundamental goal is to "advance management and policies so that government can function". Some of the various definitions which have been offered for the term are: "the management of public programs"; the "translation of politics into the reality that citizens see every day"; and "the study of government decision making, the analysis of the policies themselves, the various inputs that have produced them, and the inputs necessary to produce alternative policies."

Exam Probability: **High**

15. *Answer choices:*

(see index for correct answer)

- a. Foundry School
- b. International School of Management
- c. Open management education
- d. Public administration

Guidance: level 1

:: Business theory ::

__________ or cultural quotient is a term used in business, education, government and academic research. __________ can be understood as the capability to relate and work effectively across cultures. Originally, the term __________ and the abbreviation "CQ" was developed by the research done by Soon Ang and Linn Van Dyne as a researched-based way of measuring and predicting intercultural performance.

Exam Probability: **Low**

16. *Answer choices:*

(see index for correct answer)

- a. Communication quotient
- b. Product innovation
- c. Six forces model
- d. Robust decision-making

Guidance: level 1

:: Training ::

A _________ is commonly known as an individual taking part in a _________ program or a graduate program within a company after having graduated from university or college.

Exam Probability: **High**

17. *Answer choices:*

(see index for correct answer)

- a. Biography Work
- b. Arts Party
- c. Trainee
- d. Teletraining

Guidance: level 1

:: Human resource management ::

_________ means increasing the scope of a job through extending the range of its job duties and responsibilities generally within the same level and periphery. _________ involves combining various activities at the same level in the organization and adding them to the existing job. It is also called the horizontal expansion of job activities. This contradicts the principles of specialisation and the division of labour whereby work is divided into small units, each of which is performed repetitively by an individual worker and the responsibilities are always clear. Some motivational theories suggest that the boredom and alienation caused by the division of labour can actually cause efficiency to fall. Thus, _________ seeks to motivate workers through reversing the process of specialisation. A typical approach might be to replace assembly lines with modular work; instead of an employee repeating the same step on each product, they perform several tasks on a single item. In order for employees to be provided with _________ they will need to be retrained in new fields to understand how each field works.

Exam Probability: **Medium**

18. *Answer choices:*

(see index for correct answer)

- a. Job enlargement
- b. Mechanical aptitude

- c. Resource-based view
- d. Employment testing

Guidance: level 1

:: ::

__________ is a belief that hard work and diligence have a moral benefit and an inherent ability, virtue or value to strengthen character and individual abilities. It is a set of values centered on importance of work and manifested by determination or desire to work hard. Social ingrainment of this value is considered to enhance character through hard work that is respective to an individual`s field of work.

Exam Probability: **Medium**

19. *Answer choices:*

(see index for correct answer)

- a. open system
- b. Work ethic
- c. Character
- d. deep-level diversity

Guidance: level 1

:: Behavior ::

__________ refers to behavior-change procedures that were employed during the 1970s and early 1980s. Based on methodological behaviorism, overt behavior was modified with presumed consequences, including artificial positive and negative reinforcement contingencies to increase desirable behavior, or administering positive and negative punishment and/or extinction to reduce problematic behavior. For the treatment of phobias, habituation and punishment were the basic principles used in flooding, a subcategory of desensitization.

Exam Probability: **Medium**

20. *Answer choices:*

(see index for correct answer)

- a. Behavior modification
- b. theory of reasoned action

Guidance: level 1

:: Human resource management ::

An __________ is a diagram that shows the structure of an organization and the relationships and relative ranks of its parts and positions/jobs. The term is also used for similar diagrams, for example ones showing the different elements of a field of knowledge or a group of languages.

Exam Probability: **High**

21. *Answer choices:*

(see index for correct answer)

- a. Organizational chart
- b. Workforce planning
- c. Attendance management
- d. Domestic inquiry

Guidance: level 1

:: Training ::

__________ is the process of ensuring compliance with laws, regulations, rules, standards, or social norms. By enforcing laws and regulations, governments attempt to effectuate successful implementation of policies.

Exam Probability: **Low**

22. *Answer choices:*

(see index for correct answer)

- a. Enforcement
- b. Boardcast
- c. Instructor-led training
- d. Person Analysis

Guidance: level 1

:: Human resource management ::

__________ refers to the ratio of the number of job positions to the number of job applicants and is used in the context of selection and recruitment.

Exam Probability: **High**

23. *Answer choices:*

(see index for correct answer)

- a. Corporate Equality Index
- b. Employee value proposition
- c. Selection ratio
- d. Job sharing

Guidance: level 1

:: ::

__________ is defined by sociologist John R. Schermerhorn as the "...degree to which the people affected by decision are treated by dignity and respect. The theory focuses on the interpersonal treatment people receive when procedures are implemented.

Exam Probability: **Low**

24. *Answer choices:*

(see index for correct answer)

- a. information systems assessment
- b. Interactional justice
- c. personal values
- d. hierarchical

Guidance: level 1

:: ::

__________ consists of using generic or ad hoc methods in an orderly manner to find solutions to problems. Some of the problem-solving techniques developed and used in philosophy, artificial intelligence, computer science, engineering, mathematics, or medicine are related to mental problem-solving techniques studied in psychology.

Exam Probability: **High**

25. *Answer choices:*

(see index for correct answer)

- a. Problem solving
- b. interpersonal communication
- c. similarity-attraction theory
- d. hierarchical

Guidance: level 1

:: Management ::

__________ is the kind of knowledge that is difficult to transfer to another person by means of writing it down or verbalizing it. For example, that London is in the United Kingdom is a piece of explicit knowledge that can be written down, transmitted, and understood by a recipient. However, the ability to speak a language, ride a bicycle, knead dough, play a musical instrument, or design and use complex equipment requires all sorts of knowledge that is not always known explicitly, even by expert practitioners, and which is difficult or impossible to explicitly transfer to other people.

Exam Probability: **Low**

26. *Answer choices:*

(see index for correct answer)

- a. Statistical process control
- b. Change advisory board
- c. Investment control
- d. Tacit knowledge

Guidance: level 1

:: Occupational safety and health ::

__________ is a set of six naturally occurring silicate minerals, which all have in common their asbestiform habit: i.e., long , thin fibrous crystals, with each visible fiber composed of millions of microscopic "fibrils" that can be released by abrasion and other processes. The minerals are chrysotile, amosite, crocidolite, tremolite, anthophyllite, and actinolite.

Exam Probability: **High**

27. *Answer choices:*

(see index for correct answer)

- a. Hearing conservation program
- b. EHS Today
- c. CLP Regulation
- d. Job safety analysis

Guidance: level 1

:: Labor relations in the United States ::

In the context of U.S. labor politics, " _________ s" refers to state laws that prohibit union security agreements between companies and labor unions. Under these laws, employees in unionized workplaces are banned from negotiating contracts which require all members who benefit from the union contract to contribute to the costs of union representation.

Exam Probability: **High**

28. *Answer choices:*

(see index for correct answer)

- a. Jewish Labor Committee
- b. Jobs with Justice
- c. National Football League Players Association
- d. Right-to-work law

Guidance: level 1

:: Supply chain management terms ::

In business and finance, _________ is a system of organizations, people, activities, information, and resources involved inmoving a product or service from supplier to customer. _________ activities involve the transformation of natural resources, raw materials, and components into a finished product that is delivered to the end customer. In sophisticated _________ systems, used products may re-enter the _________ at any point where residual value is recyclable. _________ s link value chains.

Exam Probability: **High**

29. *Answer choices:*

(see index for correct answer)

- a. Supply-chain management
- b. Final assembly schedule
- c. Work in process
- d. inventory management

Guidance: level 1

:: Employee relations ::

__________ are tools used by organizational leadership to gain feedback on and measure employee engagement, employee morale, and performance. Usually answered anonymously, surveys are also used to gain a holistic picture of employees` feelings on such areas as working conditions, supervisory impact, and motivation that regular channels of communication may not. Surveys are considered effective in this regard provided they are well-designed, effectively administered, have validity, and evoke changes and improvements.

Exam Probability: **Medium**

30. *Answer choices:*

(see index for correct answer)

- a. Employee morale
- b. employee stock ownership
- c. Employee surveys
- d. Employee engagement

Guidance: level 1

:: ::

__________ is the combination of structured planning and the active management choice of one`s own professional career. __________ was first defined in a social work doctoral thesis by Mary Valentich as the implementation of a career strategy through application of career tactics in relation to chosen career orientation . Career orientation referred to the overall design or pattern of one`s career, shaped by particular goals and interests and identifiable by particular positions that embody these goals and interests. Career strategy pertains to the individual`s general approach to the realization of career goals, and to the specificity of the goals themselves. Two general strategy approaches are adaptive and planned. Career tactics are actions to maintain oneself in a satisfactory employment situation. Tactics may be more or less assertive, with assertiveness in the work situation referring to actions taken to advance one`s career interests or to exercise one`s legitimate rights while respecting the rights of others.

Exam Probability: **Low**

31. *Answer choices:*

(see index for correct answer)

- a. Career management
- b. similarity-attraction theory
- c. hierarchical perspective
- d. corporate values

Guidance: level 1

:: Human resource management ::

__________ are transactions in which the ownership of companies, other business organizations, or their operating units are transferred or consolidated with other entities. As an aspect of strategic management, M&A can allow enterprises to grow or downsize, and change the nature of their business or competitive position.

Exam Probability: **High**

32. *Answer choices:*

(see index for correct answer)

- a. Parallel running
- b. Chartered Institute of Personnel and Development
- c. Technical performance measure

- d. Organizational ethics

Guidance: level 1

:: Financial statements ::

In financial accounting, a _________ or statement of financial position or statement of financial condition is a summary of the financial balances of an individual or organization, whether it be a sole proprietorship, a business partnership, a corporation, private limited company or other organization such as Government or not-for-profit entity. Assets, liabilities and ownership equity are listed as of a specific date, such as the end of its financial year. A _________ is often described as a "snapshot of a company`s financial condition". Of the four basic financial statements, the _________ is the only statement which applies to a single point in time of a business` calendar year.

Exam Probability: **Low**

33. *Answer choices:*

(see index for correct answer)

- a. Statement on Auditing Standards No. 70: Service Organizations
- b. Balance sheet
- c. quarterly report
- d. Quarterly finance report

Guidance: level 1

:: ::

_________, also known as drug abuse, is a patterned use of a drug in which the user consumes the substance in amounts or with methods which are harmful to themselves or others, and is a form of substance-related disorder. Widely differing definitions of drug abuse are used in public health, medical and criminal justice contexts. In some cases criminal or anti-social behaviour occurs when the person is under the influence of a drug, and long term personality changes in individuals may occur as well. In addition to possible physical, social, and psychological harm, use of some drugs may also lead to criminal penalties, although these vary widely depending on the local jurisdiction.

Exam Probability: **High**

34. *Answer choices:*

(see index for correct answer)

- a. surface-level diversity
- b. similarity-attraction theory
- c. deep-level diversity
- d. interpersonal communication

Guidance: level 1

:: ::

_________ is overt or covert, often harmful, social interaction with the intention of inflicting damage or other unpleasantness upon another individual. It may occur either reactively or without provocation. In humans, frustration due to blocked goals can cause _________ . Human _________ can be classified into direct and indirect _________ ; whilst the former is characterized by physical or verbal behavior intended to cause harm to someone, the latter is characterized by behavior intended to harm the social relations of an individual or group.

Exam Probability: **High**

35. *Answer choices:*

(see index for correct answer)

- a. surface-level diversity
- b. imperative
- c. empathy
- d. Aggression

Guidance: level 1

:: Business law ::

A pre-entry _________ is a form of union security agreement under which the employer agrees to hire union members only, and employees must remain members of the union at all times in order to remain employed. This is different from a post-entry _________ , which is an agreement requiring all employees to join the union if they are not already members. In a union shop, the union must accept as a member any person hired by the employer.

Exam Probability: **High**

36. *Answer choices:*

(see index for correct answer)

- a. Novation
- b. Closed shop
- c. Forward-looking statement
- d. Consularization

Guidance: level 1

:: ::

__________ is an important topic of Human Resource Management. It helps develop the career of the individual and the prosperous growth of the organization. On the job training is a form of training provided at the workplace. During the training, employees are familiarized with the working environment they will become part of. Employees also get a hands-on experience using machinery, equipment, tools, materials, etc. Part of is to face the challenges that occur during the performance of the job. An experienced employee or a manager are executing the role of the mentor who through written, or verbal instructions and demonstrations are passing on his/her knowledge and company-specific skills to the new employee. Executing the training on at the job location, rather than the classroom, creates a stress-free environment for the employees. __________ is the most popular method of training not only in the United States but in most of the developed countries, such as the United Kingdom, China, Russia, etc. Its effectiveness is based on the use of existing workplace tools, machines, documents and equipment, and the knowledge of specialists who are working in this field. __________ is easy to arrange and manage and it simplifies the process of adapting to the new workplace.OJT is highly used for practical tasks. It is inexpensive, and it doesn't require special equipment that is normally used for a specific job. Upon satisfaction of completion of the training, the employer is expected to retain participants as regular employees.

Exam Probability: **Medium**

37. *Answer choices:*

(see index for correct answer)

- a. imperative
- b. information systems assessment
- c. corporate values
- d. personal values

Guidance: level 1

:: ::

_________ are interactive computer-mediated technologies that facilitate the creation and sharing of information, ideas, career interests and other forms of expression via virtual communities and networks. The variety of stand-alone and built-in _________ services currently available introduces challenges of definition; however, there are some common features.

Exam Probability: **Medium**

38. *Answer choices:*

(see index for correct answer)

- a. Character
- b. personal values
- c. Social media
- d. similarity-attraction theory

Guidance: level 1

:: Offshoring ::

A __________ is the temporary suspension or permanent termination of employment of an employee or, more commonly, a group of employees for business reasons, such as personnel management or downsizing an organization. Originally, __________ referred exclusively to a temporary interruption in work, or employment but this has evolved to a permanent elimination of a position in both British and US English, requiring the addition of "temporary" to specify the original meaning of the word. A __________ is not to be confused with wrongful termination. Laid off workers or displaced workers are workers who have lost or left their jobs because their employer has closed or moved, there was insufficient work for them to do, or their position or shift was abolished . Downsizing in a company is defined to involve the reduction of employees in a workforce. Downsizing in companies became a popular practice in the 1980s and early 1990s as it was seen as a way to deliver better shareholder value as it helps to reduce the costs of employers . Indeed, recent research on downsizing in the U.S., UK, and Japan suggests that downsizing is being regarded by management as one of the preferred routes to help declining organizations, cutting unnecessary costs, and improve organizational performance. Usually a __________ occurs as a cost cutting measure.

Exam Probability: **High**

39. *Answer choices:*

(see index for correct answer)

- a. Programmers Guild
- b. Offshore company
- c. Global labor arbitrage
- d. Avasant

Guidance: level 1

:: Business ethics ::

__________ is a type of harassment technique that relates to a sexual nature and the unwelcome or inappropriate promise of rewards in exchange for sexual favors. __________ includes a range of actions from mild transgressions to sexual abuse or assault. Harassment can occur in many different social settings such as the workplace, the home, school, churches, etc. Harassers or victims may be of any gender.

Exam Probability: **High**

40. *Answer choices:*

(see index for correct answer)

- a. Sherpa
- b. Destructionism
- c. Hostile work environment
- d. Sexual harassment

Guidance: level 1

:: Management ::

_________ is a technique used by some employers to rotate their employees` assigned jobs throughout their employment. Employers practice this technique for a number of reasons. It was designed to promote flexibility of employees and to keep employees interested into staying with the company/organization which employs them. There is also research that shows how _________ s help relieve the stress of employees who work in a job that requires manual labor.

Exam Probability: **High**

41. *Answer choices:*

(see index for correct answer)

- a. Manager Tools Podcast
- b. Project team builder
- c. Hierarchical organization
- d. Job rotation

Guidance: level 1

:: Types of marketing ::

In microeconomics and management, _________ is an arrangement in which the supply chain of a company is owned by that company. Usually each member of the supply chain produces a different product or service, and the products combine to satisfy a common need. It is contrasted with horizontal integration, wherein a company produces several items which are related to one another. _________ has also described management styles that bring large portions of the supply chain not only under a common ownership, but also into one corporation .

Exam Probability: **High**

42. *Answer choices:*

(see index for correct answer)

- a. Ambush marketing
- b. Consumer Generated Advertising
- c. Cause marketing
- d. Influencer marketing

Guidance: level 1

:: Validity (statistics) ::

_________ is "the degree to which a test measures what it claims, or purports, to be measuring." In the classical model of test validity, _________ is one of three main types of validity evidence, alongside content validity and criterion validity. Modern validity theory defines _________ as the overarching concern of validity research, subsuming all other types of validity evidence.

Exam Probability: **High**

43. *Answer choices:*

(see index for correct answer)

- a. External validity
- b. Statistical conclusion
- c. Face validity
- d. Construct validity

Guidance: level 1

:: United States federal labor legislation ::

The _________ of 1988 is a United States federal law that generally prevents employers from using polygraph tests, either for pre-employment screening or during the course of employment, with certain exemptions.

Exam Probability: **High**

44. *Answer choices:*

(see index for correct answer)

- a. Employment Act of 1946
- b. Employee Polygraph Protection Act
- c. Uniformed Services Employment and Reemployment Rights Act
- d. Pension Protection Act of 2006

Guidance: level 1

:: Human resource management ::

__________ is an institutional process that maximizes performance levels and competency for an organization. The process includes all the activities needed to maintain a productive workforce, such as field service management, human resource management, performance and training management, data collection, recruiting, budgeting, forecasting, scheduling and analytics.

Exam Probability: **Medium**

45. *Answer choices:*

(see index for correct answer)

- a. Experticity
- b. Workforce management
- c. Organizational culture
- d. Multiculturalism

Guidance: level 1

:: Human resource management ::

__________ is the application of information technology for both networking and supporting at least two individual or collective actors in their shared performing of HR activities.

Exam Probability: **High**

46. *Answer choices:*

(see index for correct answer)

- a. E-HRM
- b. Lego Serious Play
- c. Sham peer review
- d. Open-book management

Guidance: level 1

:: Human resource management ::

_________ is a flexible hours schedule that allows workers to alter workday start and finish times. In contrast to traditional work arrangements that require employees to work a standard 9 a.m. to 5 p.m. day, _________ typically involves a "core" period of the day during which employees are required to be at work , and a "bandwidth" period within which all required hours must be worked . The working day outside of the "core" period is "flexible time", in which employees can choose when they work, subject to achieving total daily, weekly or monthly hours within the "bandwidth" period set by employers, and subject to the necessary work being done. The total working time required of employees on _________ schedules is the same as that required under traditional work schedules. A _________ policy allows staff to determine when they will work, while a flexplace policy allows staff to determine where they will work. Advantages include allowing employees to coordinate their work hours with public transport schedules, with the schedules of their children, and with daily traffic patterns to avoid high congestion times such as rush hour. Some claim that flexible working will change the nature of the way we work. The idea of _________ was invented by Christel Kammerer.

Exam Probability: **Low**

47. *Answer choices:*

(see index for correct answer)

- a. Workplace mentoring
- b. Flextime
- c. Adecco Group North America
- d. Turnover

Guidance: level 1

:: Educational assessment and evaluation ::

An _________ is a component of a competence to do a certain kind of work at a certain level. Outstanding _________ can be considered "talent". An _________ may be physical or mental. _________ is inborn potential to do certain kinds of work whether developed or undeveloped. Ability is developed knowledge, understanding, learned or acquired abilities or attitude. The innate nature of _________ is in contrast to skills and achievement, which represent knowledge or ability that is gained through learning.

Exam Probability: **Medium**

48. *Answer choices:*

(see index for correct answer)

- a. Careerscope
- b. Central Board of Secondary Education
- c. Veterinary College Admission Test
- d. Aptitude

Guidance: level 1

:: Labour law ::

A __________ is a "shop-floor" organization representing workers that functions as a local/firm-level complement to trade unions but is independent of these at least in some countries. __________ s exist with different names in a variety of related forms in a number of European countries, including Britain ; Germany and Austria ; Luxembourg ; the Netherlands and Flanders in Belgium ; Italy ; France ; Wallonia in Belgium and Spain .

Exam Probability: **High**

49. *Answer choices:*

(see index for correct answer)

- a. Works council
- b. Negligent hiring
- c. Bosman ruling
- d. Matthew W. Finkin

Guidance: level 1

:: Training ::

__________ is a phase of training needs analysis directed at identifying which individuals within an organization should receive training.

Exam Probability: **Medium**

50. *Answer choices:*

(see index for correct answer)

- a. Training camp
- b. Person Analysis
- c. Arts Party

- d. Trainee

Guidance: level 1

:: Trade unions in the United States ::

The _________ is a labor union in the United States and Canada. Formed in 1903 by the merger of The Team Drivers International Union and The Teamsters National Union, the union now represents a diverse membership of blue-collar and professional workers in both the public and private sectors. The union had approximately 1.3 million members in 2013. Formerly known as the _________, Chauffeurs, Warehousemen and Helpers of America, the IBT is a member of the Change to Win Federation and Canadian Labour Congress.

Exam Probability: **Medium**

51. *Answer choices:*

(see index for correct answer)

- a. Tennessee Nurses Association
- b. National Building Trades Council
- c. National Education Association
- d. Rhode Island Federation of Teachers and Health Professionals

Guidance: level 1

:: Human resource management ::

_________, also known as organizational socialization, is management jargon first created in 1988 that refers to the mechanism through which new employees acquire the necessary knowledge, skills, and behaviors in order to become effective organizational members and insiders.

Exam Probability: **Medium**

52. *Answer choices:*

(see index for correct answer)

- a. Four-day week
- b. Onboarding
- c. E-HRM
- d. Reward management

Guidance: level 1

:: Unemployment benefits ::

__________ are payments made by back authorized bodies to unemployed people. In the United States, benefits are funded by a compulsory governmental insurance system, not taxes on individual citizens. Depending on the jurisdiction and the status of the person, those sums may be small, covering only basic needs, or may compensate the lost time proportionally to the previous earned salary.

Exam Probability: **High**

53. *Answer choices:*

(see index for correct answer)

- a. National Insurance Act 1911
- b. Unemployment benefits
- c. Unemployment benefits in Spain
- d. Unemployment benefits in Sweden

Guidance: level 1

:: United States employment discrimination case law ::

__________ , 524 U.S. 775 , is a US labor law case of the United States Supreme Court in which the Court identified the circumstances under which an employer may be held liable under Title VII of the Civil Rights Act of 1964 for the acts of a supervisory employee whose sexual harassment of subordinates has created a hostile work environment amounting to employment discrimination. The court held that "an employer is vicariously liable for actionable discrimination caused by a supervisor, but subject to an affirmative defense looking to the reasonableness of the employer`s conduct as well as that of a plaintiff victim."

Exam Probability: **Medium**

54. *Answer choices:*

(see index for correct answer)

- a. Faragher v. City of Boca Raton
- b. Dothard v. Rawlinson
- c. Reeves v. Sanderson Plumbing Products, Inc.
- d. Hosanna-Tabor Evangelical Lutheran Church and School v. Equal Employment Opportunity Commission

Guidance: level 1

:: Trade union legislation ::

The __________ is the name for several legislative bills on US labor law which have been proposed and sometimes introduced into one or both chambers of the U.S. Congress.

Exam Probability: **Low**

55. *Answer choices:*

(see index for correct answer)

- a. Trade Union Reform and Employment Rights Act 1993
- b. Trade Disputes Act 1906
- c. Padlock Law
- d. National Labor Relations Act

Guidance: level 1

:: Majority–minority relations ::

__________, also known as reservation in India and Nepal, positive discrimination / action in the United Kingdom, and employment equity in Canada and South Africa, is the policy of promoting the education and employment of members of groups that are known to have previously suffered from discrimination. Historically and internationally, support for __________ has sought to achieve goals such as bridging inequalities in employment and pay, increasing access to education, promoting diversity, and redressing apparent past wrongs, harms, or hindrances.

Exam Probability: **Low**

56. *Answer choices:*

(see index for correct answer)

- a. cultural Relativism
- b. cultural dissonance
- c. Affirmative action

Guidance: level 1

:: Employment compensation ::

_________ , merit increase or pay for performance, is performance-related pay, most frequently in the context of educational reform or government civil service reform . It provides bonuses for workers who perform their jobs effectively, according to easily measurable criteria. In the United States, policy makers are divided on whether _________ should be offered to public school teachers, and other public employees, as is commonly the case in the United Kingdom.

Exam Probability: **Low**

57. *Answer choices:*

(see index for correct answer)

- a. Lilly Ledbetter Fair Pay Act of 2009
- b. Streamlining Claims Processing for Federal Contractor Employees Act
- c. New York Disability Benefits Law
- d. Merit pay

Guidance: level 1

:: ::

In organizational behavior and industrial/organizational psychology, proactivity or _________ behavior by individuals refers to anticipatory, change-oriented and self-initiated behavior in situations. _________ behavior involves acting in advance of a future situation, rather than just reacting. It means taking control and making things happen rather than just adjusting to a situation or waiting for something to happen. _________ employees generally do not need to be asked to act, nor do they require detailed instructions.

Exam Probability: **High**

58. *Answer choices:*

(see index for correct answer)

- a. information systems assessment
- b. interpersonal communication
- c. Proactive
- d. similarity-attraction theory

Guidance: level 1

:: United States federal labor legislation ::

The _________ of 1967 is a US labor law that forbids employment discrimination against anyone at least 40 years of age in the United States . In 1967, the bill was signed into law by President Lyndon B. Johnson. The ADEA prevents age discrimination and provides equal employment opportunity under conditions that were not explicitly covered in Title VII of the Civil Rights Act of 1964. It also applies to the standards for pensions and benefits provided by employers, and requires that information concerning the needs of older workers be provided to the general public.

Exam Probability: **Medium**

59. *Answer choices:*

(see index for correct answer)

- a. Federal Emergency Relief Administration
- b. Age Discrimination in Employment Act
- c. Civil Rights Act of 1964
- d. National Apprenticeship Act

Guidance: level 1

Information systems

Information systems (IS) are formal, sociotechnical, organizational systems designed to collect, process, store, and distribute information. In a sociotechnical perspective Information Systems are composed by four components: technology, process, people and organizational structure.

:: Computer networking ::

A backbone is a part of computer network that interconnects various pieces of network, providing a path for the exchange of information between different LANs or subnetworks. A backbone can tie together diverse networks in the same building, in different buildings in a campus environment, or over wide areas. Normally, the backbone`s capacity is greater than the networks connected to it.

Exam Probability: **High**

1. *Answer choices:*

(see index for correct answer)

- a. DNOS
- b. Fabric computing
- c. Synchronous virtual pipe
- d. Backbone network

Guidance: level 1

:: E-commerce ::

Electronic governance or e-governance is the application of information and communication technology for delivering government services, exchange of information, communication transactions, integration of various stand-alone systems and services between government-to-citizen , _________ , government-to-government , government-to-employees as well as back-office processes and interactions within the entire government framework. Through e-governance, government services are made available to citizens in a convenient, efficient, and transparent manner. The three main target groups that can be distinguished in governance concepts are government, citizens, andbusinesses/interest groups. In e-governance, there are no distinct boundaries.

Exam Probability: **High**

2. *Answer choices:*

(see index for correct answer)

- a. ESewa
- b. Government-to-business
- c. Demandware
- d. Online insurance

Guidance: level 1

:: ::

_________ is a kind of action that occur as two or more objects have an effect upon one another. The idea of a two-way effect is essential in the concept of _________ , as opposed to a one-way causal effect. A closely related term is interconnectivity, which deals with the _________ s of _________ s within systems: combinations of many simple _________ s can lead to surprising emergent phenomena. _________ has different tailored meanings in various sciences. Changes can also involve _________ .

Exam Probability: **High**

3. *Answer choices:*

(see index for correct answer)

- a. Sarbanes-Oxley act of 2002
- b. Interaction
- c. corporate values
- d. hierarchical

Guidance: level 1

:: Data analysis ::

_________ , also referred to as text data mining, roughly equivalent to text analytics, is the process of deriving high-quality information from text. High-quality information is typically derived through the devising of patterns and trends through means such as statistical pattern learning. _________ usually involves the process of structuring the input text , deriving patterns within the structured data, and finally evaluation and interpretation of the output. `High quality` in _________ usually refers to some combination of relevance, novelty, and interest. Typical _________ tasks include text categorization, text clustering, concept/entity extraction, production of granular taxonomies, sentiment analysis, document summarization, and entity relation modeling .

Exam Probability: **Low**

4. *Answer choices:*

(see index for correct answer)

- a. Segmented regression
- b. Text mining
- c. Synqera
- d. Overdispersion

Guidance: level 1

:: ::

_________ Holdings, Inc. is an American company operating a worldwide online payments system that supports online money transfers and serves as an electronic alternative to traditional paper methods like checks and money orders. The company operates as a payment processor for online vendors, auction sites, and many other commercial users, for which it charges a fee in exchange for benefits such as one-click transactions and password memory. _________ `s payment system, also called _________ , is considered a type of payment rail.

Exam Probability: **High**

5. *Answer choices:*

(see index for correct answer)

- a. process perspective
- b. PayPal
- c. deep-level diversity
- d. co-culture

Guidance: level 1

:: ::

A _______ , sometimes called a passcode, is a memorized secret used to confirm the identity of a user. Using the terminology of the NIST Digital Identity Guidelines, the secret is memorized by a party called the claimant while the party verifying the identity of the claimant is called the verifier. When the claimant successfully demonstrates knowledge of the _______ to the verifier through an established authentication protocol, the verifier is able to infer the claimant's identity.

Exam Probability: **High**

6. *Answer choices:*

(see index for correct answer)

- a. open system
- b. co-culture
- c. hierarchical perspective
- d. Password

Guidance: level 1

:: ::

_______ is the function of specifying access rights/privileges to resources, which is related to information security and computer security in general and to access control in particular. More formally, "to authorize" is to define an access policy. For example, human resources staff are normally authorized to access employee records and this policy is usually formalized as access control rules in a computer system. During operation, the system uses the access control rules to decide whether access requests from consumers shall be approved or disapproved . Resources include individual files or an item's data, computer programs, computer devices and functionality provided by computer applications. Examples of consumers are computer users, computer Software and other Hardware on the computer.

Exam Probability: **High**

7. *Answer choices:*

(see index for correct answer)

- a. Authorization
- b. deep-level diversity
- c. hierarchical
- d. empathy

Guidance: level 1

:: Marketing by medium ::

__________ or viral advertising is a business strategy that uses existing social networks to promote a product. Its name refers to how consumers spread information about a product with other people in their social networks, much in the same way that a virus spreads from one person to another. It can be delivered by word of mouth or enhanced by the network effects of the Internet and mobile networks.

Exam Probability: **Low**

8. *Answer choices:*

(see index for correct answer)

- a. Social marketing intelligence
- b. Brand infiltration
- c. Viral marketing
- d. Social video marketing

Guidance: level 1

:: Global Positioning System ::

The __________ , originally Navstar GPS, is a satellite-based radionavigation system owned by the United States government and operated by the United States Air Force. It is a global navigation satellite system that provides geolocation and time information to a GPS receiver anywhere on or near the Earth where there is an unobstructed line of sight to four or more GPS satellites. Obstacles such as mountains and buildings block the relatively weak GPS signals.

Exam Probability: **High**

9. *Answer choices:*

(see index for correct answer)

- a. European Geostationary Navigation Overlay Service
- b. Fleetlinc
- c. GPS Tuner
- d. Wide Area GPS Enhancement

Guidance: level 1

:: Finance ::

__________ is a financial estimate intended to help buyers and owners determine the direct and indirect costs of a product or system. It is a management accounting concept that can be used in full cost accounting or even ecological economics where it includes social costs.

Exam Probability: **High**

10. *Answer choices:*

(see index for correct answer)

- a. In-house lending
- b. Total cost of ownership
- c. Debt restructuring
- d. Quantitative easing

Guidance: level 1

:: Data privacy ::

__________ is the relationship between the collection and dissemination of data, technology, the public expectation of privacy, legal and political issues surrounding them. It is also known as data privacy or data protection.

Exam Probability: **Low**

11. *Answer choices:*

(see index for correct answer)

- a. Geolocation Privacy and Surveillance Act
- b. 80/20 Thinking
- c. Christopher Graham
- d. Information privacy

Guidance: level 1

:: Information science ::

In discourse-based grammatical theory, _________ is any tracking of referential information by speakers. Information may be new, just introduced into the conversation; given, already active in the speakers` consciousness; or old, no longer active. The various types of activation, and how these are defined, are model-dependent.

Exam Probability: **Low**

12. *Answer choices:*

(see index for correct answer)

- a. Taxonomic database
- b. Overcategorization
- c. Information flow
- d. General formal ontology

Guidance: level 1

:: Internet advertising ::

_________ is software that aims to gather information about a person or organization, sometimes without their knowledge, that may send such information to another entity without the consumer`s consent, that asserts control over a device without the consumer`s knowledge, or it may send such information to another entity with the consumer`s consent, through cookies.

Exam Probability: **Low**

13. *Answer choices:*

(see index for correct answer)

- a. Directory Harvest Attack
- b. Spyware
- c. Web banner
- d. Comparison of ad servers

Guidance: level 1

:: Automatic identification and data capture ::

_________ is human–computer interaction in which a computer is expected to be transported during normal usage, which allows for transmission of data, voice and video. _________ involves mobile communication, mobile hardware, and mobile software. Communication issues include ad hoc networks and infrastructure networks as well as communication properties, protocols, data formats and concrete technologies. Hardware includes mobile devices or device components. Mobile software deals with the characteristics and requirements of mobile applications.

Exam Probability: **Low**

14. *Answer choices:*

(see index for correct answer)

- a. Mobile computing
- b. Guard tour patrol system
- c. Label printer
- d. SILVIA

Guidance: level 1

:: Credit cards ::

The _________ Company, also known as Amex, is an American multinational financial services corporation headquartered in Three World Financial Center in New York City. The company was founded in 1850 and is one of the 30 components of the Dow Jones Industrial Average. The company is best known for its charge card, credit card, and traveler's cheque businesses.

Exam Probability: **High**

15. *Answer choices:*

(see index for correct answer)

- a. Wirecard
- b. Access
- c. Netbanx
- d. Bankcard

Guidance: level 1

:: Market research ::

_________ s are many different distantly related animals that typically have a long cylindrical tube-like body and no limbs. _________ s vary in size from microscopic to over 1 metre in length for marine polychaete _________ s , 6.7 metres for the African giant earth _________ , Microchaetus rappi, and 58 metres for the marine nemertean _________ , Lineus longissimus. Various types of _________ occupy a small variety of parasitic niches, living inside the bodies of other animals. Free-living _________ species do not live on land, but instead, live in marine or freshwater environments, or underground by burrowing.In biology, " _________ " refers to an obsolete taxon, vermes, used by Carolus Linnaeus and Jean-Baptiste Lamarck for all non-arthropod invertebrate animals, now seen to be paraphyletic. The name stems from the Old English word wyrm. Most animals called " _________ s" are invertebrates, but the term is also used for the amphibian caecilians and the slow _________ Anguis, a legless burrowing lizard. Invertebrate animals commonly called " _________ s" include annelids , nematodes , platyhelminthes , marine nemertean _________ s , marine Chaetognatha , priapulid _________ s, and insect larvae such as grubs and maggots.

Exam Probability: **Low**

16. *Answer choices:*

(see index for correct answer)

- a. Friday night death slot
- b. AbsolutData
- c. Competitor analysis
- d. Worm

Guidance: level 1

:: ::

A _________ is server software, or hardware dedicated to running said software, that can satisfy World Wide Web client requests. A _________ can, in general, contain one or more websites. A _________ processes incoming network requests over HTTP and several other related protocols.

Exam Probability: **Low**

17. *Answer choices:*

(see index for correct answer)

- a. similarity-attraction theory
- b. Sarbanes-Oxley act of 2002
- c. empathy
- d. Web server

Guidance: level 1

:: Google services ::

_________ is a web mapping service developed by Google. It offers satellite imagery, aerial photography, street maps, 360° panoramic views of streets , real-time traffic conditions, and route planning for traveling by foot, car, bicycle and air , or public transportation.

Exam Probability: **Low**

18. *Answer choices:*

(see index for correct answer)

- a. Google Sites
- b. Google Personalized Search
- c. Google Chart API
- d. Google Maps

Guidance: level 1

:: Network management ::

_________ is the process of administering and managing computer networks. Services provided by this discipline include fault analysis, performance management, provisioning of networks and maintaining the quality of service. Software that enables network administrators to perform their functions is called _________ software.

Exam Probability: **Low**

19. *Answer choices:*

(see index for correct answer)

- a. Upstream server
- b. System Center Advisor
- c. Automounter
- d. Network management

Guidance: level 1

:: Geographic information systems ::

_________ is the computational process of transforming a physical address description to a location on the Earth`s surface . Reverse _________ , on the other hand, converts geographic coordinates to a description of a location, usually the name of a place or an addressable location. _________ relies on a computer representation of address points, the street / road network, together with postal and administrative boundaries.

Exam Probability: **High**

20. *Answer choices:*

(see index for correct answer)

- a. Image rectification
- b. Geographic information retrieval
- c. Geocoding
- d. Digital Earth Reference Model

Guidance: level 1

:: Automatic identification and data capture ::

_________ is the trademark for a type of matrix barcode first designed in 1994 for the automotive industry in Japan. A barcode is a machine-readable optical label that contains information about the item to which it is attached. In practice, _________ s often contain data for a locator, identifier, or tracker that points to a website or application. A _________ uses four standardized encoding modes to store data efficiently; extensions may also be used.

Exam Probability: **Medium**

21. *Answer choices:*

(see index for correct answer)

- a. Automatic number plate recognition
- b. QR code
- c. Automatic identification and data capture
- d. Wireless identification and sensing platform

Guidance: level 1

:: Reputation management ::

_________ refers to the influencing and controlling of an individual`s or group`s reputation. Originally a public relations term, the growth of the internet and social media, along with _________ companies, have made search results a core part of an individual`s or group`s reputation. Online _________ , sometimes abbreviated as ORM, focuses on the management of product and service search website results. Ethical grey areas include mug shot removal sites, astroturfing customer review sites, censoring negative complaints, and using search engine optimization tactics to influence results.

Exam Probability: **Medium**

22. *Answer choices:*

(see index for correct answer)

- a. Raph Levien
- b. Star
- c. Reputation management
- d. Infamy

Guidance: level 1

:: Big data ::

_________ is the discovery, interpretation, and communication of meaningful patterns in data; and the process of applying those patterns towards effective decision making. In other words, _________ can be understood as the connective tissue between data and effective decision making, within an organization. Especially valuable in areas rich with recorded information, _________ relies on the simultaneous application of statistics, computer programming and operations research to quantify performance.

Exam Probability: **Medium**

23. *Answer choices:*

(see index for correct answer)

- a. Sumo Logic
- b. Attivio
- c. Analytics
- d. Continuuity

Guidance: level 1

:: Computer access control ::

_________ is the act of confirming the truth of an attribute of a single piece of data claimed true by an entity. In contrast with identification, which refers to the act of stating or otherwise indicating a claim purportedly attesting to a person or thing`s identity, _________ is the process of actually confirming that identity. It might involve confirming the identity of a person by validating their identity documents, verifying the authenticity of a website with a digital certificate, determining the age of an artifact by carbon dating, or ensuring that a product is what its packaging and labeling claim to be. In other words, _________ often involves verifying the validity of at least one form of identification.

Exam Probability: **High**

24. *Answer choices:*

(see index for correct answer)

- a. Universal controls
- b. Security token
- c. Security question
- d. Authentication

Guidance: level 1

:: Teams ::

A _________ usually refers to a group of individuals who work together from different geographic locations and rely on communication technology such as email, FAX, and video or voice conferencing services in order to collaborate. The term can also refer to groups or teams that work together asynchronously or across organizational levels. Powell, Piccoli and Ives define _________ s as "groups of geographically, organizationally and/or time dispersed workers brought together by information and telecommunication technologies to accomplish one or more organizational tasks." According to Ale Ebrahim et. al. , _________ s can also be defined as "small temporary groups of geographically, organizationally and/or time dispersed knowledge workers who coordinate their work predominantly with electronic information and communication technologies in order to accomplish one or more organization tasks."

Exam Probability: **High**

25. *Answer choices:*

(see index for correct answer)

- a. Virtual team
- b. Team-building

Guidance: level 1

:: Data management ::

" _________ " is a field that treats ways to analyze, systematically extract information from, or otherwise deal with data sets that are too large or complex to be dealt with by traditional data-processing application software. Data with many cases offer greater statistical power, while data with higher complexity may lead to a higher false discovery rate. _________ challenges include capturing data, data storage, data analysis, search, sharing, transfer, visualization, querying, updating, information privacy and data source. _________ was originally associated with three key concepts: volume, variety, and velocity. Other concepts later attributed with _________ are veracity and value.

Exam Probability: **High**

26. *Answer choices:*

(see index for correct answer)

- a. Inverted index
- b. Storage area network
- c. Microsoft SQL Server Master Data Services
- d. Big data

Guidance: level 1

:: Cryptography ::

In cryptography, _________ is the process of encoding a message or information in such a way that only authorized parties can access it and those who are not authorized cannot. _________ does not itself prevent interference, but denies the intelligible content to a would-be interceptor. In an _________ scheme, the intended information or message, referred to as plaintext, is encrypted using an _________ algorithm – a cipher – generating ciphertext that can be read only if decrypted. For technical reasons, an _________ scheme usually uses a pseudo-random _________ key generated by an algorithm. It is in principle possible to decrypt the message without possessing the key, but, for a well-designed _________ scheme, considerable computational resources and skills are required. An authorized recipient can easily decrypt the message with the key provided by the originator to recipients but not to unauthorized users.

Exam Probability: **Low**

27. *Answer choices:*

(see index for correct answer)

- a. Electronic Signature
- b. cryptosystem
- c. Encryption
- d. Anonymous matching

Guidance: level 1

:: Payment systems ::

_________ s are part of a payment system issued by financial institutions, such as a bank, to a customer that enables its owner to access the funds in the customer`s designated bank accounts, or through a credit account and make payments by electronic funds transfer and access automated teller machines . Such cards are known by a variety of names including bank cards, ATM cards, MAC , client cards, key cards or cash cards.

Exam Probability: **Low**

28. *Answer choices:*

(see index for correct answer)

- a. Amazon Coin
- b. Interac
- c. Payment card

- d. Tabbedout

Guidance: level 1

:: Asset ::

In financial accounting, an _________ is any resource owned by the business. Anything tangible or intangible that can be owned or controlled to produce value and that is held by a company to produce positive economic value is an _________ . Simply stated, _________ s represent value of ownership that can be converted into cash . The balance sheet of a firm records the monetary value of the _________ s owned by that firm. It covers money and other valuables belonging to an individual or to a business.

Exam Probability: **High**

29. *Answer choices:*

(see index for correct answer)

- a. Fixed asset
- b. Asset

Guidance: level 1

:: Transaction processing ::

Transaction processing is information processing in computer science that is divided into individual, indivisible operations called transactions. Each transaction must succeed or fail as a complete unit; it can never be only partially complete.

Exam Probability: **High**

30. *Answer choices:*

(see index for correct answer)

- a. Transaction log
- b. CloudTran
- c. Consistency model
- d. Transaction processing

Guidance: level 1

:: E-commerce ::

__________ generally refer to payment services operated under financial regulation and performed from or via a mobile device. Instead of paying with cash, cheque, or credit cards, a consumer can use a mobile to pay for a wide range of services and digital or hard goods. Although the concept of using non-coin-based currency systems has a long history, it is only recently that the technology to support such systems has become widely available.

Exam Probability: **Low**

31. *Answer choices:*

(see index for correct answer)

- a. Seja online
- b. Digital currency
- c. Mobile payment
- d. Electronic Commerce Directive

Guidance: level 1

:: Data management ::

__________ means protecting digital data, such as those in a database, from destructive forces and from the unwanted actions of unauthorized users, such as a cyberattack or a data breach.

Exam Probability: **Medium**

32. *Answer choices:*

(see index for correct answer)

- a. Australian National Data Service
- b. Paper data storage
- c. RSD
- d. Data security

Guidance: level 1

:: Data management ::

Given organizations` increasing dependency on information technology to run their operations, Business continuity planning covers the entire organization, and Disaster recovery focuses on IT.

Exam Probability: **Low**

33. *Answer choices:*

(see index for correct answer)

- a. Online complex processing
- b. Parchive
- c. Computer-aided software engineering
- d. Disaster recovery plan

Guidance: level 1

:: Production economics ::

In microeconomics, _________ are the cost advantages that enterprises obtain due to their scale of operation , with cost per unit of output decreasing with increasing scale.

Exam Probability: **Low**

34. *Answer choices:*

(see index for correct answer)

- a. Learning-by-doing
- b. Industrial production index
- c. Capitalist mode of production
- d. Cost-of-production theory of value

Guidance: level 1

:: Information technology management ::

_________ within quality management systems and information technology systems is a process—either formal or informal—used to ensure that changes to a product or system are introduced in a controlled and coordinated manner. It reduces the possibility that unnecessary changes will be introduced to a system without forethought, introducing faults into the system or undoing changes made by other users of software. The goals of a _________ procedure usually include minimal disruption to services, reduction in back-out activities, and cost-effective utilization of resources involved in implementing change.

Exam Probability: **Medium**

35. *Answer choices:*

(see index for correct answer)

- a. Run Book Automation
- b. Change control
- c. IT risk
- d. Knowledge balance sheet

Guidance: level 1

:: ::

A __________ is a published declaration of the intentions, motives, or views of the issuer, be it an individual, group, political party or government. A __________ usually accepts a previously published opinion or public consensus or promotes a new idea with prescriptive notions for carrying out changes the author believes should be made. It often is political or artistic in nature, but may present an individual`s life stance. __________ s relating to religious belief are generally referred to as creeds.

Exam Probability: **High**

36. *Answer choices:*

(see index for correct answer)

- a. similarity-attraction theory
- b. Manifesto
- c. process perspective
- d. hierarchical

Guidance: level 1

:: Data management ::

__________ involves combining data residing in different sources and providing users with a unified view of them. This process becomes significant in a variety of situations, which include both commercial and scientific domains. __________ appears with increasing frequency as the volume and the need to share existing data explodes. It has become the focus of extensive theoretical work, and numerous open problems remain unsolved. __________ encourages collaboration between internal as well as external users

Exam Probability: **Medium**

37. *Answer choices:*

(see index for correct answer)

- a. Bitmap index
- b. Data integration
- c. Serializability
- d. Retention period

Guidance: level 1

:: Industrial automation ::

_________ is the technology by which a process or procedure is performed with minimal human assistance. _________ or automatic control is the use of various control systems for operating equipment such as machinery, processes in factories, boilers and heat treating ovens, switching on telephone networks, steering and stabilization of ships, aircraft and other applications and vehicles with minimal or reduced human intervention.

Exam Probability: **Medium**

38. *Answer choices:*

(see index for correct answer)

- a. Automation surprise
- b. Distributed control system
- c. Automation
- d. CODESYS

Guidance: level 1

:: Big data ::

_________ refers to the skills, technologies, practices for continuous iterative exploration and investigation of past business performance to gain insight and drive business planning. _________ focuses on developing new insights and understanding of business performance based on data and statistical methods. In contrast, business intelligence traditionally focuses on using a consistent set of metrics to both measure past performance and guide business planning, which is also based on data and statistical methods.

Exam Probability: **Low**

39. *Answer choices:*

(see index for correct answer)

- a. Business analytics

- b. Analytics
- c. Talend
- d. Medio

Guidance: level 1

:: Infographics ::

A _________ is a graphical representation of data, in which "the data is represented by symbols, such as bars in a bar _________, lines in a line _________, or slices in a pie _________". A _________ can represent tabular numeric data, functions or some kinds of qualitative structure and provides different info.

Exam Probability: **Medium**

40. *Answer choices:*

(see index for correct answer)

- a. Tube map
- b. Chart
- c. Transit map
- d. Motion chart

Guidance: level 1

:: Information systems ::

A _________ manages the creation and modification of digital content. It typically supports multiple users in a collaborative environment.

Exam Probability: **Medium**

41. *Answer choices:*

(see index for correct answer)

- a. Marine Life Information Network
- b. Content management system
- c. Trust management
- d. Automated information system

Guidance: level 1

:: Virtual reality ::

A _________ is a computer-based simulated environment which may be populated by many users who can create a personal avatar, and simultaneously and independently explore the _________ , participate in its activities and communicate with others. These avatars can be textual, two or three-dimensional graphical representations, or live video avatars with auditory and touch sensations. In general, _________ s allow for multiple users but single player computer games, such as Skyrim, can also be considered a type of _________ .

Exam Probability: **Low**

42. *Answer choices:*

(see index for correct answer)

- a. Virtual world
- b. QuickTime VR
- c. XVROS
- d. Uru: Ages Beyond Myst

Guidance: level 1

:: Metadata ::

_________ s usage can be discovered by inspection of software applications or application data files through a process of manual or automated Application Discovery and Understanding. Once _________ s are discovered they can be registered in a metadata registry.

Exam Probability: **Low**

43. *Answer choices:*

(see index for correct answer)

- a. Synonym ring
- b. AES31
- c. Mail Isolation Control and Tracking
- d. Vorbis comment

Guidance: level 1

:: Data management ::

_________ , or IG, is the management of information at an organization. _________ balances the use and security of information. _________ helps with legal compliance, operational transparency, and reducing expenditures associated with legal discovery. An organization can establish a consistent and logical framework for employees to handle data through their _________ policies and procedures. These policies guide proper behavior regarding how organizations and their employees handle electronically stored information .

Exam Probability: **Medium**

44. *Answer choices:*

(see index for correct answer)

- a. Data Transformation Services
- b. Wiping
- c. XLDB
- d. Information governance

Guidance: level 1

:: Network analyzers ::

A _________ , meaning "meat eater" , is an organism that derives its energy and nutrient requirements from a diet consisting mainly or exclusively of animal tissue, whether through predation or scavenging. Animals that depend solely on animal flesh for their nutrient requirements are called obligate _________ s while those that also consume non-animal food are called facultative _________ s. Omnivores also consume both animal and non-animal food, and, apart from the more general definition, there is no clearly defined ratio of plant to animal material that would distinguish a facultative _________ from an omnivore. A _________ at the top of the food chain, not preyed upon by other animals, is termed an apex predator.

Exam Probability: **High**

45. *Answer choices:*

(see index for correct answer)

- a. Carnivore
- b. Ettercap
- c. OmniPeek
- d. Network intelligence

Guidance: level 1

:: Data management ::

_________ is a data management concept concerning the capability that enables an organization to ensure that high data quality exists throughout the complete lifecycle of the data. The key focus areas of _________ include availability, usability, consistency, data integrity and data security and includes establishing processes to ensure effective data management throughout the enterprise such as accountability for the adverse effects of poor data quality and ensuring that the data which an enterprise has can be used by the entire organization.

Exam Probability: **High**

46. *Answer choices:*

(see index for correct answer)

- a. Data virtualization
- b. Data governance
- c. White pages schema
- d. Paper data storage

Guidance: level 1

:: Virtual reality ::

_________ is an experience taking place within simulated and immersive environments that can be similar to or completely different from the real world. Applications of _________ can include entertainment and educational purposes . Other, distinct types of VR style technology include augmented reality and mixed reality.

Exam Probability: **Low**

47. *Answer choices:*

(see index for correct answer)

- a. Virtual reality
- b. Aspen Movie Map
- c. Twinity
- d. Stroker Serpentine

Guidance: level 1

:: Information technology ::

_________ is the use of computers to store, retrieve, transmit, and manipulate data, or information, often in the context of a business or other enterprise. IT is considered to be a subset of information and communications technology . An _________ system is generally an information system, a communications system or, more specifically speaking, a computer system – including all hardware, software and peripheral equipment – operated by a limited group of users.

Exam Probability: **Low**

48. *Answer choices:*

(see index for correct answer)

- a. Henry Bakis
- b. Consumerization
- c. Information and communications technology
- d. Information technology

Guidance: level 1

:: ::

_________ , Inc. was a company that provided human resource management systems , Financial Management Solutions , supply chain management , customer relationship management , and enterprise performance management software, as well as software for manufacturing, and student administration to large corporations, governments, and organizations. It existed as an independent corporation until its acquisition by Oracle Corporation in 2005. The _________ name and product line are now marketed by Oracle.

Exam Probability: **Medium**

49. *Answer choices:*

(see index for correct answer)

- a. PeopleSoft
- b. Character
- c. open system
- d. interpersonal communication

Guidance: level 1

:: Computer security standards ::

The _________ for Information Technology Security Evaluation is an international standard for computer security certification. It is currently in version 3.1 revision 5.

Exam Probability: **Low**

50. *Answer choices:*

(see index for correct answer)

- a. Blacker
- b. FIPS 199
- c. IEEE 802.10
- d. Common Criteria

Guidance: level 1

:: Systems theory ::

A _________ is a group of interacting or interrelated entities that form a unified whole. A _________ is delineated by its spatial and temporal boundaries, surrounded and influenced by its environment, described by its structure and purpose and expressed in its functioning.

Exam Probability: **Medium**

51. *Answer choices:*

(see index for correct answer)

- a. decentralized system
- b. management system
- c. Viable System Model
- d. equifinality

Guidance: level 1

:: Information retrieval ::

_________ is the practice of making content from multiple enterprise-type sources, such as databases and intranets, searchable to a defined audience .

Exam Probability: **Medium**

52. *Answer choices:*

(see index for correct answer)

- a. Schoolr
- b. Poison words
- c. Enterprise search
- d. Noisy text analytics

Guidance: level 1

:: Internet marketing ::

__________ is the process of increasing the quality and quantity of website traffic, increasing visibility of a website or a web page to users of a web search engine.SEO refers to the improvement of unpaid results , and excludes the purchase of paid placement.

Exam Probability: **High**

53. *Answer choices:*

(see index for correct answer)

- a. Run of network
- b. HubSpot
- c. Search engine optimization
- d. Dynamic keyword insertion

Guidance: level 1

:: Information systems ::

In artificial intelligence, an _________ is a computer system that emulates the decision-making ability of a human expert. _________ s are designed to solve complex problems by reasoning through bodies of knowledge, represented mainly as if–then rules rather than through conventional procedural code. The first _________ s were created in the 1970s and then proliferated in the 1980s. _________ s were among the first truly successful forms of artificial intelligence software. However, some experts point out that _________ s were not part of true artificial intelligence since they lack the ability to learn autonomously from external data.An _________ is divided into two subsystems: the inference engine and the knowledge base. The knowledge base represents facts and rules. The inference engine applies the rules to the known facts to deduce new facts. Inference engines can also include explanation and debugging abilities.

Exam Probability: **Low**

54. *Answer choices:*

(see index for correct answer)

- a. Reason maintenance
- b. European Research Center for Information Systems
- c. CountrySTAT
- d. Expert system

Guidance: level 1

:: Payment systems ::

A _________ is any system used to settle financial transactions through the transfer of monetary value. This includes the institutions, instruments, people, rules, procedures, standards, and technologies that make it exchange possible. A common type of _________ is called an operational network that links bank accounts and provides for monetary exchange using bank deposits. Some _________ s also include credit mechanisms, which are essentially a different aspect of payment.

Exam Probability: **Medium**

55. *Answer choices:*

(see index for correct answer)

- a. Payment system
- b. Net Element

- c. International Payments Framework
- d. Cheque truncation system

Guidance: level 1

:: ::

The ________ , commonly known as the Web, is an information system where documents and other web resources are identified by Uniform Resource Locators , which may be interlinked by hypertext, and are accessible over the Internet. The resources of the WWW may be accessed by users by a software application called a web browser.

Exam Probability: **Medium**

56. *Answer choices:*

(see index for correct answer)

- a. deep-level diversity
- b. levels of analysis
- c. Sarbanes-Oxley act of 2002
- d. co-culture

Guidance: level 1

:: E-commerce ::

________ is a type of performance-based marketing in which a business rewards one or more affiliates for each visitor or customer brought by the affiliate`s own marketing efforts.

Exam Probability: **Low**

57. *Answer choices:*

(see index for correct answer)

- a. Payza
- b. Affiliate marketing
- c. TRANZ 330
- d. Tor

Guidance: level 1

:: Computer access control protocols ::

An __________ is a type of computer communications protocol or cryptographic protocol specifically designed for transfer of authentication data between two entities. It allows the receiving entity to authenticate the connecting entity as well as authenticate itself to the connecting entity by declaring the type of information needed for authentication as well as syntax. It is the most important layer of protection needed for secure communication within computer networks.

Exam Probability: **Medium**

58. *Answer choices:*

(see index for correct answer)

- a. Authentication protocol
- b. LAN Manager
- c. POP before SMTP
- d. Ticket Granting Ticket

Guidance: level 1

:: Marketing ::

__________ is a business model in which consumers create value and businesses consume that value. For example, when a consumer writes reviews or when a consumer gives a useful idea for new product development then that consumer is creating value for the business if the business adopts the input. In the C2B model, a reverse auction or demand collection model, enables buyers to name or demand their own price, which is often binding, for a specific good or service. Inside of a consumer to business market the roles involved in the transaction must be established and the consumer must offer something of value to the business.

Exam Probability: **Medium**

59. *Answer choices:*

(see index for correct answer)

- a. Cross merchandising
- b. Joseph E. Grosberg
- c. LIDA
- d. Marchitecture

Guidance: level 1

Marketing

Marketing is the study and management of exchange relationships. Marketing is the business process of creating relationships with and satisfying customers. With its focus on the customer, marketing is one of the premier components of business management.
Marketing is defined by the American Marketing Association as "the activity, set of institutions, and processes for creating, communicating, delivering, and exchanging offerings that have value for customers, clients, partners, and society at large."

:: Product development ::

In business and engineering, __________ covers the complete process of bringing a new product to market. A central aspect of NPD is product design, along with various business considerations. __________ is described broadly as the transformation of a market opportunity into a product available for sale. The product can be tangible or intangible , though sometimes services and other processes are distinguished from "products." NPD requires an understanding of customer needs and wants, the competitive environment, and the nature of the market.Cost, time and quality are the main variables that drive customer needs. Aiming at these three variables, innovative companies develop continuous practices and strategies to better satisfy customer requirements and to increase their own market share by a regular development of new products. There are many uncertainties and challenges which companies must face throughout the process. The use of best practices and the elimination of barriers to communication are the main concerns for the management of the NPD .

Exam Probability: **High**

1. *Answer choices:*

(see index for correct answer)

- a. Virtual prototyping
- b. Design brief
- c. Engineering design management
- d. New product development

Guidance: level 1

:: Marketing ::

A _________ is the quantity of payment or compensation given by one party to another in return for one unit of goods or services.. A _________ is influenced by both production costs and demand for the product. A _________ may be determined by a monopolist or may be imposed on the firm by market conditions.

Exam Probability: **Low**

2. *Answer choices:*

(see index for correct answer)

- a. Double-loop marketing
- b. Price
- c. Corporate anniversary
- d. Product naming convention

Guidance: level 1

:: ::

An _________ is the production of goods or related services within an economy. The major source of revenue of a group or company is the indicator of its relevant _________. When a large group has multiple sources of revenue generation, it is considered to be working in different industries. Manufacturing _________ became a key sector of production and labour in European and North American countries during the Industrial Revolution, upsetting previous mercantile and feudal economies. This came through many successive rapid advances in technology, such as the production of steel and coal.

Exam Probability: **Low**

3. *Answer choices:*

(see index for correct answer)

- a. empathy
- b. Industry
- c. information systems assessment
- d. functional perspective

Guidance: level 1

:: Marketing ::

__________, in marketing, manufacturing, call centres and management, is the use of flexible computer-aided manufacturing systems to produce custom output. Such systems combine the low unit costs of mass production processes with the flexibility of individual customization.

Exam Probability: **Low**

4. *Answer choices:*

(see index for correct answer)

- a. MaxDiff
- b. Party plan
- c. Mass customization
- d. Content Curation Marketing

Guidance: level 1

:: Costs ::

In economics, __________ is the total economic cost of production and is made up of variable cost, which varies according to the quantity of a good produced and includes inputs such as labour and raw materials, plus fixed cost, which is independent of the quantity of a good produced and includes inputs that cannot be varied in the short term: fixed costs such as buildings and machinery, including sunk costs if any. Since cost is measured per unit of time, it is a flow variable.

Exam Probability: **Medium**

5. *Answer choices:*

(see index for correct answer)

- a. Manufacturing cost
- b. Economic cost
- c. Search cost
- d. Total cost

Guidance: level 1

:: Credit cards ::

The __________ Company, also known as Amex, is an American multinational financial services corporation headquartered in Three World Financial Center in New York City. The company was founded in 1850 and is one of the 30 components of the Dow Jones Industrial Average. The company is best known for its charge card, credit card, and traveler`s cheque businesses.

Exam Probability: **Low**

6. *Answer choices:*

(see index for correct answer)

- a. Cashplus
- b. EnRoute
- c. HSBC
- d. American Express

Guidance: level 1

:: Business planning ::

__________ is an organization`s process of defining its strategy, or direction, and making decisions on allocating its resources to pursue this strategy. It may also extend to control mechanisms for guiding the implementation of the strategy. __________ became prominent in corporations during the 1960s and remains an important aspect of strategic management. It is executed by strategic planners or strategists, who involve many parties and research sources in their analysis of the organization and its relationship to the environment in which it competes.

Exam Probability: **High**

7. *Answer choices:*

(see index for correct answer)

- a. Strategic planning
- b. Customer Demand Planning
- c. Joint decision trap
- d. Exit planning

Guidance: level 1

:: ::

Business is the activity of making one`s living or making money by producing or buying and selling products . Simply put, it is "any activity or enterprise entered into for profit. It does not mean it is a company, a corporation, partnership, or have any such formal organization, but it can range from a street peddler to General Motors."

Exam Probability: **Low**

8. *Answer choices:*

(see index for correct answer)

- a. Character
- b. cultural
- c. surface-level diversity
- d. Firm

Guidance: level 1

:: Consumer behaviour ::

Convenient procedures, products and services are those intended to increase ease in accessibility, save resources and decrease frustration. A modern _________ is a labor-saving device, service or substance which make a task easier or more efficient than a traditional method. _________ is a relative concept, and depends on context. For example, automobiles were once considered a _________ , yet today are regarded as a normal part of life.

Exam Probability: **Low**

9. *Answer choices:*

(see index for correct answer)

- a. Consumer behaviour
- b. Convenience
- c. Demographic profile
- d. Customer retention

Guidance: level 1

:: Production economics ::

In microeconomics, _________ are the cost advantages that enterprises obtain due to their scale of operation , with cost per unit of output decreasing with increasing scale.

Exam Probability: **Low**

10. *Answer choices:*

(see index for correct answer)

- a. Transaction cost
- b. Robinson Crusoe economy
- c. Economies of scale
- d. Sectoral output

Guidance: level 1

:: Supply chain management ::

The _________ is a barcode symbology that is widely used in the United States, Canada, United Kingdom, Australia, New Zealand, in Europe and other countries for tracking trade items in stores.

Exam Probability: **Medium**

11. *Answer choices:*

(see index for correct answer)

- a. Distribution software
- b. Supplier enablement
- c. Universal Product Code
- d. Materials management

Guidance: level 1

:: Market research ::

_________ is the action of defining, gathering, analyzing, and distributing intelligence about products, customers, competitors, and any aspect of the environment needed to support executives and managers in strategic decision making for an organization.

Exam Probability: **Medium**

12. *Answer choices:*

(see index for correct answer)

- a. Mendelsohn Affluent Survey
- b. DIY research
- c. Customer satisfaction research
- d. Consumer neuroscience

Guidance: level 1

:: Consumer theory ::

__________ is the quantity of a good that consumers are willing and able to purchase at various prices during a given period of time.

Exam Probability: **Medium**

13. *Answer choices:*

(see index for correct answer)

- a. Elasticity of substitution
- b. Rational addiction
- c. Hicksian demand function
- d. Demand

Guidance: level 1

:: Industrial design ::

In physics and mathematics, the __________ of a mathematical space is informally defined as the minimum number of coordinates needed to specify any point within it. Thus a line has a __________ of one because only one coordinate is needed to specify a point on it for example, the point at 5 on a number line. A surface such as a plane or the surface of a cylinder or sphere has a __________ of two because two coordinates are needed to specify a point on it for example, both a latitude and longitude are required to locate a point on the surface of a sphere. The inside of a cube, a cylinder or a sphere is three- __________ al because three coordinates are needed to locate a point within these spaces.

Exam Probability: **Low**

14. *Answer choices:*

(see index for correct answer)

- a. Design for X
- b. Dimension
- c. Pilot experiment
- d. Diffus Design

Guidance: level 1

:: ::

A _________ is a person who trades in commodities produced by other people. Historically, a _________ is anyone who is involved in business or trade. _________s have operated for as long as industry, commerce, and trade have existed. During the 16th-century, in Europe, two different terms for _________ s emerged: One term, meerseniers, described local traders such as bakers, grocers, etc.; while a new term, koopman (Dutch: koopman, described _________ s who operated on a global stage, importing and exporting goods over vast distances, and offering added-value services such as credit and finance.

Exam Probability: **Medium**

15. *Answer choices:*

(see index for correct answer)

- a. Merchant
- b. empathy
- c. personal values
- d. hierarchical

Guidance: level 1

:: Marketing ::

A _________ is a group of customers within a business`s serviceable available market at which a business aims its marketing efforts and resources. A _________ is a subset of the total market for a product or service. The _________ typically consists of consumers who exhibit similar characteristics and are considered most likely to buy a business`s market offerings or are likely to be the most profitable segments for the business to service.

Exam Probability: **Low**

16. *Answer choices:*

(see index for correct answer)

- a. Cult brand
- b. Discounting
- c. Demand signal repository
- d. Target market

Guidance: level 1

:: Problem solving ::

In other words, _________ is a situation where a group of people meet to generate new ideas and solutions around a specific domain of interest by removing inhibitions. People are able to think more freely and they suggest as many spontaneous new ideas as possible. All the ideas are noted down and those ideas are not criticized and after _________ session the ideas are evaluated.The term was popularized by Alex Faickney Osborn in the 1953 book Applied Imagination.

Exam Probability: **Low**

17. *Answer choices:*

(see index for correct answer)

- a. Self-organising heuristic
- b. Computational thinking
- c. Social heuristics
- d. Community method

Guidance: level 1

:: ::

_________ , known in Europe as research and technological development , refers to innovative activities undertaken by corporations or governments in developing new services or products, or improving existing services or products. _________ constitutes the first stage of development of a potential new service or the production process.

Exam Probability: **High**

18. *Answer choices:*

(see index for correct answer)

- a. imperative
- b. Research and development
- c. surface-level diversity

- d. hierarchical perspective

Guidance: level 1

:: ::

__________ , also referred to as orthostasis, is a human position in which the body is held in an upright position and supported only by the feet.

Exam Probability: **Medium**

19. *Answer choices:*

(see index for correct answer)

- a. personal values
- b. process perspective
- c. interpersonal communication
- d. levels of analysis

Guidance: level 1

:: Belief ::

__________ is an umbrella term of influence. __________ can attempt to influence a person`s beliefs, attitudes, intentions, motivations, or behaviors. In business, __________ is a process aimed at changing a person`s attitude or behavior toward some event, idea, object, or other person, by using written, spoken words or visual tools to convey information, feelings, or reasoning, or a combination thereof. __________ is also an often used tool in the pursuit of personal gain, such as election campaigning, giving a sales pitch, or in trial advocacy. __________ can also be interpreted as using one`s personal or positional resources to change people`s behaviors or attitudes.Systematic __________ is the process through which attitudes or beliefs are leveraged by appeals to logic and reason. Heuristic __________ on the other hand is the process through which attitudes or beliefs are leveraged by appeals to habit or emotion.

Exam Probability: **Medium**

20. *Answer choices:*

(see index for correct answer)

- a. Persuasion
- b. Transubstantiation

- c. Philosophy of happiness
- d. Reality tunnel

Guidance: level 1

:: Marketing ::

The _________ is a foundation model for businesses. The _________ has been defined as the "set of marketing tools that the firm uses to pursue its marketing objectives in the target market". Thus the _________ refers to four broad levels of marketing decision, namely: product, price, place, and promotion. Marketing practice has been occurring for millennia, but marketing theory emerged in the early twentieth century. The contemporary _________ , or the 4 Ps, which has become the dominant framework for marketing management decisions, was first published in 1960. In services marketing, an extended _________ is used, typically comprising 7 Ps, made up of the original 4 Ps extended by process, people, and physical evidence. Occasionally service marketers will refer to 8 Ps, comprising these 7 Ps plus performance.

Exam Probability: **Medium**

21. *Answer choices:*

(see index for correct answer)

- a. Earned media
- b. Marketing myopia
- c. Joseph E. Grosberg
- d. Marketing mix

Guidance: level 1

:: Direct selling ::

_________ consists of two main business models: single-level marketing, in which a direct seller makes money by buying products from a parent organization and selling them directly to customers, and multi-level marketing , in which the direct seller may earn money from both direct sales to customers and by sponsoring new direct sellers and potentially earning a commission from their efforts.

Exam Probability: **Low**

22. *Answer choices:*

(see index for correct answer)

- a. The Longaberger Company
- b. Direct Selling News
- c. Direct Selling Association
- d. CVSL

Guidance: level 1

:: ::

Competition arises whenever at least two parties strive for a goal which cannot be shared: where one`s gain is the other`s loss .

Exam Probability: **Medium**

23. *Answer choices:*

(see index for correct answer)

- a. interpersonal communication
- b. process perspective
- c. similarity-attraction theory
- d. Competitor

Guidance: level 1

:: Debt ::

_________ is the trust which allows one party to provide money or resources to another party wherein the second party does not reimburse the first party immediately , but promises either to repay or return those resources at a later date. In other words, _________ is a method of making reciprocity formal, legally enforceable, and extensible to a large group of unrelated people.

Exam Probability: **Medium**

24. *Answer choices:*

(see index for correct answer)

- a. Zombie company
- b. Credit
- c. Debt adjustment
- d. Extendible bond

Guidance: level 1

:: Marketing ::

__________ , sometimes called trigger-based or event-driven marketing, is a marketing strategy that uses two-way communication channels to allow consumers to connect with a company directly. Although this exchange can take place in person, in the last decade it has increasingly taken place almost exclusively online through email, social media, and blogs.

Exam Probability: **Medium**

25. *Answer choices:*

(see index for correct answer)

- a. Generic trademark
- b. Interactive marketing
- c. Digital billboard
- d. Customer insight

Guidance: level 1

:: Basic financial concepts ::

__________ is a sustained increase in the general price level of goods and services in an economy over a period of time.When the general price level rises, each unit of currency buys fewer goods and services; consequently, __________ reflects a reduction in the purchasing power per unit of money a loss of real value in the medium of exchange and unit of account within the economy. The measure of __________ is the __________ rate, the annualized percentage change in a general price index, usually the consumer price index, over time. The opposite of __________ is deflation.

Exam Probability: **Medium**

26. *Answer choices:*

(see index for correct answer)

- a. Present value of benefits
- b. Forward guidance
- c. Inflation
- d. Tax shield

Guidance: level 1

:: Services management and marketing ::

_________ is a specialised branch of marketing. _________ emerged as a separate field of study in the early 1980s, following the recognition that the unique characteristics of services required different strategies compared with the marketing of physical goods.

Exam Probability: **Low**

27. *Answer choices:*

(see index for correct answer)

- a. Service design
- b. Services marketing
- c. Functional branding
- d. Night service

Guidance: level 1

:: ::

The _________ is a U.S. business-focused, English-language international daily newspaper based in New York City. The Journal, along with its Asian and European editions, is published six days a week by Dow Jones & Company, a division of News Corp. The newspaper is published in the broadsheet format and online. The Journal has been printed continuously since its inception on July 8, 1889, by Charles Dow, Edward Jones, and Charles Bergstresser.

Exam Probability: **High**

28. *Answer choices:*

(see index for correct answer)

- a. interpersonal communication
- b. levels of analysis
- c. empathy
- d. Wall Street Journal

Guidance: level 1

:: Project management ::

A _________ is a source or supply from which a benefit is produced and it has some utility. _________ s can broadly be classified upon their availability—they are classified into renewable and non-renewable _________ s.Examples of non renewable _________ s are coal ,crude oil natural gas nuclear energy etc. Examples of renewable _________ s are air,water,wind,solar energy etc. They can also be classified as actual and potential on the basis of level of development and use, on the basis of origin they can be classified as biotic and abiotic, and on the basis of their distribution, as ubiquitous and localized . An item becomes a _________ with time and developing technology. Typically, _________ s are materials, energy, services, staff, knowledge, or other assets that are transformed to produce benefit and in the process may be consumed or made unavailable. Benefits of _________ utilization may include increased wealth, proper functioning of a system, or enhanced well-being. From a human perspective a natural _________ is anything obtained from the environment to satisfy human needs and wants. From a broader biological or ecological perspective a _________ satisfies the needs of a living organism .

Exam Probability: **Low**

29. *Answer choices:*

(see index for correct answer)

- a. Scope statement
- b. The Chicken and the Pig
- c. Resource
- d. Operational bill

Guidance: level 1

:: Reputation management ::

A _________ is an astronomical object consisting of a luminous spheroid of plasma held together by its own gravity. The nearest _________ to Earth is the Sun. Many other _________ s are visible to the naked eye from Earth during the night, appearing as a multitude of fixed luminous points in the sky due to their immense distance from Earth. Historically, the most prominent _________ s were grouped into constellations and asterisms, the brightest of which gained proper names. Astronomers have assembled _________ catalogues that identify the known _________ s and provide standardized stellar designations. However, most of the estimated 300 sextillion _________ s in the Universe are invisible to the naked eye from Earth, including all _________ s outside our galaxy, the Milky Way.

Exam Probability: **Low**

30. *Answer choices:*

(see index for correct answer)

- a. The Economy of Esteem
- b. Sybil attack
- c. Advogato
- d. Star

Guidance: level 1

:: ::

A _________ is an organization, usually a group of people or a company, authorized to act as a single entity and recognized as such in law. Early incorporated entities were established by charter . Most jurisdictions now allow the creation of new _________ s through registration.

Exam Probability: **Medium**

31. *Answer choices:*

(see index for correct answer)

- a. levels of analysis
- b. process perspective
- c. Corporation
- d. hierarchical

Guidance: level 1

:: Debt ::

_________ , in finance and economics, is payment from a borrower or deposit-taking financial institution to a lender or depositor of an amount above repayment of the principal sum , at a particular rate. It is distinct from a fee which the borrower may pay the lender or some third party. It is also distinct from dividend which is paid by a company to its shareholders from its profit or reserve, but not at a particular rate decided beforehand, rather on a pro rata basis as a share in the reward gained by risk taking entrepreneurs when the revenue earned exceeds the total costs.

Exam Probability: **Medium**

32. *Answer choices:*

(see index for correct answer)

- a. Interest
- b. Default trap
- c. Christians Against Poverty
- d. Debt-lag

Guidance: level 1

:: Product development ::

_________ is the understanding of the dynamics of the product in order to showcase the best qualities and maximum features of the product. Marketers spend a lot of time and research in order to target their attended audience. Marketers will look into a _________ before marketing a product towards their customers.

Exam Probability: **High**

33. *Answer choices:*

(see index for correct answer)

- a. Embedded intelligence
- b. Product optimization
- c. Product concept
- d. Design for assembly

Guidance: level 1

:: Brand management ::

In marketing, _________ is the analysis and planning on how a brand is perceived in the market. Developing a good relationship with the target market is essential for _________ . Tangible elements of _________ include the product itself; its look, price, and packaging, etc. The intangible elements are the experiences that the consumers share with the brand, and also the relationships they have with the brand. A brand manager would oversee all aspects of the consumer`s brand association as well as relationships with members of the supply chain.

Exam Probability: **High**

34. *Answer choices:*

(see index for correct answer)

- a. Brand strength analysis
- b. Brand management
- c. E3 Agency Network
- d. Superbrands

Guidance: level 1

:: ::

_________ are interactive computer-mediated technologies that facilitate the creation and sharing of information, ideas, career interests and other forms of expression via virtual communities and networks. The variety of stand-alone and built-in _________ services currently available introduces challenges of definition; however, there are some common features.

Exam Probability: **High**

35. *Answer choices:*

(see index for correct answer)

- a. Social media
- b. surface-level diversity
- c. cultural
- d. Character

Guidance: level 1

:: ::

In the broadest sense, _________ is any practice which contributes to the sale of products to a retail consumer. At a retail in-store level, _________ refers to the variety of products available for sale and the display of those products in such a way that it stimulates interest and entices customers to make a purchase.

Exam Probability: **High**

36. *Answer choices:*

(see index for correct answer)

- a. Merchandising
- b. Character
- c. co-culture
- d. information systems assessment

Guidance: level 1

:: Marketing ::

_________ is a market strategy in which a firm decides to ignore market segment differences and appeal the whole market with one offer or one strategy, which supports the idea of broadcasting a message that will reach the largest number of people possible. Traditionally _________ has focused on radio, television and newspapers as the media used to reach this broad audience. By reaching the largest audience possible, exposure to the product is maximized, and in theory this would directly correlate with a larger number of sales or buys into the product.

Exam Probability: **Medium**

37. *Answer choices:*

(see index for correct answer)

- a. Geomarketing
- b. Product naming convention
- c. Cause-related loyalty marketing
- d. Digital native

Guidance: level 1

:: ::

An ________, often referred to as a creative agency or an ad agency, is a business dedicated to creating, planning, and handling advertising and sometimes other forms of promotion and marketing for its clients. An ad agency is generally independent from the client; it may be an internal department or agency that provides an outside point of view to the effort of selling the client`s products or services, or an outside firm. An agency can also handle overall marketing and branding strategies promotions for its clients, which may include sales as well.

Exam Probability: **Medium**

38. *Answer choices:*

(see index for correct answer)

- a. hierarchical perspective
- b. Advertising agency
- c. corporate values
- d. personal values

Guidance: level 1

:: Marketing ::

________ is the percentage of a market accounted for by a specific entity. In a survey of nearly 200 senior marketing managers, 67% responded that they found the revenue- "dollar ________" metric very useful, while 61% found "unit ________" very useful.

Exam Probability: **High**

39. *Answer choices:*

(see index for correct answer)

- a. Demand signal repository
- b. Market share
- c. Official statistics
- d. Content Curation Marketing

Guidance: level 1

:: ::

__________ is the production of products for use or sale using labour and machines, tools, chemical and biological processing, or formulation. The term may refer to a range of human activity, from handicraft to high tech, but is most commonly applied to industrial design, in which raw materials are transformed into finished goods on a large scale. Such finished goods may be sold to other manufacturers for the production of other, more complex products, such as aircraft, household appliances, furniture, sports equipment or automobiles, or sold to wholesalers, who in turn sell them to retailers, who then sell them to end users and consumers.

Exam Probability: **Low**

40. *Answer choices:*

(see index for correct answer)

- a. levels of analysis
- b. corporate values
- c. process perspective
- d. Character

Guidance: level 1

:: Marketing ::

__________ is multi-channel online marketing technique focused at reaching a specific audience on their smartphones, tablets, or any other related devices through websites, E-mail, SMS and MMS, social media, or mobile applications. __________ can provide customers with time and location sensitive, personalized information that promotes goods, services and ideas. In a more theoretical manner, academic Andreas Kaplan defines __________ as "any marketing activity conducted through a ubiquitous network to which consumers are constantly connected using a personal mobile device".

Exam Probability: **Low**

41. *Answer choices:*

(see index for correct answer)

- a. Markup
- b. Global Center for Health Innovation
- c. Interactive collateral management
- d. Mobile marketing

Guidance: level 1

:: Income ::

In business and accounting, net income is an entity's income minus cost of goods sold, expenses and taxes for an accounting period. It is computed as the residual of all revenues and gains over all expenses and losses for the period, and has also been defined as the net increase in shareholders' equity that results from a company's operations. In the context of the presentation of financial statements, the IFRS Foundation defines net income as synonymous with profit and loss. The difference between revenue and the cost of making a product or providing a service, before deducting overheads, payroll, taxation, and interest payments. This is different from operating income .

Exam Probability: **Low**

42. *Answer choices:*

(see index for correct answer)

- a. Bottom line
- b. Aggregate income
- c. Implied level of government service
- d. National average salary

Guidance: level 1

:: ::

In law, a _________ is a coming together of parties to a dispute, to present information in a tribunal, a formal setting with the authority to adjudicate claims or disputes. One form of tribunal is a court. The tribunal, which may occur before a judge, jury, or other designated trier of fact, aims to achieve a resolution to their dispute.

Exam Probability: **Low**

43. *Answer choices:*

(see index for correct answer)

- a. levels of analysis
- b. cultural
- c. hierarchical
- d. Trial

Guidance: level 1

:: Commerce ::

_________ relates to "the exchange of goods and services, especially on a large scale". It includes legal, economic, political, social, cultural and technological systems that operate in a country or in international trade.

Exam Probability: **Low**

44. *Answer choices:*

(see index for correct answer)

- a. RFM
- b. Recommerce
- c. Agio
- d. Organ trade

Guidance: level 1

:: ::

In law, an _________ is the process in which cases are reviewed, where parties request a formal change to an official decision. _________ s function both as a process for error correction as well as a process of clarifying and interpreting law. Although appellate courts have existed for thousands of years, common law countries did not incorporate an affirmative right to _________ into their jurisprudence until the 19th century.

Exam Probability: **High**

45. *Answer choices:*

(see index for correct answer)

- a. Appeal
- b. personal values
- c. Character
- d. process perspective

Guidance: level 1

:: Consumer behaviour ::

_________ is an activity in which a customer browses the available goods or services presented by one or more retailers with the potential intent to purchase a suitable selection of them. A typology of shopper types has been developed by scholars which identifies one group of shoppers as recreational shoppers, that is, those who enjoy _________ and view it as a leisure activity.

Exam Probability: **Medium**

46. *Answer choices:*

(see index for correct answer)

- a. Buzz monitoring
- b. Mociology
- c. Shopping
- d. Visual merchandising

Guidance: level 1

:: Marketing ::

_________ is based on a marketing concept which can be adopted by an organization as a strategy for business expansion. Where implemented, a franchisor licenses its know-how, procedures, intellectual property, use of its business model, brand, and rights to sell its branded products and services to a franchisee. In return the franchisee pays certain fees and agrees to comply with certain obligations, typically set out in a Franchise Agreement.

Exam Probability: **High**

47. *Answer choices:*

(see index for correct answer)

- a. Audience screen
- b. Franchising
- c. Double bottom line
- d. Lead management

Guidance: level 1

:: Management ::

A _________ is a comprehensive document or blueprint that outlines the advertising and marketing efforts for the coming year. It describes business activities involved in accomplishing specific marketing objectives within a set time frame. A _________ also includes a description of the current marketing position of a business, a discussion of the target market and a description of the marketing mix that a business will use to achieve their marketing goals. A _________ has a formal structure, but can be used as a formal or informal document which makes it very flexible. It contains some historical data, future predictions, and methods or strategies to achieve the marketing objectives. _________s start with the identification of customer needs through a market research and how the business can satisfy these needs while generating an acceptable return. This includes processes such as market situation analysis, action programs, budgets, sales forecasts, strategies and projected financial statements. A _________ can also be described as a technique that helps a business to decide on the best use of its resources to achieve corporate objectives. It can also contain a full analysis of the strengths and weaknesses of a company, its organization and its products.

Exam Probability: **Medium**

48. *Answer choices:*

(see index for correct answer)

- a. Lead scoring
- b. Supply management
- c. Marketing management
- d. Marketing plan

Guidance: level 1

:: ::

_________ is a marketing communication that employs an openly sponsored, non-personal message to promote or sell a product, service or idea. Sponsors of _________ are typically businesses wishing to promote their products or services. _________ is differentiated from public relations in that an advertiser pays for and has control over the message. It differs from personal selling in that the message is non-personal, i.e., not directed to a particular individual. _________ is communicated through various mass media, including traditional media such as newspapers, magazines, television, radio, outdoor _________ or direct mail; and new media such as search results, blogs, social media, websites or text messages. The actual presentation of the message in a medium is referred to as an advertisement, or "ad" or advert for short.

Exam Probability: **Low**

49. *Answer choices:*

(see index for correct answer)

- a. functional perspective
- b. similarity-attraction theory
- c. deep-level diversity
- d. Advertising

Guidance: level 1

:: ::

In _________ relations and communication science, _________ s are groups of individual people, and the _________ is the totality of such groupings. This is a different concept to the sociological concept of the Öffentlichkeit or _________ sphere. The concept of a _________ has also been defined in political science, psychology, marketing, and advertising. In _________ relations and communication science, it is one of the more ambiguous concepts in the field. Although it has definitions in the theory of the field that have been formulated from the early 20th century onwards, it has suffered in more recent years from being blurred, as a result of conflation of the idea of a _________ with the notions of audience, market segment, community, constituency, and stakeholder.

Exam Probability: **High**

50. *Answer choices:*

(see index for correct answer)

- a. Public
- b. Sarbanes-Oxley act of 2002
- c. cultural
- d. deep-level diversity

Guidance: level 1

:: bad_topic ::

Sponsoring something is the act of supporting an event, activity, person, or organization financially or through the provision of products or services. The individual or group that provides the support, similar to a benefactor, is known as sponsor.

Exam Probability: **Medium**

51. *Answer choices:*

(see index for correct answer)

- a. Caremark Rx
- b. Priceearnings ratio
- c. Sponsorship
- d. Nynex

Guidance: level 1

:: Asset ::

In financial accounting, an _________ is any resource owned by the business. Anything tangible or intangible that can be owned or controlled to produce value and that is held by a company to produce positive economic value is an _________. Simply stated, _________s represent value of ownership that can be converted into cash . The balance sheet of a firm records the monetary value of the _________s owned by that firm. It covers money and other valuables belonging to an individual or to a business.

Exam Probability: **Low**

52. *Answer choices:*

(see index for correct answer)

- a. Asset
- b. Fixed asset

Guidance: level 1

:: ::

_________ is the process whereby a business sets the price at which it will sell its products and services, and may be part of the business`s marketing plan. In setting prices, the business will take into account the price at which it could acquire the goods, the manufacturing cost, the market place, competition, market condition, brand, and quality of product.

Exam Probability: **Medium**

53. *Answer choices:*

(see index for correct answer)

- a. Pricing
- b. hierarchical perspective
- c. deep-level diversity
- d. imperative

Guidance: level 1

:: Management ::

The term _________ refers to measures designed to increase the degree of autonomy and self-determination in people and in communities in order to enable them to represent their interests in a responsible and self-determined way, acting on their own authority. It is the process of becoming stronger and more confident, especially in controlling one`s life and claiming one`s rights. _________ as action refers both to the process of self- _________ and to professional support of people, which enables them to overcome their sense of powerlessness and lack of influence, and to recognize and use their resources. To do work with power.

Exam Probability: **High**

54. *Answer choices:*

(see index for correct answer)

- a. Marketing science
- b. Twelve leverage points
- c. Empowerment
- d. Value proposition

Guidance: level 1

:: Generally Accepted Accounting Principles ::

Expenditure is an outflow of money to another person or group to pay for an item or service, or for a category of costs. For a tenant, rent is an _________ . For students or parents, tuition is an _________ . Buying food, clothing, furniture or an automobile is often referred to as an _________ . An _________ is a cost that is "paid" or "remitted", usually in exchange for something of value. Something that seems to cost a great deal is "expensive". Something that seems to cost little is "inexpensive". " _________ s of the table" are _________ s of dining, refreshments, a feast, etc.

Exam Probability: **High**

55. *Answer choices:*

(see index for correct answer)

- a. deferred revenue
- b. Operating profit
- c. Income statement
- d. Fixed investment

Guidance: level 1

:: Management ::

_________ is the organizational discipline which focuses on the practical application of marketing orientation, techniques and methods inside enterprises and organizations and on the management of a firm`s marketing resources and activities.

Exam Probability: **Low**

56. *Answer choices:*

(see index for correct answer)

- a. Marketing management
- b. Records manager
- c. Just in time
- d. Empowerment

Guidance: level 1

:: ::

A _________ is the process of presenting a topic to an audience. It is typically a demonstration, introduction, lecture, or speech meant to inform, persuade, inspire, motivate, or to build good will or to present a new idea or product. The term can also be used for a formal or ritualized introduction or offering, as with the _________ of a debutante. _________ s in certain formats are also known as keynote address.

Exam Probability: **Low**

57. *Answer choices:*

(see index for correct answer)

- a. Presentation
- b. personal values
- c. imperative
- d. cultural

Guidance: level 1

:: ::

_________ is the administration of an organization, whether it is a business, a not-for-profit organization, or government body. _________ includes the activities of setting the strategy of an organization and coordinating the efforts of its employees to accomplish its objectives through the application of available resources, such as financial, natural, technological, and human resources. The term " _________ " may also refer to those people who manage an organization.

Exam Probability: **Low**

58. *Answer choices:*

(see index for correct answer)

- a. co-culture
- b. levels of analysis
- c. interpersonal communication
- d. empathy

Guidance: level 1

:: Business models ::

A _________ is "an autonomous association of persons united voluntarily to meet their common economic, social, and cultural needs and aspirations through a jointly-owned and democratically-controlled enterprise". _________ s may include.

Exam Probability: **High**

59. *Answer choices:*

(see index for correct answer)

- a. Lawyers on Demand
- b. Defensive patent aggregation
- c. Cooperative
- d. Business networking

Guidance: level 1

Manufacturing

Manufacturing is the production of merchandise for use or sale using labor and machines, tools, chemical and biological processing, or formulation. The term may refer to a range of human activity, from handicraft to high tech, but is most commonly applied to industrial design , in which raw materials are transformed into finished goods on a large scale. Such finished goods may be sold to other manufacturers for the production of other, more complex products, such as aircraft, household appliances, furniture, sports equipment or automobiles, or sold to wholesalers, who in turn sell them to retailers, who then sell them to end users and consumers.

:: Industrial design ::

In physics and mathematics, the _________ of a mathematical space is informally defined as the minimum number of coordinates needed to specify any point within it. Thus a line has a _________ of one because only one coordinate is needed to specify a point on it for example, the point at 5 on a number line. A surface such as a plane or the surface of a cylinder or sphere has a _________ of two because two coordinates are needed to specify a point on it for example, both a latitude and longitude are required to locate a point on the surface of a sphere. The inside of a cube, a cylinder or a sphere is three- _________ al because three coordinates are needed to locate a point within these spaces.

Exam Probability: **High**

1. *Answer choices:*

(see index for correct answer)

- a. Bauhaus
- b. Dimension
- c. AxSTREAM
- d. Electronic packaging

Guidance: level 1

:: Marketing ::

__________ or stock is the goods and materials that a business holds for the ultimate goal of resale .

Exam Probability: **High**

2. *Answer choices:*

(see index for correct answer)

- a. Multicultural marketing
- b. Marketing activation
- c. Horizontal integration
- d. Pink money

Guidance: level 1

:: Industrial processes ::

__________ is a technique involving the condensation of vapors and the return of this condensate to the system from which it originated. It is used in industrial and laboratory distillations. It is also used in chemistry to supply energy to reactions over a long period of time.

Exam Probability: **Low**

3. *Answer choices:*

(see index for correct answer)

- a. Tinning
- b. Peroxide process
- c. Quartz tube furnace
- d. Reflux

Guidance: level 1

:: Production and manufacturing ::

Automatic ________ in continuous production processes is a combination of control engineering and chemical engineering disciplines that uses industrial control systems to achieve a production level of consistency, economy and safety which could not be achieved purely by human manual control. It is implemented widely in industries such as oil refining, pulp and paper manufacturing, chemical processing and power generating plants.

Exam Probability: **High**

4. *Answer choices:*

(see index for correct answer)

- a. Process control
- b. Report generator
- c. Assembly line
- d. Reverse engineering

Guidance: level 1

:: Consortia ::

A ________ is an association of two or more individuals, companies, organizations or governments with the objective of participating in a common activity or pooling their resources for achieving a common goal.

Exam Probability: **Low**

5. *Answer choices:*

(see index for correct answer)

- a. Open Solutions Alliance
- b. Consortium
- c. EuroTorp
- d. Builder homesite

Guidance: level 1

:: Costs ::

__________ is the process used by companies to reduce their costs and increase their profits. Depending on a company's services or product, the strategies can vary. Every decision in the product development process affects cost.

Exam Probability: **High**

6. *Answer choices:*

(see index for correct answer)

- a. Cost reduction
- b. Incremental cost-effectiveness ratio
- c. Social cost
- d. labor cost

Guidance: level 1

:: Information systems ::

__________ is the process of creating, sharing, using and managing the knowledge and information of an organisation. It refers to a multidisciplinary approach to achieving organisational objectives by making the best use of knowledge.

Exam Probability: **Medium**

7. *Answer choices:*

(see index for correct answer)

- a. Management information system
- b. Spatial intelligence of cities
- c. Knowledge management
- d. Spatial decision support system

Guidance: level 1

:: Distribution, retailing, and wholesaling ::

__________ measures the performance of a system. Certain goals are defined and the __________ gives the percentage to which those goals should be achieved. Fill rate is different from __________.

Exam Probability: **Low**

8. *Answer choices:*

(see index for correct answer)

- a. National
- b. Distribution center management system
- c. Fast Fiction
- d. Concession

Guidance: level 1

:: Project management ::

Contemporary business and science treat as a _________ any undertaking, carried out individually or collaboratively and possibly involving research or design, that is carefully planned to achieve a particular aim.

Exam Probability: **Medium**

9. *Answer choices:*

(see index for correct answer)

- a. Resource leveling
- b. Team performance management
- c. Project
- d. Stakeholder analysis

Guidance: level 1

:: Commercial item transport and distribution ::

_________ in logistics and supply chain management is an organization`s use of third-party businesses to outsource elements of its distribution, warehousing, and fulfillment services.

Exam Probability: **High**

10. *Answer choices:*

(see index for correct answer)

- a. Third-party logistics
- b. Common carrier
- c. Parcel
- d. Haulage

Guidance: level 1

:: Product development ::

In business and engineering, __________ covers the complete process of bringing a new product to market. A central aspect of NPD is product design, along with various business considerations. __________ is described broadly as the transformation of a market opportunity into a product available for sale. The product can be tangible or intangible , though sometimes services and other processes are distinguished from "products." NPD requires an understanding of customer needs and wants, the competitive environment, and the nature of the market.Cost, time and quality are the main variables that drive customer needs. Aiming at these three variables, innovative companies develop continuous practices and strategies to better satisfy customer requirements and to increase their own market share by a regular development of new products. There are many uncertainties and challenges which companies must face throughout the process. The use of best practices and the elimination of barriers to communication are the main concerns for the management of the NPD .

Exam Probability: **High**

11. *Answer choices:*

(see index for correct answer)

- a. New product development
- b. Specification tree
- c. Embedded intelligence
- d. Product line extension

Guidance: level 1

:: Packaging ::

In work place, _________ or job _________ means good ranking with the hypothesized conception of requirements of a role. There are two types of job _________ s: contextual and task. Task _________ is related to cognitive ability while contextual _________ is dependent upon personality. Task _________ are behavioral roles that are recognized in job descriptions and by remuneration systems, they are directly related to organizational _________ , whereas, contextual _________ are value based and additional behavioral roles that are not recognized in job descriptions and covered by compensation; they are extra roles that are indirectly related to organizational _________ . Citizenship _________ like contextual _________ means a set of individual activity/contribution that supports the organizational culture.

Exam Probability: **Medium**

12. *Answer choices:*

(see index for correct answer)

- a. Performance
- b. Digipak
- c. Tamper resistance
- d. Multi-pack

Guidance: level 1

:: Project management ::

_________ is a process of setting goals, planning and/or controlling the organizing and leading the execution of any type of activity, such as.

Exam Probability: **Low**

13. *Answer choices:*

(see index for correct answer)

- a. LibrePlan
- b. Participatory impact pathways analysis
- c. Management process
- d. Site survey

Guidance: level 1

:: Mereology ::

_________ , in the abstract, is what belongs to or with something, whether as an attribute or as a component of said thing. In the context of this article, it is one or more components , whether physical or incorporeal, of a person`s estate; or so belonging to, as in being owned by, a person or jointly a group of people or a legal entity like a corporation or even a society. Depending on the nature of the _________ , an owner of _________ has the right to consume, alter, share, redefine, rent, mortgage, pawn, sell, exchange, transfer, give away or destroy it, or to exclude others from doing these things, as well as to perhaps abandon it; whereas regardless of the nature of the _________ , the owner thereof has the right to properly use it , or at the very least exclusively keep it.

Exam Probability: **High**

14. *Answer choices:*

(see index for correct answer)

- a. Mereology
- b. Meronomy
- c. Property
- d. Non-wellfounded mereology

Guidance: level 1

:: Project management ::

_________ is the right to exercise power, which can be formalized by a state and exercised by way of judges, appointed executives of government, or the ecclesiastical or priestly appointed representatives of a God or other deities.

Exam Probability: **Low**

15. *Answer choices:*

(see index for correct answer)

- a. Scope
- b. Authority
- c. Akihabara syndrome
- d. TimeTac

Guidance: level 1

:: Project management ::

A __________ is a team whose members usually belong to different groups, functions and are assigned to activities for the same project. A team can be divided into sub-teams according to need. Usually __________ s are only used for a defined period of time. They are disbanded after the project is deemed complete. Due to the nature of the specific formation and disbandment, __________ s are usually in organizations.

Exam Probability: **Low**

16. *Answer choices:*

(see index for correct answer)

- a. Logical framework approach
- b. Project team
- c. Product flow diagram
- d. Constructability

Guidance: level 1

:: Supply chain management ::

A __________ is a type of auction in which the traditional roles of buyer and seller are reversed. Thus, there is one buyer and many potential sellers. In an ordinary auction , buyers compete to obtain goods or services by offering increasingly higher prices. In contrast, in a __________ , the sellers compete to obtain business from the buyer and prices will typically decrease as the sellers underbid each other.

Exam Probability: **Medium**

17. *Answer choices:*

(see index for correct answer)

- a. Stock depth
- b. Astra Resources Plc
- c. Interorganizational system
- d. Reverse auction

Guidance: level 1

:: Lean manufacturing ::

__________ is the Sino-Japanese word for "improvement". In business, __________ refers to activities that continuously improve all functions and involve all employees from the CEO to the assembly line workers. It also applies to processes, such as purchasing and logistics, that cross organizational boundaries into the supply chain. It has been applied in healthcare, psychotherapy, life-coaching, government, and banking.

Exam Probability: **Medium**

18. *Answer choices:*

(see index for correct answer)

- a. Kanban
- b. Poka-yoke
- c. Frequent deliveries
- d. Kaizen

Guidance: level 1

:: Business ::

The seller, or the provider of the goods or services, completes a sale in response to an acquisition, appropriation, requisition or a direct interaction with the buyer at the point of sale. There is a passing of title of the item, and the settlement of a price, in which agreement is reached on a price for which transfer of ownership of the item will occur. The seller, not the purchaser typically executes the sale and it may be completed prior to the obligation of payment. In the case of indirect interaction, a person who sells goods or service on behalf of the owner is known as a __________ man or __________ woman or __________ person, but this often refers to someone selling goods in a store/shop, in which case other terms are also common, including __________ clerk, shop assistant, and retail clerk.

Exam Probability: **High**

19. *Answer choices:*

(see index for correct answer)

- a. Ha Van Tham
- b. Relationship Science
- c. Sales
- d. Architecture of Interoperable Information Systems

Guidance: level 1

:: Data interchange standards ::

_________ is the concept of businesses electronically communicating information that was traditionally communicated on paper, such as purchase orders and invoices. Technical standards for EDI exist to facilitate parties transacting such instruments without having to make special arrangements.

Exam Probability: **Low**

20. *Answer choices:*
(see index for correct answer)

- a. Electronic data interchange
- b. Interaction protocol
- c. Domain Application Protocol
- d. ASC X12

Guidance: level 1

:: Production and manufacturing ::

_________ is a concept in purchasing and project management for securing the quality and timely delivery of goods and components.

Exam Probability: **Medium**

21. *Answer choices:*
(see index for correct answer)

- a. Beltweigher
- b. Expediting
- c. Transfer line
- d. Variable rate feeder

Guidance: level 1

:: Unit operations ::

__________ is the process of separating the components or substances from a liquid mixture by using selective boiling and condensation. __________ may result in essentially complete separation , or it may be a partial separation that increases the concentration of selected components in the mixture. In either case, the process exploits differences in the volatility of the mixture`s components. In industrial chemistry, __________ is a unit operation of practically universal importance, but it is a physical separation process, not a chemical reaction.

Exam Probability: **Low**

22. *Answer choices:*

(see index for correct answer)

- a. Sedimentation coefficient
- b. Theoretical plate
- c. Distillation
- d. Settling

Guidance: level 1

:: Project management ::

In political science, an __________ is a means by which a petition signed by a certain minimum number of registered voters can force a government to choose to either enact a law or hold a public vote in parliament in what is called indirect __________ , or under direct __________ , the proposition is immediately put to a plebiscite or referendum, in what is called a Popular initiated Referendum or citizen-initiated referendum).

Exam Probability: **Medium**

23. *Answer choices:*

(see index for correct answer)

- a. Multidisciplinary approach
- b. Social project management
- c. Initiative
- d. Axelos

Guidance: level 1

:: Planning ::

_________ is a high level plan to achieve one or more goals under conditions of uncertainty. In the sense of the "art of the general," which included several subsets of skills including tactics, siegecraft, logistics etc., the term came into use in the 6th century C.E. in East Roman terminology, and was translated into Western vernacular languages only in the 18th century. From then until the 20th century, the word " _________ " came to denote "a comprehensive way to try to pursue political ends, including the threat or actual use of force, in a dialectic of wills" in a military conflict, in which both adversaries interact.

Exam Probability: **Low**

24. *Answer choices:*

(see index for correct answer)

- a. Strategy
- b. Concept driven strategy
- c. Group information management
- d. Territorialist School

Guidance: level 1

:: Direct marketing ::

_________ Inc. is an American privately owned multi-level marketing company. According to Direct Selling News, _________ was the sixth largest network marketing company in the world in 2018, with a wholesale volume of US$3.25 billion. _________ is based in Addison, Texas, outside Dallas. The company was founded by _________ Ash in 1963. Richard Rogers, _________ `s son, is the chairman, and David Holl is president and was named CEO in 2006.

Exam Probability: **Medium**

25. *Answer choices:*

(see index for correct answer)

- a. International Masters Publishers
- b. Mary Kay
- c. Direct marketing
- d. Direct mail fundraising

Guidance: level 1

:: Project management ::

Some scenarios associate "this kind of planning" with learning "life skills". _________ s are necessary, or at least useful, in situations where individuals need to know what time they must be at a specific location to receive a specific service, and where people need to accomplish a set of goals within a set time period.

Exam Probability: **Medium**

26. *Answer choices:*

(see index for correct answer)

- a. Concurrent engineering
- b. Association for Project Management
- c. Operational bill
- d. Schedule

Guidance: level 1

:: Project management ::

A _________ is the approximation of the cost of a program, project, or operation. The _________ is the product of the cost estimating process. The _________ has a single total value and may have identifiable component values. A problem with a cost overrun can be avoided with a credible, reliable, and accurate _________. A cost estimator is the professional who prepares _________ s. There are different types of cost estimators, whose title may be preceded by a modifier, such as building estimator, or electrical estimator, or chief estimator. Other professionals such as quantity surveyors and cost engineers may also prepare _________ s or contribute to _________ s. In the US, according to the Bureau of Labor Statistics, there were 185,400 cost estimators in 2010. There are around 75,000 professional quantity surveyors working in the UK.

Exam Probability: **High**

27. *Answer choices:*

(see index for correct answer)

- a. Project Management Professional
- b. Cost estimate
- c. Mandated lead arranger
- d. Outcomes theory

Guidance: level 1

:: Product management ::

__________ s, also known as Shewhart charts or process-behavior charts, are a statistical process control tool used to determine if a manufacturing or business process is in a state of control.

Exam Probability: **Medium**

28. *Answer choices:*

(see index for correct answer)

- a. Trademark look
- b. Product information
- c. Discontinuation
- d. Control chart

Guidance: level 1

:: Industrial engineering ::

The __________ is the design of any task that aims to describe or explain the variation of information under conditions that are hypothesized to reflect the variation. The term is generally associated with experiments in which the design introduces conditions that directly affect the variation, but may also refer to the design of quasi-experiments, in which natural conditions that influence the variation are selected for observation.

Exam Probability: **High**

29. *Answer choices:*

(see index for correct answer)

- a. Design of experiments
- b. Richard Muther
- c. Therblig
- d. Inspection in manufacturing

Guidance: level 1

:: Production and manufacturing ::

A BOM can define products as they are designed , as they are ordered , as they are built , or as they are maintained . The different types of BOMs depend on the business need and use for which they are intended. In process industries, the BOM is also known as the formula, recipe, or ingredients list. The phrase "bill of material" is frequently used by engineers as an adjective to refer not to the literal bill, but to the current production configuration of a product, to distinguish it from modified or improved versions under study or in test.

Exam Probability: **Low**

30. *Answer choices:*

(see index for correct answer)

- a. Piece work
- b. Six Sigma
- c. Cycle time variation
- d. Bill of materials

Guidance: level 1

:: Time management ::

__________ is the process of planning and exercising conscious control of time spent on specific activities, especially to increase effectiveness, efficiency, and productivity. It involves a juggling act of various demands upon a person relating to work, social life, family, hobbies, personal interests and commitments with the finiteness of time. Using time effectively gives the person "choice" on spending/managing activities at their own time and expediency.

Exam Probability: **High**

31. *Answer choices:*

(see index for correct answer)

- a. Sufficient unto the day is the evil thereof
- b. Maestro concept
- c. Time management
- d. Time Trek

Guidance: level 1

:: Decision theory ::

_________ is a method developed in Japan beginning in 1966 to help transform the voice of the customer into engineering characteristics for a product. Yoji Akao, the original developer, described QFD as a "method to transform qualitative user demands into quantitative parameters, to deploy the functions forming quality, and to deploy methods for achieving the design quality into subsystems and component parts, and ultimately to specific elements of the manufacturing process." The author combined his work in quality assurance and quality control points with function deployment used in value engineering.

Exam Probability: **Medium**

32. *Answer choices:*

(see index for correct answer)

- a. Analysis paralysis
- b. Flipism
- c. Rational Focal Point
- d. Quality function deployment

Guidance: level 1

:: Management accounting ::

_________ are costs that are not directly accountable to a cost object . _________ may be either fixed or variable. _________ include administration, personnel and security costs. These are those costs which are not directly related to production. Some _________ may be overhead. But some overhead costs can be directly attributed to a project and are direct costs.

Exam Probability: **Low**

33. *Answer choices:*

(see index for correct answer)

- a. Indirect costs
- b. Cost driver
- c. Revenue center
- d. Certified Management Accountants of Canada

Guidance: level 1

:: Project management ::

In general usage, a _________ is a comprehensive evaluation of an individual`s current pay and future financial state by using current known variables to predict future income, asset values and withdrawal plans. This often includes a budget which organizes an individual`s finances and sometimes includes a series of steps or specific goals for spending and saving in the future. This plan allocates future income to various types of expenses, such as rent or utilities, and also reserves some income for short-term and long-term savings. A _________ is sometimes referred to as an investment plan, but in personal finance a _________ can focus on other specific areas such as risk management, estates, college, or retirement.

Exam Probability: **Low**

34. *Answer choices:*

(see index for correct answer)

- a. Integrated product team
- b. Theme-centered interaction
- c. Project network
- d. Financial plan

Guidance: level 1

:: Management ::

In organizational studies, _________ is the efficient and effective development of an organization`s resources when they are needed. Such resources may include financial resources, inventory, human skills, production resources, or information technology and natural resources.

Exam Probability: **Low**

35. *Answer choices:*

(see index for correct answer)

- a. Integrated master plan
- b. Business rule
- c. Resource management
- d. Failure demand

Guidance: level 1

:: Management ::

An _________ is a loosely coupled, self-organizing network of firms that combine their economic output to provide products and services offerings to the market. Firms in the _________ may operate independently, for example, through market mechanisms, or cooperatively through agreements and contracts. They provide value added service or product to the OEM .

Exam Probability: **Low**

36. *Answer choices:*
(see index for correct answer)

- a. Logistics support analysis
- b. Jarratt report
- c. Formula for change
- d. Social business model

Guidance: level 1

:: Production and manufacturing ::

_________ consists of organization-wide efforts to "install and make permanent climate where employees continuously improve their ability to provide on demand products and services that customers will find of particular value." "Total" emphasizes that departments in addition to production are obligated to improve their operations; "management" emphasizes that executives are obligated to actively manage quality through funding, training, staffing, and goal setting. While there is no widely agreed-upon approach, TQM efforts typically draw heavily on the previously developed tools and techniques of quality control. TQM enjoyed widespread attention during the late 1980s and early 1990s before being overshadowed by ISO 9000, Lean manufacturing, and Six Sigma.

Exam Probability: **Low**

37. *Answer choices:*
(see index for correct answer)

- a. ERPNEXT
- b. Production plan
- c. Feeder line
- d. Nuffield Tools and Gauges

Guidance: level 1

:: Fault-tolerant computer systems ::

__________ decision-making is a group decision-making process in which group members develop, and agree to support a decision in the best interest of the whole group or common goal. __________ may be defined professionally as an acceptable resolution, one that can be supported, even if not the "favourite" of each individual. It has its origin in the Latin word consensus , which is from consentio meaning literally feel together. It is used to describe both the decision and the process of reaching a decision. __________ decision-making is thus concerned with the process of deliberating and finalizing a decision, and the social, economic, legal, environmental and political effects of applying this process.

Exam Probability: **High**

38. *Answer choices:*

(see index for correct answer)

- a. Single point of failure
- b. RAID
- c. Processor array
- d. Consensus

Guidance: level 1

:: Metal heat treatments ::

__________ is a group of industrial and metalworking processes used to alter the physical, and sometimes chemical, properties of a material. The most common application is metallurgical. Heat treatments are also used in the manufacture of many other materials, such as glass. Heat treatment involves the use of heating or chilling, normally to extreme temperatures, to achieve a desired result such as hardening or softening of a material. Heat treatment techniques include annealing, case hardening, precipitation strengthening, tempering, carburizing, normalizing and quenching. It is noteworthy that while the term heat treatment applies only to processes where the heating and cooling are done for the specific purpose of altering properties intentionally, heating and cooling often occur incidentally during other manufacturing processes such as hot forming or welding.

Exam Probability: **Low**

39. *Answer choices:*

(see index for correct answer)

- a. Heat treating
- b. Carburizing
- c. Austempering
- d. Induction hardening

Guidance: level 1

:: ::

Catalysis is the process of increasing the rate of a chemical reaction by adding a substance known as a _________ , which is not consumed in the catalyzed reaction and can continue to act repeatedly. Because of this, only very small amounts of _________ are required to alter the reaction rate in principle.

Exam Probability: **Low**

40. *Answer choices:*

(see index for correct answer)

- a. hierarchical perspective
- b. empathy
- c. Catalyst
- d. similarity-attraction theory

Guidance: level 1

:: Gas technologies ::

A _________ is a device used to transfer heat between two or more fluids. _________ s are used in both cooling and heating processes. The fluids may be separated by a solid wall to prevent mixing or they may be in direct contact. They are widely used in space heating, refrigeration, air conditioning, power stations, chemical plants, petrochemical plants, petroleum refineries, natural-gas processing, and sewage treatment. The classic example of a _________ is found in an internal combustion engine in which a circulating fluid known as engine coolant flows through radiator coils and air flows past the coils, which cools the coolant and heats the incoming air. Another example is the heat sink, which is a passive _________ that transfers the heat generated by an electronic or a mechanical device to a fluid medium, often air or a liquid coolant.

Exam Probability: **High**

41. *Answer choices:*

(see index for correct answer)

- a. Gas lighting
- b. Wobbe index
- c. Mass flow sensor
- d. Heat exchanger

Guidance: level 1

:: Lean manufacturing ::

_________ is a Japanese term that means "mistake-proofing" or "inadvertent error prevention". A _________ is any mechanism in any process that helps an equipment operator avoid mistakes . Its purpose is to eliminate product defects by preventing, correcting, or drawing attention to human errors as they occur. The concept was formalised, and the term adopted, by Shigeo Shingo as part of the Toyota Production System. It was originally described as baka-yoke, but as this means "fool-proofing" the name was changed to the milder _________ .

Exam Probability: **Medium**

42. *Answer choices:*

(see index for correct answer)

- a. Lean accounting
- b. Poka-yoke
- c. Lean software development
- d. Manufacturing supermarket

Guidance: level 1

:: Management ::

_________ is the process of thinking about the activities required to achieve a desired goal. It is the first and foremost activity to achieve desired results. It involves the creation and maintenance of a plan, such as psychological aspects that require conceptual skills. There are even a couple of tests to measure someone's capability of _________ well. As such, _________ is a fundamental property of intelligent behavior. An important further meaning, often just called " _________ " is the legal context of permitted building developments.

Exam Probability: **Medium**

43. *Answer choices:*
(see index for correct answer)

- a. Planning
- b. Supplier performance management
- c. Semiconductor consolidation
- d. DMSMS

Guidance: level 1

:: ::

Some scenarios associate "this kind of planning" with learning "life skills". Schedules are necessary, or at least useful, in situations where individuals need to know what time they must be at a specific location to receive a specific service, and where people need to accomplish a set of goals within a set time period.

Exam Probability: **High**

44. *Answer choices:*
(see index for correct answer)

- a. functional perspective
- b. Scheduling
- c. personal values
- d. levels of analysis

Guidance: level 1

:: Debt ::

__________ is the trust which allows one party to provide money or resources to another party wherein the second party does not reimburse the first party immediately , but promises either to repay or return those resources at a later date. In other words, __________ is a method of making reciprocity formal, legally enforceable, and extensible to a large group of unrelated people.

Exam Probability: **Medium**

45. *Answer choices:*

(see index for correct answer)

- a. Debt-lag
- b. Credit cycle
- c. Teacher Loan Forgiveness
- d. Vulture fund

Guidance: level 1

:: Management ::

__________ is a category of business activity made possible by software tools that aim to provide customers with both independence from vendors and better means for engaging with vendors. These same tools can also apply to individuals` relations with other institutions and organizations.

Exam Probability: **Low**

46. *Answer choices:*

(see index for correct answer)

- a. Business-oriented architecture
- b. Visual learning
- c. Vendor relationship management
- d. Business process improvement

Guidance: level 1

:: Management ::

A process is a unique combination of tools, materials, methods, and people engaged in producing a measurable output; for example a manufacturing line for machine parts. All processes have inherent statistical variability which can be evaluated by statistical methods.

Exam Probability: **High**

47. *Answer choices:*

(see index for correct answer)

- a. Quick response manufacturing
- b. Court of Assistants
- c. Logistics support analysis
- d. Process capability

Guidance: level 1

:: Knowledge representation ::

__________ s are causal diagrams created by Kaoru Ishikawa that show the causes of a specific event.

Exam Probability: **High**

48. *Answer choices:*

(see index for correct answer)

- a. Knowledge value chain
- b. OntoCAPE
- c. Ishikawa diagram
- d. Futures wheel

Guidance: level 1

:: Quality awards ::

The __________ recognizes U.S. organizations in the business, health care, education, and nonprofit sectors for performance excellence. The Baldrige Award is the only formal recognition of the performance excellence of both public and private U.S. organizations given by the President of the United States. It is administered by the Baldrige Performance Excellence Program, which is based at and managed by the National Institute of Standards and Technology , an agency of the U.S. Department of Commerce.

Exam Probability: **Medium**

49. *Answer choices:*

(see index for correct answer)

- a. Rajiv Gandhi National Quality Award
- b. Philippine Quality Award
- c. Malcolm Baldrige National Quality Award
- d. Canada Awards for Excellence

Guidance: level 1

:: Natural resources ::

__________ s are resources that exist without actions of humankind. This includes all valued characteristics such as magnetic, gravitational, electrical properties and forces etc. On Earth it includes sunlight, atmosphere, water, land along with all vegetation, crops and animal life that naturally subsists upon or within the heretofore identified characteristics and substances.

Exam Probability: **Medium**

50. *Answer choices:*

(see index for correct answer)

- a. QEMSCAN
- b. Natural resource
- c. Exploitation of natural resources
- d. Soil

Guidance: level 1

:: Outsourcing ::

_________ is the practice of sourcing from the global market for goods and services across geopolitical boundaries. _________ often aims to exploit global efficiencies in the delivery of a product or service. These efficiencies include low cost skilled labor, low cost raw material and other economic factors like tax breaks and low trade tariffs. A large number of Information Technology projects and Services, including IS Applications and Mobile Apps and database services are outsourced globally to countries like Pakistan and India for more economical pricing.

Exam Probability: **Medium**

51. *Answer choices:*

(see index for correct answer)

- a. Harvey Nash
- b. Service review
- c. Transition methodology
- d. Minacs

Guidance: level 1

:: Alchemical processes ::

In chemistry, a _________ is a special type of homogeneous mixture composed of two or more substances. In such a mixture, a solute is a substance dissolved in another substance, known as a solvent. The mixing process of a _________ happens at a scale where the effects of chemical polarity are involved, resulting in interactions that are specific to solvation. The _________ assumes the phase of the solvent when the solvent is the larger fraction of the mixture, as is commonly the case. The concentration of a solute in a _________ is the mass of that solute expressed as a percentage of the mass of the whole _________. The term aqueous _________ is when one of the solvents is water.

Exam Probability: **Medium**

52. *Answer choices:*

(see index for correct answer)

- a. Fermentation in food processing
- b. Sublimation apparatus
- c. Putrefying bacteria
- d. Congelation

Guidance: level 1

:: Data management ::

_________ refers to a data-driven improvement cycle used for improving, optimizing and stabilizing business processes and designs. The _________ improvement cycle is the core tool used to drive Six Sigma projects. However, _________ is not exclusive to Six Sigma and can be used as the framework for other improvement applications.

Exam Probability: **Medium**

53. *Answer choices:*

(see index for correct answer)

- a. Match report
- b. Global concurrency control
- c. Record linkage
- d. Metadata

Guidance: level 1

:: Procurement ::

A _________ is a standard business process whose purpose is to invite suppliers into a bidding process to bid on specific products or services. RfQ generally means the same thing as Call for bids and Invitation for bid .

Exam Probability: **Low**

54. *Answer choices:*

(see index for correct answer)

- a. Euromethod
- b. Swiss challenge
- c. Request for quotation
- d. Best value procurement

Guidance: level 1

:: Supply chain management terms ::

In business and finance, _________ is a system of organizations, people, activities, information, and resources involved inmoving a product or service from supplier to customer. _________ activities involve the transformation of natural resources, raw materials, and components into a finished product that is delivered to the end customer. In sophisticated _________ systems, used products may re-enter the _________ at any point where residual value is recyclable. _________ s link value chains.

Exam Probability: **Low**

55. *Answer choices:*

(see index for correct answer)

- a. Overstock
- b. Consumables
- c. Most valuable customers
- d. inventory management

Guidance: level 1

:: Risk analysis ::

Supply-chain risk management is "the implementation of strategies to manage both everyday and exceptional risks along the supply chain based on continuous risk assessment with the objective of reducing vulnerability and ensuring continuity".

Exam Probability: **High**

56. *Answer choices:*

(see index for correct answer)

- a. Supply chain risk management
- b. MOSAIC Threat Assessment Systems
- c. The PRS Group, Inc.
- d. Wilderness Risk Management Conference

Guidance: level 1

:: Production and manufacturing ::

_________ is a comprehensive and rigorous industrial process by which a previously sold, leased, used, worn or non-functional product or part is returned to a 'like-new' or 'better-than-new' condition, from both a quality and performance perspective, through a controlled, reproducible and sustainable process.

Exam Probability: **Medium**

57. *Answer choices:*
(see index for correct answer)

- a. Remanufacturing
- b. Computer-aided process planning
- c. Six Sigma
- d. Piece work

Guidance: level 1

:: Marketing techniques ::

A _________ is an award to be given to a person, a group of people like a sports team, or organization to recognise and reward actions or achievements. Official _________ s often involve monetary rewards as well as the fame that comes with them. Some _________ s are also associated with extravagant awarding ceremonies, such as the Academy Awards.

Exam Probability: **Low**

58. *Answer choices:*
(see index for correct answer)

- a. Beauty whitewash
- b. Stunt casting
- c. Faith-based marketing
- d. As seen on TV

Guidance: level 1

:: Industrial organization ::

In economics, specifically general equilibrium theory, a perfect market is defined by several idealizing conditions, collectively called _________ . In theoretical models where conditions of _________ hold, it has been theoretically demonstrated that a market will reach an equilibrium in which the quantity supplied for every product or service, including labor, equals the quantity demanded at the current price. This equilibrium would be a Pareto optimum.

Exam Probability: **High**

59. *Answer choices:*

(see index for correct answer)

- a. Tapered integration
- b. Switching cost
- c. Organizational studies
- d. Perfect competition

Guidance: level 1

Commerce

Commerce relates to "the exchange of goods and services, especially on a large scale." It includes legal, economic, political, social, cultural and technological systems that operate in any country or internationally.

:: Market structure and pricing ::

_________ has historically emerged in two separate types of discussions in economics, that of Adam Smith on the one hand, and that of Karl Marx on the other hand. Adam Smith in his writing on economics stressed the importance of laissez-faire principles outlining the operation of the market in the absence of dominant political mechanisms of control, while Karl Marx discussed the working of the market in the presence of a controlled economy sometimes referred to as a command economy in the literature. Both types of _________ have been in historical evidence throughout the twentieth century and twenty-first century.

Exam Probability: **Medium**

1. *Answer choices:*

(see index for correct answer)

- a. Installed base
- b. industry concentration
- c. Open source
- d. Market structure

Guidance: level 1

:: Business models ::

A _________ is "an autonomous association of persons united voluntarily to meet their common economic, social, and cultural needs and aspirations through a jointly-owned and democratically-controlled enterprise". _________ s may include.

Exam Probability: **High**

2. *Answer choices:*

(see index for correct answer)

- a. Cooperative
- b. Strategy map
- c. Micro-enterprise
- d. Volatility, uncertainty, complexity and ambiguity

Guidance: level 1

:: Fraud ::

In law, _________ is intentional deception to secure unfair or unlawful gain, or to deprive a victim of a legal right. _________ can violate civil law , a criminal law , or it may cause no loss of money, property or legal right but still be an element of another civil or criminal wrong. The purpose of _________ may be monetary gain or other benefits, for example by obtaining a passport, travel document, or driver`s license, or mortgage _________ , where the perpetrator may attempt to qualify for a mortgage by way of false statements.

Exam Probability: **Medium**

3. *Answer choices:*

(see index for correct answer)

- a. Fraud
- b. Wangiri
- c. Lottery scam
- d. Shell corporation

Guidance: level 1

:: Auctioneering ::

Unlike sealed-bid auctions , an _________ is "open" or fully transparent, as the identity of all bidders is disclosed to each other during the auction. More generally, an auction mechanism is considered "English" if it involves an iterative process of adjusting the price in a direction that is unfavorable to the bidders . In contrast, a Dutch auction would adjust the price in a direction that favored the bidders .

Exam Probability: **High**

4. *Answer choices:*

(see index for correct answer)

- a. English auction
- b. Auction chant
- c. The Ohio Auction School
- d. Dutch auction

Guidance: level 1

:: ::

_________ is the exchange of capital, goods, and services across international borders or territories.

Exam Probability: **Low**

5. *Answer choices:*

(see index for correct answer)

- a. similarity-attraction theory
- b. Sarbanes-Oxley act of 2002
- c. hierarchical
- d. International trade

Guidance: level 1

:: ::

The Walt _________ Company, commonly known as Walt _________ or simply _________ , is an American diversified multinational mass media and entertainment conglomerate headquartered at the Walt _________ Studios in Burbank, California.

Exam Probability: **Low**

6. *Answer choices:*

(see index for correct answer)

- a. interpersonal communication
- b. Disney
- c. process perspective
- d. hierarchical perspective

Guidance: level 1

:: Stock market ::

The _________ of a corporation is all of the shares into which ownership of the corporation is divided. In American English, the shares are commonly known as " _________ s". A single share of the _________ represents fractional ownership of the corporation in proportion to the total number of shares. This typically entitles the _________ holder to that fraction of the company's earnings, proceeds from liquidation of assets , or voting power, often dividing these up in proportion to the amount of money each _________ holder has invested. Not all _________ is necessarily equal, as certain classes of _________ may be issued for example without voting rights, with enhanced voting rights, or with a certain priority to receive profits or liquidation proceeds before or after other classes of shareholders.

Exam Probability: **High**

7. *Answer choices:*

(see index for correct answer)

- a. Correlation trading
- b. Registered share
- c. No-par stock
- d. Stock

Guidance: level 1

:: ::

Walter Elias Disney was an American entrepreneur, animator, voice actor and film producer. A pioneer of the American animation industry, he introduced several developments in the production of cartoons. As a film producer, Disney holds the record for most Academy Awards earned by an individual, having won 22 Oscars from 59 nominations. He was presented with two Golden Globe Special Achievement Awards and an Emmy Award, among other honors. Several of his films are included in the National Film Registry by the Library of Congress.

Exam Probability: **Medium**

8. *Answer choices:*

(see index for correct answer)

- a. Walt Disney
- b. surface-level diversity
- c. levels of analysis
- d. functional perspective

Guidance: level 1

:: Dot-com bubble ::

Yahoo! _________ was a web hosting service. It was founded in November 1994 by David Bohnett and John Rezner, and was called Beverly Hills Internet for a very short time before being named _________ .

Exam Probability: **High**

9. *Answer choices:*

(see index for correct answer)

- a. Dot-com bubble
- b. Excite
- c. Beenz
- d. GeoCities

Guidance: level 1

:: Costs ::

In economics, _________ is the total economic cost of production and is made up of variable cost, which varies according to the quantity of a good produced and includes inputs such as labour and raw materials, plus fixed cost, which is independent of the quantity of a good produced and includes inputs that cannot be varied in the short term: fixed costs such as buildings and machinery, including sunk costs if any. Since cost is measured per unit of time, it is a flow variable.

Exam Probability: **High**

10. *Answer choices:*

(see index for correct answer)

- a. Khozraschyot
- b. Total cost
- c. Total cost of acquisition
- d. Average variable cost

Guidance: level 1

:: ::

A _________ is a professional who provides expert advice in a particular area such as security , management, education, accountancy, law, human resources, marketing , finance, engineering, science or any of many other specialized fields.

Exam Probability: **Low**

11. *Answer choices:*

(see index for correct answer)

- a. cultural
- b. Consultant
- c. imperative
- d. Sarbanes-Oxley act of 2002

Guidance: level 1

:: Computer access control ::

_________ is the act of confirming the truth of an attribute of a single piece of data claimed true by an entity. In contrast with identification, which refers to the act of stating or otherwise indicating a claim purportedly attesting to a person or thing`s identity, _________ is the process of actually confirming that identity. It might involve confirming the identity of a person by validating their identity documents, verifying the authenticity of a website with a digital certificate, determining the age of an artifact by carbon dating, or ensuring that a product is what its packaging and labeling claim to be. In other words, _________ often involves verifying the validity of at least one form of identification.

Exam Probability: **Medium**

12. *Answer choices:*

(see index for correct answer)

- a. Delegated administration
- b. OAuth
- c. Identity provider
- d. Mutual authentication

Guidance: level 1

:: ::

_________ is a concept of English common law and is a necessity for simple contracts but not for special contracts . The concept has been adopted by other common law jurisdictions, including the US.

Exam Probability: **Low**

13. *Answer choices:*

(see index for correct answer)

- a. Consideration
- b. hierarchical
- c. personal values
- d. deep-level diversity

Guidance: level 1

:: Marketing ::

_________ is the percentage of a market accounted for by a specific entity. In a survey of nearly 200 senior marketing managers, 67% responded that they found the revenue- "dollar _________ " metric very useful, while 61% found "unit _________ " very useful.

Exam Probability: **High**

14. *Answer choices:*

(see index for correct answer)

- a. Mass customization
- b. Place branding
- c. Business stature
- d. Pick and pack

Guidance: level 1

:: Supply chain management ::

A _________ is a type of auction in which the traditional roles of buyer and seller are reversed. Thus, there is one buyer and many potential sellers. In an ordinary auction , buyers compete to obtain goods or services by offering increasingly higher prices. In contrast, in a _________ , the sellers compete to obtain business from the buyer and prices will typically decrease as the sellers underbid each other.

Exam Probability: **High**

15. *Answer choices:*

(see index for correct answer)

- a. Reverse auction
- b. Keith Oliver
- c. Pacific Access
- d. Supply-chain operations reference

Guidance: level 1

:: Economic globalization ::

__________ is an agreement in which one company hires another company to be responsible for a planned or existing activity that is or could be done internally,and sometimes involves transferring employees and assets from one firm to another.

Exam Probability: **Low**

16. *Answer choices:*

(see index for correct answer)

- a. global financial
- b. reshoring

Guidance: level 1

:: ::

Advertising is a marketing communication that employs an openly sponsored, non-personal message to promote or sell a product, service or idea. Sponsors of advertising are typically businesses wishing to promote their products or services. Advertising is differentiated from public relations in that an advertiser pays for and has control over the message. It differs from personal selling in that the message is non-personal, i.e., not directed to a particular individual.Advertising is communicated through various mass media, including traditional media such as newspapers, magazines, television, radio, outdoor advertising or direct mail; and new media such as search results, blogs, social media, websites or text messages. The actual presentation of the message in a medium is referred to as an __________, or "ad" or advert for short.

Exam Probability: **Low**

17. *Answer choices:*

(see index for correct answer)

- a. open system
- b. hierarchical
- c. information systems assessment
- d. Advertisement

Guidance: level 1

:: Income ::

In business and accounting, net income is an entity`s income minus cost of goods sold, expenses and taxes for an accounting period. It is computed as the residual of all revenues and gains over all expenses and losses for the period, and has also been defined as the net increase in shareholders` equity that results from a company`s operations. In the context of the presentation of financial statements, the IFRS Foundation defines net income as synonymous with profit and loss. The difference between revenue and the cost of making a product or providing a service, before deducting overheads, payroll, taxation, and interest payments. This is different from operating income .

Exam Probability: **High**

18. *Answer choices:*

(see index for correct answer)

- a. Implied level of government service
- b. Return of investment
- c. Signing bonus
- d. Bottom line

Guidance: level 1

:: Credit cards ::

The ________ Company, also known as Amex, is an American multinational financial services corporation headquartered in Three World Financial Center in New York City. The company was founded in 1850 and is one of the 30 components of the Dow Jones Industrial Average. The company is best known for its charge card, credit card, and traveler`s cheque businesses.

Exam Probability: **High**

19. *Answer choices:*

(see index for correct answer)

- a. Centurion Card
- b. American Express
- c. CardIt
- d. Payoneer

Guidance: level 1

:: ::

_________ is an American restaurant chain and international franchise which was founded in 1958 by Dan and Frank Carney. The company is known for its Italian-American cuisine menu, including pizza and pasta, as well as side dishes and desserts. _________ has 18,431 restaurants worldwide as of December 31, 2018, making it the world`s largest pizza chain in terms of locations. It is a subsidiary of Yum! Brands, Inc., one of the world`s largest restaurant companies.

Exam Probability: **High**

20. *Answer choices:*

(see index for correct answer)

- a. imperative
- b. Pizza Hut
- c. process perspective
- d. co-culture

Guidance: level 1

:: Business terms ::

The _________ or reception is an area where visitors arrive and first encounter a staff at a place of business. _________ staff will deal with whatever question the visitor has and put them in contact with a relevant person at the company. Broadly speaking, the _________ includes roles that affect the revenues of the business. The term _________ is in contrast to the term back office which refers to a company`s operations, personnel, accounting, payroll and financial departments which do not interact directly with customers.

Exam Probability: **Medium**

21. *Answer choices:*

(see index for correct answer)

- a. Mission statement
- b. Strategic partner
- c. back office
- d. Front office

Guidance: level 1

:: ::

A _________ is a sworn body of people convened to render an impartial verdict officially submitted to them by a court, or to set a penalty or judgment. Modern juries tend to be found in courts to ascertain the guilt or lack thereof in a crime. In Anglophone jurisdictions, the verdict may be guilty or not guilty . The old institution of grand juries still exists in some places, particularly the United States, to investigate whether enough evidence of a crime exists to bring someone to trial.

Exam Probability: **Low**

22. *Answer choices:*

(see index for correct answer)

- a. deep-level diversity
- b. Character
- c. hierarchical perspective
- d. Jury

Guidance: level 1

:: ::

A _________ is an individual or institution that legally owns one or more shares of stock in a public or private corporation. _________ s may be referred to as members of a corporation. Legally, a person is not a _________ in a corporation until their name and other details are entered in the corporation`s register of _________ s or members.

Exam Probability: **Low**

23. *Answer choices:*

(see index for correct answer)

- a. similarity-attraction theory
- b. Sarbanes-Oxley act of 2002
- c. functional perspective
- d. surface-level diversity

Guidance: level 1

:: ::

In law, a __________ is a coming together of parties to a dispute, to present information in a tribunal, a formal setting with the authority to adjudicate claims or disputes. One form of tribunal is a court. The tribunal, which may occur before a judge, jury, or other designated trier of fact, aims to achieve a resolution to their dispute.

Exam Probability: **High**

24. *Answer choices:*

(see index for correct answer)

- a. co-culture
- b. Sarbanes-Oxley act of 2002
- c. process perspective
- d. personal values

Guidance: level 1

:: ::

__________, or auditory perception, is the ability to perceive sounds by detecting vibrations, changes in the pressure of the surrounding medium through time, through an organ such as the ear. The academic field concerned with __________ is auditory science.

Exam Probability: **Low**

25. *Answer choices:*

(see index for correct answer)

- a. cultural
- b. open system
- c. hierarchical
- d. empathy

Guidance: level 1

:: Minimum wage ::

A _________ is the lowest remuneration that employers can legally pay their workers—the price floor below which workers may not sell their labor. Most countries had introduced _________ legislation by the end of the 20th century.

Exam Probability: **Low**

26. *Answer choices:*

(see index for correct answer)

- a. Minimum Wage Fairness Act
- b. Minimum wage
- c. Guaranteed minimum income
- d. Minimum wage in the United States

Guidance: level 1

:: Human resource management ::

_________ are the people who make up the workforce of an organization, business sector, or economy. "Human capital" is sometimes used synonymously with " _________ ", although human capital typically refers to a narrower effect . Likewise, other terms sometimes used include manpower, talent, labor, personnel, or simply people.

Exam Probability: **Medium**

27. *Answer choices:*

(see index for correct answer)

- a. Human resource consulting
- b. Contractor management
- c. Talent management system
- d. Cross-training

Guidance: level 1

:: ::

_________ refers to a business or organization attempting to acquire goods or services to accomplish its goals. Although there are several organizations that attempt to set standards in the _________ process, processes can vary greatly between organizations. Typically the word " _________ " is not used interchangeably with the word "procurement", since procurement typically includes expediting, supplier quality, and transportation and logistics in addition to _________ .

Exam Probability: **High**

28. *Answer choices:*

(see index for correct answer)

- a. deep-level diversity
- b. levels of analysis
- c. information systems assessment
- d. functional perspective

Guidance: level 1

:: Stock market ::

_________ is freedom from, or resilience against, potential harm caused by others. Beneficiaries of _________ may be of persons and social groups, objects and institutions, ecosystems or any other entity or phenomenon vulnerable to unwanted change by its environment.

Exam Probability: **High**

29. *Answer choices:*

(see index for correct answer)

- a. House stock
- b. Security
- c. Follow-on offering
- d. All or none

Guidance: level 1

:: Monopoly (economics) ::

A _________ exists when a specific person or enterprise is the only supplier of a particular commodity. This contrasts with a monopsony which relates to a single entity`s control of a market to purchase a good or service, and with oligopoly which consists of a few sellers dominating a market. Monopolies are thus characterized by a lack of economic competition to produce the good or service, a lack of viable substitute goods, and the possibility of a high _________ price well above the seller`s marginal cost that leads to a high _________ profit. The verb monopolise or monopolize refers to the process by which a company gains the ability to raise prices or exclude competitors. In economics, a _________ is a single seller. In law, a _________ is a business entity that has significant market power, that is, the power to charge overly high prices. Although monopolies may be big businesses, size is not a characteristic of a _________ . A small business may still have the power to raise prices in a small industry .

Exam Probability: **Medium**

30. *Answer choices:*

(see index for correct answer)

- a. Dominance
- b. Monopoly
- c. Herfindahl index
- d. Concentration ratio

Guidance: level 1

:: ::

A _________ is a person who trades in commodities produced by other people. Historically, a _________ is anyone who is involved in business or trade. _________ s have operated for as long as industry, commerce, and trade have existed. During the 16th-century, in Europe, two different terms for _________ s emerged: One term, meerseniers, described local traders such as bakers, grocers, etc.; while a new term, koopman (Dutch: koopman, described _________ s who operated on a global stage, importing and exporting goods over vast distances, and offering added-value services such as credit and finance.

Exam Probability: **Low**

31. *Answer choices:*

(see index for correct answer)

- a. process perspective
- b. functional perspective
- c. interpersonal communication
- d. corporate values

Guidance: level 1

:: ::

The __________ is a political and economic union of 28 member states that are located primarily in Europe. It has an area of 4,475,757 km2 and an estimated population of about 513 million. The EU has developed an internal single market through a standardised system of laws that apply in all member states in those matters, and only those matters, where members have agreed to act as one. EU policies aim to ensure the free movement of people, goods, services and capital within the internal market, enact legislation in justice and home affairs and maintain common policies on trade, agriculture, fisheries and regional development. For travel within the Schengen Area, passport controls have been abolished. A monetary union was established in 1999 and came into full force in 2002 and is composed of 19 EU member states which use the euro currency.

Exam Probability: **High**

32. *Answer choices:*

(see index for correct answer)

- a. cultural
- b. Character
- c. functional perspective
- d. empathy

Guidance: level 1

:: Price fixing convictions ::

_________ is the flag carrier airline of the United Kingdom, headquartered at Waterside, Harmondsworth. It is the second largest airline in the United Kingdom, based on fleet size and passengers carried, behind easyJet. The airline is based in Waterside near its main hub at London Heathrow Airport. In January 2011 BA merged with Iberia, creating the International Airlines Group , a holding company registered in Madrid, Spain. IAG is the world's third-largest airline group in terms of annual revenue and the second-largest in Europe. It is listed on the London Stock Exchange and in the FTSE 100 Index. _________ is the first passenger airline to have generated more than $1 billion on a single air route in a year .

Exam Probability: **Low**

33. *Answer choices:*

(see index for correct answer)

- a. Christmas tree production in Denmark
- b. Hoffmann-La Roche
- c. British Airways
- d. Heineken International

Guidance: level 1

:: ::

In legal terminology, a _________ is any formal legal document that sets out the facts and legal reasons that the filing party or parties believes are sufficient to support a claim against the party or parties against whom the claim is brought that entitles the plaintiff to a remedy . For example, the Federal Rules of Civil Procedure that govern civil litigation in United States courts provide that a civil action is commenced with the filing or service of a pleading called a _________ . Civil court rules in states that have incorporated the Federal Rules of Civil Procedure use the same term for the same pleading.

Exam Probability: **High**

34. *Answer choices:*

(see index for correct answer)

- a. Character
- b. cultural
- c. corporate values

- d. Complaint

Guidance: level 1

:: Business law ::

A __________ is a business entity created by two or more parties, generally characterized by shared ownership, shared returns and risks, and shared governance. Companies typically pursue __________ s for one of four reasons: to access a new market, particularly emerging markets; to gain scale efficiencies by combining assets and operations; to share risk for major investments or projects; or to access skills and capabilities.

Exam Probability: **Low**

35. *Answer choices:*

(see index for correct answer)

- a. Joint venture
- b. Practicing without a license
- c. Limited liability company
- d. OHADA

Guidance: level 1

:: Information retrieval ::

__________ is a technique used by recommender systems. __________ has two senses, a narrow one and a more general one.

Exam Probability: **Low**

36. *Answer choices:*

(see index for correct answer)

- a. Binary Independence Model
- b. Cosine similarity
- c. GLIMPSE
- d. Collaborative filtering

Guidance: level 1

:: Information technology management ::

__________ s or pop-ups are forms of online advertising on the World Wide Web. A pop-up is a graphical user interface display area, usually a small window, that suddenly appears in the foreground of the visual interface. The pop-up window containing an advertisement is usually generated by JavaScript that uses cross-site scripting , sometimes with a secondary payload that uses Adobe Flash. They can also be generated by other vulnerabilities/security holes in browser security.

Exam Probability: **High**

37. *Answer choices:*

(see index for correct answer)

- a. Knowledge management software
- b. Pop-up ad
- c. Electronic document and records management system
- d. Trustworthy computing

Guidance: level 1

:: Management ::

__________ is a process by which entities review the quality of all factors involved in production. ISO 9000 defines __________ as "A part of quality management focused on fulfilling quality requirements".

Exam Probability: **Medium**

38. *Answer choices:*

(see index for correct answer)

- a. Defensive expenditures
- b. Complementary assets
- c. Power structure
- d. Quality control

Guidance: level 1

:: ::

According to the philosopher Piyush Mathur , "Tangibility is the property that a phenomenon exhibits if it has and/or transports mass and/or energy and/or momentum".

Exam Probability: **Low**

39. *Answer choices:*

(see index for correct answer)

- a. Sarbanes-Oxley act of 2002
- b. Tangible
- c. Character
- d. information systems assessment

Guidance: level 1

:: Management accounting ::

__________ , or dollar contribution per unit, is the selling price per unit minus the variable cost per unit. "Contribution" represents the portion of sales revenue that is not consumed by variable costs and so contributes to the coverage of fixed costs. This concept is one of the key building blocks of break-even analysis.

Exam Probability: **Medium**

40. *Answer choices:*

(see index for correct answer)

- a. Contribution margin
- b. Double counting
- c. Direct material usage variance
- d. Cost driver

Guidance: level 1

:: E-commerce ::

__________ is the business-to-business or business-to-consumer or business-to-government purchase and sale of supplies, work, and services through the Internet as well as other information and networking systems, such as electronic data interchange and enterprise resource planning.

Exam Probability: **High**

41. *Answer choices:*

(see index for correct answer)

- a. Debit card
- b. Virtual workplace
- c. Video commerce
- d. Mobile commerce

Guidance: level 1

:: Hospitality industry ::

_________ refers to the relationship between a guest and a host, wherein the host receives the guest with goodwill, including the reception and entertainment of guests, visitors, or strangers. Louis, chevalier de Jaucourt describes _________ in the Encyclopédie as the virtue of a great soul that cares for the whole universe through the ties of humanity.

Exam Probability: **High**

42. *Answer choices:*

(see index for correct answer)

- a. Cover charge
- b. Restaurant rating
- c. Restaurant ware
- d. Hospitality

Guidance: level 1

:: Auctioneering ::

A _________ is one of several similar kinds of auctions. Most commonly, it means an auction in which the auctioneer begins with a high asking price, and lowers it until some participant accepts the price, or it reaches a predetermined reserve price. This has also been called a clock auction or open-outcry descending-price auction. This type of auction is good for auctioning goods quickly, since a sale never requires more than one bid. Strategically, it`s similar to a first-price sealed-bid auction.

Exam Probability: **Low**

43. *Answer choices:*

(see index for correct answer)

- a. Online trading community
- b. Dutch auction
- c. Auction
- d. How Much Wood Would a Woodchuck Chuck

Guidance: level 1

:: Summary statistics ::

_________ is the number of occurrences of a repeating event per unit of time. It is also referred to as temporal _________ , which emphasizes the contrast to spatial _________ and angular _________ . The period is the duration of time of one cycle in a repeating event, so the period is the reciprocal of the _________ . For example: if a newborn baby's heart beats at a _________ of 120 times a minute, its period—the time interval between beats—is half a second . _________ is an important parameter used in science and engineering to specify the rate of oscillatory and vibratory phenomena, such as mechanical vibrations, audio signals , radio waves, and light.

Exam Probability: **High**

44. *Answer choices:*

(see index for correct answer)

- a. weighted mean
- b. Generalized entropy index
- c. Summary statistics
- d. Scan statistic

Guidance: level 1

:: Management ::

In business, a _________ is the attribute that allows an organization to outperform its competitors. A _________ may include access to natural resources, such as high-grade ores or a low-cost power source, highly skilled labor, geographic location, high entry barriers, and access to new technology.

Exam Probability: **High**

45. *Answer choices:*

(see index for correct answer)

- a. Outrage constraint
- b. Oriental management
- c. Records manager
- d. Quality, cost, delivery

Guidance: level 1

:: Production economics ::

In microeconomics, _________ are the cost advantages that enterprises obtain due to their scale of operation , with cost per unit of output decreasing with increasing scale.

Exam Probability: **Low**

46. *Answer choices:*

(see index for correct answer)

- a. Foundations of Economic Analysis
- b. Total factor productivity
- c. Economies of scale
- d. Socially optimal firm size

Guidance: level 1

:: E-commerce ::

_________ is the activity of buying or selling of products on online services or over the Internet. Electronic commerce draws on technologies such as mobile commerce, electronic funds transfer, supply chain management, Internet marketing, online transaction processing, electronic data interchange , inventory management systems, and automated data collection systems.

Exam Probability: **High**

47. *Answer choices:*

(see index for correct answer)

- a. Social commerce
- b. Triton
- c. Online locator service
- d. Center for the Connected Consumer

Guidance: level 1

:: Production economics ::

In economics and related disciplines, a _________ is a cost in making any economic trade when participating in a market.

Exam Probability: **Low**

48. *Answer choices:*

(see index for correct answer)

- a. Transaction cost
- b. Total factor productivity
- c. Factor price
- d. Limiting factor

Guidance: level 1

:: ::

_________ s is the linguistic and philosophical study of meaning, in language, programming languages, formal logics, and semiotics. It is concerned with the relationship between signifiers—like words, phrases, signs, and symbols—and what they stand for in reality, their denotation.

Exam Probability: **Medium**

49. *Answer choices:*

(see index for correct answer)

- a. empathy
- b. Sarbanes-Oxley act of 2002
- c. process perspective
- d. surface-level diversity

Guidance: level 1

:: Marketing ::

_________ or stock is the goods and materials that a business holds for the ultimate goal of resale .

Exam Probability: **Medium**

50. *Answer choices:*

(see index for correct answer)

- a. Inventory
- b. Interactive collateral management
- c. Digital omnivore
- d. Content marketing

Guidance: level 1

:: Debt ::

__________ , in finance and economics, is payment from a borrower or deposit-taking financial institution to a lender or depositor of an amount above repayment of the principal sum , at a particular rate. It is distinct from a fee which the borrower may pay the lender or some third party. It is also distinct from dividend which is paid by a company to its shareholders from its profit or reserve, but not at a particular rate decided beforehand, rather on a pro rata basis as a share in the reward gained by risk taking entrepreneurs when the revenue earned exceeds the total costs.

Exam Probability: **High**

51. *Answer choices:*

(see index for correct answer)

- a. Paid outside closing
- b. Interest
- c. Debit note
- d. Cohort default rate

Guidance: level 1

:: ::

__________ is both a research area and a practical skill encompassing the ability of an individual or organization to "lead" or guide other individuals, teams, or entire organizations. Specialist literature debates various viewpoints, contrasting Eastern and Western approaches to __________ , and also United States versus European approaches. U.S. academic environments define __________ as "a process of social influence in which a person can enlist the aid and support of others in the accomplishment of a common task".

Exam Probability: **Low**

52. *Answer choices:*

(see index for correct answer)

- a. functional perspective
- b. Leadership
- c. corporate values
- d. information systems assessment

Guidance: level 1

:: ::

In financial markets, a share is a unit used as mutual funds, limited partnerships, and real estate investment trusts. The owner of _________ in the corporation/company is a shareholder of the corporation. A share is an indivisible unit of capital, expressing the ownership relationship between the company and the shareholder. The denominated value of a share is its face value, and the total of the face value of issued _________ represent the capital of a company, which may not reflect the market value of those _________ .

Exam Probability: **Medium**

53. *Answer choices:*

(see index for correct answer)

- a. imperative
- b. Shares
- c. functional perspective
- d. open system

Guidance: level 1

:: ::

_________ is the administration of an organization, whether it is a business, a not-for-profit organization, or government body. _________ includes the activities of setting the strategy of an organization and coordinating the efforts of its employees to accomplish its objectives through the application of available resources, such as financial, natural, technological, and human resources. The term " _________ " may also refer to those people who manage an organization.

Exam Probability: **Medium**

54. *Answer choices:*

(see index for correct answer)

- a. process perspective
- b. Management
- c. cultural
- d. levels of analysis

Guidance: level 1

:: Free market ::

In economics, a _________ is a system in which the prices for goods and services are determined by the open market and by consumers. In a _________ , the laws and forces of supply and demand are free from any intervention by a government or other authority and from all forms of economic privilege, monopolies and artificial scarcities. Proponents of the concept of _________ contrast it with a regulated market in which a government intervenes in supply and demand through various methods, such as tariffs, used to restrict trade and to protect the local economy. In an idealized free-market economy, prices for goods and services are set freely by the forces of supply and demand and are allowed to reach their point of equilibrium without intervention by government policy.

Exam Probability: **High**

55. *Answer choices:*

(see index for correct answer)

- a. Piece rate
- b. Regulated market

Guidance: level 1

:: Statutory law ::

_________ or statute law is written law set down by a body of legislature or by a singular legislator . This is as opposed to oral or customary law; or regulatory law promulgated by the executive or common law of the judiciary. Statutes may originate with national, state legislatures or local municipalities.

Exam Probability: **Medium**

56. *Answer choices:*

(see index for correct answer)

- a. Statutory law
- b. ratification
- c. Statute of repose
- d. statute law

Guidance: level 1

:: Decision theory ::

Within economics the concept of _________ is used to model worth or value, but its usage has evolved significantly over time. The term was introduced initially as a measure of pleasure or satisfaction within the theory of utilitarianism by moral philosophers such as Jeremy Bentham and John Stuart Mill. But the term has been adapted and reapplied within neoclassical economics, which dominates modern economic theory, as a _________ function that represents a consumer's preference ordering over a choice set. As such, it is devoid of its original interpretation as a measurement of the pleasure or satisfaction obtained by the consumer from that choice.

Exam Probability: **High**

57. *Answer choices:*

(see index for correct answer)

- a. Expected value of perfect information
- b. Utility
- c. Risk function
- d. Rational planning model

Guidance: level 1

:: ::

In logic and philosophy, an _________ is a series of statements , called the premises or premisses , intended to determine the degree of truth of another statement, the conclusion. The logical form of an _________ in a natural language can be represented in a symbolic formal language, and independently of natural language formally defined " _________ s" can be made in math and computer science.

Exam Probability: **Low**

58. *Answer choices:*

(see index for correct answer)

- a. Argument
- b. similarity-attraction theory
- c. process perspective
- d. deep-level diversity

Guidance: level 1

:: ::

An _________ is a systematic and independent examination of books, accounts, statutory records, documents and vouchers of an organization to ascertain how far the financial statements as well as non-financial disclosures present a true and fair view of the concern. It also attempts to ensure that the books of accounts are properly maintained by the concern as required by law. _________ ing has become such a ubiquitous phenomenon in the corporate and the public sector that academics started identifying an " _________ Society". The _________ or perceives and recognises the propositions before them for examination, obtains evidence, evaluates the same and formulates an opinion on the basis of his judgement which is communicated through their _________ ing report.

Exam Probability: **Low**

59. *Answer choices:*

(see index for correct answer)

- a. Audit
- b. corporate values
- c. hierarchical
- d. cultural

Guidance: level 1

Business ethics

Business ethics (also known as corporate ethics) is a form of applied ethics or professional ethics, that examines ethical principles and moral or ethical problems that can arise in a business environment. It applies to all aspects of business conduct and is relevant to the conduct of individuals and entire organizations. These ethics originate from individuals, organizational statements or from the legal system. These norms, values, ethical, and unethical practices are what is used to guide business. They help those businesses maintain a better connection with their stakeholders.

:: ::

Bernard Lawrence _________ is an American former market maker, investment advisor, financier, fraudster, and convicted felon, who is currently serving a federal prison sentence for offenses related to a massive Ponzi scheme. He is the former non-executive chairman of the NASDAQ stock market, the confessed operator of the largest Ponzi scheme in world history, and the largest financial fraud in U.S. history. Prosecutors estimated the fraud to be worth $64.8 billion based on the amounts in the accounts of _________ `s 4,800 clients as of November 30, 2008.

Exam Probability: **High**

1. *Answer choices:*

(see index for correct answer)

- a. surface-level diversity
- b. cultural
- c. Madoff
- d. imperative

Guidance: level 1

:: Workplace ::

In business management, _________ is a management style whereby a manager closely observes and/or controls the work of his/her subordinates or employees.

Exam Probability: **High**

2. *Answer choices:*

(see index for correct answer)

- a. Workplace revenge
- b. Control freak
- c. Feminisation of the workplace
- d. 360-degree feedback

Guidance: level 1

:: ::

_________ is a product prepared from the leaves of the _________ plant by curing them. The plant is part of the genus Nicotiana and of the Solanaceae family. While more than 70 species of _________ are known, the chief commercial crop is N. tabacum. The more potent variant N. rustica is also used around the world.

Exam Probability: **Low**

3. *Answer choices:*

(see index for correct answer)

- a. Sarbanes-Oxley act of 2002
- b. co-culture
- c. Tobacco
- d. imperative

Guidance: level 1

:: Anti-Revisionism ::

__________ , officially the German Democratic Republic , was a country that existed from 1949 to 1990, when the eastern portion of Germany was part of the Eastern Bloc during the Cold War. It described itself as a socialist "workers` and peasants` state", and the territory was administered and occupied by Soviet forces at the end of World War II — the Soviet Occupation Zone of the Potsdam Agreement, bounded on the east by the Oder–Neisse line. The Soviet zone surrounded West Berlin but did not include it; as a result, West Berlin remained outside the jurisdiction of the GDR.

Exam Probability: **Low**

4. *Answer choices:*

(see index for correct answer)

- a. Hoxhaism
- b. Chilean Communist Party
- c. Ho Chi Minh Thought
- d. East Germany

Guidance: level 1

:: Majority–minority relations ::

It was established as axiomatic in anthropological research by Franz Boas in the first few decades of the 20th century and later popularized by his students. Boas first articulated the idea in 1887: "civilization is not something absolute, but ... is relative, and ... our ideas and conceptions are true only so far as our civilization goes". However, Boas did not coin the term.

Exam Probability: **Medium**

5. *Answer choices:*

(see index for correct answer)

- a. cultural dissonance
- b. Affirmative action
- c. positive discrimination

Guidance: level 1

:: ::

The Catholic Church, also known as the Roman Catholic Church, is the largest Christian church, with approximately 1.3 billion baptised Catholics worldwide as of 2017. As the world's oldest continuously functioning international institution, it has played a prominent role in the history and development of Western civilisation. The church is headed by the Bishop of Rome, known as the pope. Its central administration, the Holy See, is in the Vatican City, an enclave within the city of Rome in Italy.

Exam Probability: **Medium**

6. *Answer choices:*

(see index for correct answer)

- a. co-culture
- b. information systems assessment
- c. Catholicism
- d. surface-level diversity

Guidance: level 1

:: Public relations terminology ::

_________ , also called "green sheen", is a form of spin in which green PR or green marketing is deceptively used to promote the perception that an organization's products, aims or policies are environmentally friendly. Evidence that an organization is _________ often comes from pointing out the spending differences: when significantly more money or time has been spent advertising being "green" , than is actually spent on environmentally sound practices. _________ efforts can range from changing the name or label of a product to evoke the natural environment on a product that contains harmful chemicals to multimillion-dollar marketing campaigns portraying highly polluting energy companies as eco-friendly.Publicized accusations of _________ have contributed to the term's increasing use.

Exam Probability: **Medium**

7. *Answer choices:*

(see index for correct answer)

- a. PR Gallery
- b. Junk science
- c. Greenwashing
- d. Corporate pathos

Guidance: level 1

:: ::

The _________ of 1977 is a United States federal law known primarily for two of its main provisions: one that addresses accounting transparency requirements under the Securities Exchange Act of 1934 and another concerning bribery of foreign officials. The Act was amended in 1988 and in 1998, and has been subject to continued congressional concerns, namely whether its enforcement discourages U.S. companies from investing abroad.

Exam Probability: **Low**

8. *Answer choices:*

(see index for correct answer)

- a. Foreign Corrupt Practices Act
- b. co-culture
- c. hierarchical
- d. interpersonal communication

Guidance: level 1

:: Environmental economics ::

__________ is an institutional arrangement designed to help producers in developing countries achieve better trading conditions. Members of the __________ movement advocate the payment of higher prices to exporters, as well as improved social and environmental standards. The movement focuses in particular on commodities, or products which are typically exported from developing countries to developed countries, but also consumed in domestic markets most notably handicrafts, coffee, cocoa, wine, sugar, fresh fruit, chocolate, flowers and gold. The movement seeks to promote greater equity in international trading partnerships through dialogue, transparency, and respect. It promotes sustainable development by offering better trading conditions to, and securing the rights of, marginalized producers and workers in developing countries. __________ is grounded in three core beliefs; first, producers have the power to express unity with consumers. Secondly, the world trade practices that currently exist promote the unequal distribution of wealth between nations. Lastly, buying products from producers in developing countries at a fair price is a more efficient way of promoting sustainable development than traditional charity and aid.

Exam Probability: **Medium**

9. *Answer choices:*
(see index for correct answer)

- a. Forests Now Declaration
- b. Futures techniques
- c. Design impact measures
- d. Fair trade

Guidance: level 1

:: Data management ::

__________ is a form of intellectual property that grants the creator of an original creative work an exclusive legal right to determine whether and under what conditions this original work may be copied and used by others, usually for a limited term of years. The exclusive rights are not absolute but limited by limitations and exceptions to __________ law, including fair use. A major limitation on __________ on ideas is that __________ protects only the original expression of ideas, and not the underlying ideas themselves.

Exam Probability: **Low**

10. *Answer choices:*

(see index for correct answer)

- a. Data Transformation Services
- b. Database transaction
- c. Copyright
- d. Reference data

Guidance: level 1

:: Writs ::

In common law, a writ of _________ is a writ whereby a private individual who assists a prosecution can receive all or part of any penalty imposed. Its name is an abbreviation of the Latin phrase _________ pro domino rege quam pro se ipso in hac parte sequitur, meaning "[he] who sues in this matter for the king as well as for himself."

Exam Probability: **Low**

11. *Answer choices:*

(see index for correct answer)

- a. Writ of execution
- b. Qui tam

Guidance: level 1

:: ::

_________ is the study and management of exchange relationships. _________ is the business process of creating relationships with and satisfying customers. With its focus on the customer, _________ is one of the premier components of business management.

Exam Probability: **Low**

12. *Answer choices:*

(see index for correct answer)

- a. Marketing
- b. deep-level diversity
- c. personal values
- d. open system

Guidance: level 1

:: Patent law ::

A _________ is generally any statement intended to specify or delimit the scope of rights and obligations that may be exercised and enforced by parties in a legally recognized relationship. In contrast to other terms for legally operative language, the term _________ usually implies situations that involve some level of uncertainty, waiver, or risk.

Exam Probability: **Low**

13. *Answer choices:*

(see index for correct answer)

- a. Triadic patent
- b. Technological alliance
- c. Disclaimer
- d. Offensive patent aggregation

Guidance: level 1

:: Management ::

A _________ describes the rationale of how an organization creates, delivers, and captures value, in economic, social, cultural or other contexts. The process of _________ construction and modification is also called _________ innovation and forms a part of business strategy.

Exam Probability: **High**

14. *Answer choices:*

(see index for correct answer)

- a. Continuous-flow manufacturing
- b. Defensive expenditures
- c. Business model
- d. Cross ownership

Guidance: level 1

:: Product certification ::

__________ is food produced by methods that comply with the standards of organic farming. Standards vary worldwide, but organic farming features practices that cycle resources, promote ecological balance, and conserve biodiversity. Organizations regulating organic products may restrict the use of certain pesticides and fertilizers in the farming methods used to produce such products. __________ s typically are not processed using irradiation, industrial solvents, or synthetic food additives.

Exam Probability: **Low**

15. *Answer choices:*

(see index for correct answer)

- a. Organic Crop Improvement Association
- b. Organic food
- c. Product certification
- d. Hardware certification

Guidance: level 1

:: Environmental economics ::

__________ is the process of people maintaining change in a balanced environment, in which the exploitation of resources, the direction of investments, the orientation of technological development and institutional change are all in harmony and enhance both current and future potential to meet human needs and aspirations. For many in the field, __________ is defined through the following interconnected domains or pillars: environment, economic and social, which according to Fritjof Capra is based on the principles of Systems Thinking. Sub-domains of sustainable development have been considered also: cultural, technological and political. While sustainable development may be the organizing principle for __________ for some, for others, the two terms are paradoxical . Sustainable development is the development that meets the needs of the present without compromising the ability of future generations to meet their own needs. Brundtland Report for the World Commission on Environment and Development introduced the term of sustainable development.

Exam Probability: **High**

16. *Answer choices:*

(see index for correct answer)

- a. Envirofit International
- b. Sustainability
- c. Adaptive capacity
- d. Free-market environmentalism

Guidance: level 1

:: Confidence tricks ::

A __________ is a business model that recruits members via a promise of payments or services for enrolling others into the scheme, rather than supplying investments or sale of products. As recruiting multiplies, recruiting becomes quickly impossible, and most members are unable to profit; as such, __________ s are unsustainable and often illegal.

Exam Probability: **Low**

17. *Answer choices:*
(see index for correct answer)

- a. Black money scam
- b. Pyramid scheme
- c. Thai zig zag scam
- d. Blessing scam

Guidance: level 1

:: Commercial crimes ::

__________ is an agreement between participants on the same side in a market to buy or sell a product, service, or commodity only at a fixed price, or maintain the market conditions such that the price is maintained at a given level by controlling supply and demand.

Exam Probability: **Low**

18. *Answer choices:*
(see index for correct answer)

- a. Skimming
- b. Commercial bribery
- c. Terrorism financing
- d. Fraudulent conveyance

Guidance: level 1

:: Socialism ::

_________ is a label used to define the first currents of modern socialist thought as exemplified by the work of Henri de Saint-Simon, Charles Fourier, Étienne Cabet and Robert Owen.

Exam Probability: **High**

19. *Answer choices:*

(see index for correct answer)

- a. Frankfurt Declaration
- b. Haringey Solidarity Group
- c. Real socialism
- d. Common Agricultural Policy

Guidance: level 1

:: ::

The _________ , founded in 1912, is a private, nonprofit organization whose self-described mission is to focus on advancing marketplace trust, consisting of 106 independently incorporated local BBB organizations in the United States and Canada, coordinated under the Council of _________ s in Arlington, Virginia.

Exam Probability: **Medium**

20. *Answer choices:*

(see index for correct answer)

- a. information systems assessment
- b. Sarbanes-Oxley act of 2002
- c. deep-level diversity
- d. levels of analysis

Guidance: level 1

:: Parental leave ::

_________ , or family leave, is an employee benefit available in almost all countries. The term " _________ " may include maternity, paternity, and adoption leave; or may be used distinctively from "maternity leave" and "paternity leave" to describe separate family leave available to either parent to care for small children. In some countries and jurisdictions, "family leave" also includes leave provided to care for ill family members. Often, the minimum benefits and eligibility requirements are stipulated by law.

Exam Probability: **Low**

21. *Answer choices:*

(see index for correct answer)

- a. Sara Hlupekile Longwe
- b. Additional Paternity Leave Regulations 2010
- c. Cleveland Board of Education v. LaFleur
- d. Parental leave

Guidance: level 1

:: Corporate scandals ::

Exxon Mobil Corporation, doing business as _________ , is an American multinational oil and gas corporation headquartered in Irving, Texas. It is the largest direct descendant of John D. Rockefeller`s Standard Oil Company, and was formed on November 30, 1999 by the merger of Exxon and Mobil . _________ `s primary brands are Exxon, Mobil, Esso, and _________ Chemical.

Exam Probability: **Low**

22. *Answer choices:*

(see index for correct answer)

- a. Polly Peck
- b. Central Energy Italian Gas Holding
- c. Hafskip
- d. ExxonMobil

Guidance: level 1

:: Utilitarianism ::

_________ is a family of consequentialist ethical theories that promotes actions that maximize happiness and well-being for the majority of a population. Although different varieties of _________ admit different characterizations, the basic idea behind all of them is to in some sense maximize utility, which is often defined in terms of well-being or related concepts. For instance, Jeremy Bentham, the founder of _________, described utility as

Exam Probability: **High**

23. *Answer choices:*

(see index for correct answer)

- a. Mere addition paradox
- b. Utilitarianism
- c. Average and total utilitarianism
- d. Act utilitarianism

Guidance: level 1

:: Renewable energy ::

A _________ is a fuel that is produced through contemporary biological processes, such as agriculture and anaerobic digestion, rather than a fuel produced by geological processes such as those involved in the formation of fossil fuels, such as coal and petroleum, from prehistoric biological matter. If the source biomatter can regrow quickly, the resulting fuel is said to be a form of renewable energy.

Exam Probability: **Medium**

24. *Answer choices:*

(see index for correct answer)

- a. Army Energy Initiatives Task Force
- b. Solar cooker
- c. Biofuel
- d. PaveGen

Guidance: level 1

:: ::

_________ refers to a business initiative to increase the access between a company and their current and potential customers through the use of the Internet. The Internet allows the company to market themselves and attract new customers to their website where they can provide product information and better customer service. Customers can place orders electronically, therefore reducing expensive long distant phone calls and postage costs of placing orders, while saving time on behalf of the customer and company.

Exam Probability: **Low**

25. *Answer choices:*

(see index for correct answer)

- a. interpersonal communication
- b. Character
- c. similarity-attraction theory
- d. open system

Guidance: level 1

:: ::

The _________ was a severe worldwide economic depression that took place mostly during the 1930s, beginning in the United States. The timing of the _________ varied across nations; in most countries it started in 1929 and lasted until the late-1930s. It was the longest, deepest, and most widespread depression of the 20th century. In the 21st century, the _________ is commonly used as an example of how intensely the world`s economy can decline.

Exam Probability: **Low**

26. *Answer choices:*

(see index for correct answer)

- a. information systems assessment
- b. corporate values
- c. co-culture
- d. Great Depression

Guidance: level 1

:: Office work ::

__________ is the process and behavior in human interactions involving power and authority. It is also a tool to assess the operational capacity and to balance diverse views of interested parties. It is also known as office politics and organizational politics.It is the use of power and social networking within an organization to achieve changes that benefit the organization or individuals within it. Influence by individuals may serve personal interests without regard to their effect on the organization itself. Some of the personal advantages may include access to tangible assets, or intangible benefits such as status or pseudo-authority that influences the behavior of others. On the other hand, organizational politics can increase efficiency, form interpersonal relationships, expedite change, and profit the organization and its members simultaneously.Both individuals and groups may engage in office politics which can be highly destructive, as people focus on personal gains at the expense of the organization. "Self-serving political actions can negatively influence our social groupings, cooperation, information sharing, and many other organizational functions." Thus, it is vital to pay attention to organizational politics and create the right political landscape. "Politics is the lubricant that oils your organization`s internal gears." Office politics has also been described as "simply how power gets worked out on a practical, day-to-day basis."

Exam Probability: **High**

27. *Answer choices:*
(see index for correct answer)

- a. Workplace politics
- b. Executive suite
- c. Pink-collar worker
- d. Paperless office

Guidance: level 1

:: Nepotism ::

_________ is the granting of favour to relatives in various fields, including business, politics, entertainment, sports, religion and other activities. The term originated with the assignment of nephews to important positions by Catholic popes and bishops. Trading parliamentary employment for favors is a modern-day example of _________ . Criticism of _________ , however, can be found in ancient Indian texts such as the Kural literature.

Exam Probability: **Medium**

28. *Answer choices:*

(see index for correct answer)

- a. Wasta
- b. Nepotism
- c. Monklandsgate
- d. Crachach

Guidance: level 1

:: Carbon finance ::

The _________ is an international treaty which extends the 1992 United Nations Framework Convention on Climate Change that commits state parties to reduce greenhouse gas emissions, based on the scientific consensus that global warming is occurring and it is extremely likely that human-made CO2 emissions have predominantly caused it. The _________ was adopted in Kyoto, Japan on 11 December 1997 and entered into force on 16 February 2005. There are currently 192 parties to the Protocol.

Exam Probability: **High**

29. *Answer choices:*

(see index for correct answer)

- a. Joint Implementation
- b. Emissions Reduction Currency System
- c. Kyoto Protocol
- d. Solar Renewable Energy Certificate

Guidance: level 1

:: Market-based policy instruments ::

Cause marketing is defined as a type of corporate social responsibility, in which a company's promotional campaign has the dual purpose of increasing profitability while bettering society.

Exam Probability: **Low**

30. *Answer choices:*

(see index for correct answer)

- a. Feebate
- b. Public choice
- c. Cobra effect
- d. Cause-related marketing

Guidance: level 1

:: ::

The __________ is an institution of the European Union, responsible for proposing legislation, implementing decisions, upholding the EU treaties and managing the day-to-day business of the EU. Commissioners swear an oath at the European Court of Justice in Luxembourg City, pledging to respect the treaties and to be completely independent in carrying out their duties during their mandate. Unlike in the Council of the European Union, where members are directly and indirectly elected, and the European Parliament, where members are directly elected, the Commissioners are proposed by the Council of the European Union, on the basis of suggestions made by the national governments, and then appointed by the European Council after the approval of the European Parliament.

Exam Probability: **High**

31. *Answer choices:*

(see index for correct answer)

- a. corporate values
- b. surface-level diversity
- c. personal values
- d. imperative

Guidance: level 1

:: Dutch inventions ::

The Fairtrade certification initiative was created to form a new method for economic trade. This method takes an ethical standpoint, and considers the producers first.

Exam Probability: **Low**

32. *Answer choices:*

(see index for correct answer)

- a. Fair Trade Certified
- b. Dijkstra's algorithm

Guidance: level 1

:: ::

The _________ to Fight AIDS, Tuberculosis and Malaria is an international financing organization that aims to "attract, leverage and invest additional resources to end the epidemics of HIV/AIDS, tuberculosis and malaria to support attainment of the Sustainable Development Goals established by the United Nations." A public-private partnership, the organization maintains its secretariat in Geneva, Switzerland. The organization began operations in January 2002. Microsoft founder Bill Gates was one of the first private foundations among many bilateral donors to provide seed money for the partnership.

Exam Probability: **High**

33. *Answer choices:*

(see index for correct answer)

- a. open system
- b. hierarchical perspective
- c. empathy
- d. Global Fund

Guidance: level 1

:: Fraud ::

In law, _________ is intentional deception to secure unfair or unlawful gain, or to deprive a victim of a legal right. _________ can violate civil law , a criminal law , or it may cause no loss of money, property or legal right but still be an element of another civil or criminal wrong. The purpose of _________ may be monetary gain or other benefits, for example by obtaining a passport, travel document, or driver`s license, or mortgage _________ , where the perpetrator may attempt to qualify for a mortgage by way of false statements.

Exam Probability: **High**

34. *Answer choices:*

(see index for correct answer)

- a. Swatting
- b. Fraud
- c. Statute of frauds
- d. Misleading or deceptive conduct

Guidance: level 1

:: Natural gas ::

_________ is a naturally occurring hydrocarbon gas mixture consisting primarily of methane, but commonly including varying amounts of other higher alkanes, and sometimes a small percentage of carbon dioxide, nitrogen, hydrogen sulfide, or helium. It is formed when layers of decomposing plant and animal matter are exposed to intense heat and pressure under the surface of the Earth over millions of years. The energy that the plants originally obtained from the sun is stored in the form of chemical bonds in the gas.

Exam Probability: **Low**

35. *Answer choices:*

(see index for correct answer)

- a. Moisture analysis
- b. Natural gas
- c. Gas contractor
- d. Liquefied natural gas

Guidance: level 1

:: ::

The Ethics & Compliance Initiative was formed in 2015 and consists of three nonprofit organizations: the Ethics Research Center, the Ethics & Compliance Association, and the Ethics & Compliance Certification Institute. Based in Arlington, Virginia, United States, ECI is devoted to the advancement of high ethical standards and practices in public and private institutions, and provides research about ethical standards, workplace integrity, and compliance practices and processes.

Exam Probability: **High**

36. *Answer choices:*

(see index for correct answer)

- a. Ethics Resource Center
- b. levels of analysis
- c. interpersonal communication
- d. Sarbanes-Oxley act of 2002

Guidance: level 1

:: United States law ::

The ABA _________ , created by the American Bar Association , are a set of rules that prescribe baseline standards of legal ethics and professional responsibility for lawyers in the United States. They were promulgated by the ABA House of Delegates upon the recommendation of the Kutak Commission in 1983. The rules are merely recommendations, or models, and are not themselves binding. However, having a common set of Model Rules facilitates a common discourse on legal ethics, and simplifies professional responsibility training as well as the day-to-day application of such rules. As of 2015, 49 states and four territories have adopted the rules in whole or in part, of which the most recent to do so was the Commonwealth of the Northern Mariana Islands in March 2015. California is the only state that has not adopted the ABA Model Rules, while Puerto Rico is the only U.S. jurisdiction outside of confederation has not adopted them but instead has its own Código de Ética Profesional.

Exam Probability: **Medium**

37. *Answer choices:*

(see index for correct answer)

- a. Pro se

- b. judgment notwithstanding the verdict

Guidance: level 1

:: Separation of investment and commercial banking ::

The _________ refers to § 619 of the Dodd–Frank Wall Street Reform and Consumer Protection Act . The rule was originally proposed by American economist and former United States Federal Reserve Chairman Paul Volcker to restrict United States banks from making certain kinds of speculative investments that do not benefit their customers. Volcker argued that such speculative activity played a key role in the financial crisis of 2007–2008. The rule is often referred to as a ban on proprietary trading by commercial banks, whereby deposits are used to trade on the bank`s own accounts, although a number of exceptions to this ban were included in the Dodd-Frank law.

Exam Probability: **Low**

38. *Answer choices:*

(see index for correct answer)

- a. Commercial bank
- b. Merchant bank
- c. Volcker Rule
- d. Bank holding company

Guidance: level 1

:: Renewable energy ::

_________ is the conversion of energy from sunlight into electricity, either directly using photovoltaics , indirectly using concentrated _________ , or a combination. Concentrated _________ systems use lenses or mirrors and tracking systems to focus a large area of sunlight into a small beam. Photovoltaic cells convert light into an electric current using the photovoltaic effect.

Exam Probability: **Medium**

39. *Answer choices:*

(see index for correct answer)

- a. Energy hierarchy

- b. Grid balancing
- c. Renewable energy debate
- d. Algaculture

Guidance: level 1

:: ::

In ecology, a _________ is the type of natural environment in which a particular species of organism lives. It is characterized by both physical and biological features. A species` _________ is those places where it can find food, shelter, protection and mates for reproduction.

Exam Probability: **High**

40. *Answer choices:*

(see index for correct answer)

- a. functional perspective
- b. process perspective
- c. Habitat
- d. personal values

Guidance: level 1

:: ::

_________ is the introduction of contaminants into the natural environment that cause adverse change. _________ can take the form of chemical substances or energy, such as noise, heat or light. Pollutants, the components of _________, can be either foreign substances/energies or naturally occurring contaminants. _________ is often classed as point source or nonpoint source _________ .In 2015, _________ killed 9 million people in the world.

Exam Probability: **Low**

41. *Answer choices:*

(see index for correct answer)

- a. hierarchical
- b. Pollution
- c. empathy
- d. deep-level diversity

Guidance: level 1

:: Corporate scandals ::

_________ was a bank based in the Caribbean, which operated from 1986 to 2009 when it went into receivership. It was an affiliate of the Stanford Financial Group and failed when the its parent was seized by United States authorities in early 2009 as part of the investigation into Allen Stanford.

Exam Probability: **Low**

42. *Answer choices:*

(see index for correct answer)

- a. Stanford International Bank
- b. Opes Prime
- c. Enron scandal
- d. Overseas Trust Bank

Guidance: level 1

:: Trade unions ::

A _________ was a group formed of private citizens to administer law and order where they considered governmental structures to be inadequate. The term is commonly associated with the frontier areas of the American West in the mid-19th century, where groups attacked cattle rustlers and gangs, and people at gold mining claims. As non-state organizations no functioning checks existed to protect against excessive force or safeguard due process from the committees. In the years prior to the Civil War, some committees worked to free slaves and transport them to freedom.

Exam Probability: **Medium**

43. *Answer choices:*

(see index for correct answer)

- a. Unionized cooperative
- b. Vigilance committee
- c. TU
- d. Churn and burn

Guidance: level 1

:: ::

Oriental Nicety, formerly _________ , Exxon Mediterranean, SeaRiver Mediterranean, S/R Mediterranean, Mediterranean, and Dong Fang Ocean, was an oil tanker that gained notoriety after running aground in Prince William Sound spilling hundreds of thousands of barrels of crude oil in Alaska. On March 24, 1989, while owned by the former Exxon Shipping Company, and captained by Joseph Hazelwood and First Mate James Kunkel bound for Long Beach, California, the vessel ran aground on the Bligh Reef resulting in the second largest oil spill in United States history. The size of the spill is estimated to have been 40,900 to 120,000 m3 , or 257,000 to 750,000 barrels. In 1989, the _________ oil spill was listed as the 54th largest spill in history.

Exam Probability: **High**

44. *Answer choices:*

(see index for correct answer)

- a. levels of analysis
- b. empathy
- c. functional perspective
- d. Exxon Valdez

Guidance: level 1

:: Social philosophy ::

The " _________ " is a method of determining the morality of issues. It asks a decision-maker to make a choice about a social or moral issue, and assumes that they have enough information to know the consequences of their possible decisions for everyone but would not know, or would not take into account, which person he or she is. The theory contends that not knowing one`s ultimate position in society would lead to the creation of a just system, as the decision-maker would not want to make decisions which benefit a certain group at the expense of another, because the decision-maker could theoretically end up in either group. The idea has been present in moral philosophy at least since the eighteenth century. The _________ is part of a long tradition of thinking in terms of a social contract that includes the writings of Immanuel Kant, Thomas Hobbes, John Locke, Jean Jacques Rousseau, and Thomas Jefferson. Prominent modern names attached to it are John Harsanyi and John Rawls.

Exam Probability: **Low**

45. *Answer choices:*
(see index for correct answer)

- a. Veil of ignorance
- b. Invisible hand
- c. Freedom to contract
- d. vacancy chain

Guidance: level 1

:: Competition regulators ::

The _________ is an independent agency of the United States government, established in 1914 by the _________ Act. Its principal mission is the promotion of consumer protection and the elimination and prevention of anticompetitive business practices, such as coercive monopoly. It is headquartered in the _________ Building in Washington, D.C.

Exam Probability: **High**

46. *Answer choices:*
(see index for correct answer)

- a. Competition Appeal Tribunal
- b. Competition and Markets Authority
- c. Australian Competition and Consumer Commission
- d. Federal Trade Commission

Guidance: level 1

:: ::

A _________ service is an online platform which people use to build social networks or social relationship with other people who share similar personal or career interests, activities, backgrounds or real-life connections.

Exam Probability: **Medium**

47. *Answer choices:*
(see index for correct answer)

- a. functional perspective
- b. Social networking
- c. cultural
- d. Character

Guidance: level 1

:: Fraud ::

In the United States, _________ is the claiming of Medicare health care reimbursement to which the claimant is not entitled. There are many different types of _________ , all of which have the same goal: to collect money from the Medicare program illegitimately.

Exam Probability: **High**

48. *Answer choices:*

(see index for correct answer)

- a. Medicare fraud
- b. Emil Rupp
- c. Pious fraud
- d. Address fraud

Guidance: level 1

:: Toxicology ::

_________ or lead-based paint is paint containing lead. As pigment, lead chromate , Lead oxide, , and lead carbonate are the most common forms. Lead is added to paint to accelerate drying, increase durability, maintain a fresh appearance, and resist moisture that causes corrosion. It is one of the main health and environmental hazards associated with paint. In some countries, lead continues to be added to paint intended for domestic use, whereas countries such as the U.S. and the UK have regulations prohibiting this, although _________ may still be found in older properties painted prior to the introduction of such regulations. Although lead has been banned from household paints in the United States since 1978, paint used in road markings may still contain it. Alternatives such as water-based, lead-free traffic paint are readily available, and many states and federal agencies have changed their purchasing contracts to buy these instead.

Exam Probability: **High**

49. *Answer choices:*

(see index for correct answer)

- a. Lead paint

- b. Maximum Acceptable Toxicant Concentration
- c. Barium
- d. Dose

Guidance: level 1

:: False advertising law ::

The Lanham Act is the primary federal trademark statute of law in the United States. The Act prohibits a number of activities, including trademark infringement, trademark dilution, and false advertising.

Exam Probability: **Low**

50. *Answer choices:*

(see index for correct answer)

- a. Lanham Act
- b. Rebecca Tushnet

Guidance: level 1

:: Coal ::

_________ is a combustible black or brownish-black sedimentary rock, formed as rock strata called _________ seams. _________ is mostly carbon with variable amounts of other elements; chiefly hydrogen, sulfur, oxygen, and nitrogen. _________ is formed if dead plant matter decays into peat and over millions of years the heat and pressure of deep burial converts the peat into _________ . Vast deposits of _________ originates in former wetlands—called _________ forests—that covered much of the Earth`s tropical land areas during the late Carboniferous and Permian times.

Exam Probability: **Low**

51. *Answer choices:*

(see index for correct answer)

- a. Coal
- b. Carbolineum
- c. Azienda Nazionale Idrogenazione Combustibili
- d. Pulverised fuel ash

Guidance: level 1

:: Types of marketing ::

_________ is an advertisement strategy in which a company uses surprise and/or unconventional interactions in order to promote a product or service. It is a type of publicity. The term was popularized by Jay Conrad Levinson's 1984 book _________ .

Exam Probability: **Medium**

52. *Answer choices:*

(see index for correct answer)

- a. Guerrilla Marketing
- b. Evangelism marketing
- c. Association of Publishing Agencies
- d. Shopper marketing

Guidance: level 1

:: ::

_________ is a non-governmental environmental organization with offices in over 39 countries and an international coordinating body in Amsterdam, the Netherlands. _________ was founded in 1971 by Irving Stowe, and Dorothy Stowe, Canadian and US ex-pat environmental activists. _________ states its goal is to "ensure the ability of the Earth to nurture life in all its diversity" and focuses its campaigning on worldwide issues such as climate change, deforestation, overfishing, commercial whaling, genetic engineering, and anti-nuclear issues. It uses direct action, lobbying, research, and ecotage to achieve its goals. The global organization does not accept funding from governments, corporations, or political parties, relying on three million individual supporters and foundation grants. _________ has a general consultative status with the United Nations Economic and Social Council and is a founding member of the INGO Accountability Charter, an international non-governmental organization that intends to foster accountability and transparency of non-governmental organizations.

Exam Probability: **High**

53. *Answer choices:*

(see index for correct answer)

- a. Greenpeace

- b. deep-level diversity
- c. empathy
- d. similarity-attraction theory

Guidance: level 1

:: Euthenics ::

_________ is an ethical framework and suggests that an entity, be it an organization or individual, has an obligation to act for the benefit of society at large. _________ is a duty every individual has to perform so as to maintain a balance between the economy and the ecosystems. A trade-off may exist between economic development, in the material sense, and the welfare of the society and environment, though this has been challenged by many reports over the past decade. _________ means sustaining the equilibrium between the two. It pertains not only to business organizations but also to everyone whose any action impacts the environment. This responsibility can be passive, by avoiding engaging in socially harmful acts, or active, by performing activities that directly advance social goals. _________ must be intergenerational since the actions of one generation have consequences on those following.

Exam Probability: **Low**

54. *Answer choices:*

(see index for correct answer)

- a. Home economics
- b. Euthenics
- c. Family and consumer science
- d. Minnie Cumnock Blodgett

Guidance: level 1

:: ::

_________ in the United States is a federal and state program that helps with medical costs for some people with limited income and resources. _________ also offers benefits not normally covered by Medicare, including nursing home care and personal care services. The Health Insurance Association of America describes _________ as "a government insurance program for persons of all ages whose income and resources are insufficient to pay for health care." _________ is the largest source of funding for medical and health-related services for people with low income in the United States, providing free health insurance to 74 million low-income and disabled people as of 2017. It is a means-tested program that is jointly funded by the state and federal governments and managed by the states, with each state currently having broad leeway to determine who is eligible for its implementation of the program. States are not required to participate in the program, although all have since 1982. _________ recipients must be U.S. citizens or qualified non-citizens, and may include low-income adults, their children, and people with certain disabilities. Poverty alone does not necessarily qualify someone for _________ .

Exam Probability: **High**

55. *Answer choices:*

(see index for correct answer)

- a. Medicaid
- b. co-culture
- c. hierarchical
- d. interpersonal communication

Guidance: level 1

:: Leadership ::

_________ is a theory of leadership where a leader works with teams to identify needed change, creating a vision to guide the change through inspiration, and executing the change in tandem with committed members of a group; it is an integral part of the Full Range Leadership Model. _________ serves to enhance the motivation, morale, and job performance of followers through a variety of mechanisms; these include connecting the follower`s sense of identity and self to a project and to the collective identity of the organization; being a role model for followers in order to inspire them and to raise their interest in the project; challenging followers to take greater ownership for their work, and understanding the strengths and weaknesses of followers, allowing the leader to align followers with tasks that enhance their performance.

Exam Probability: **Medium**

56. *Answer choices:*

(see index for correct answer)

- a. Transformational leadership
- b. Sex differences in leadership
- c. Maintenance actions
- d. BTS Group

Guidance: level 1

:: Labour law ::

An _________ is special or specified circumstances that partially or fully exempt a person or organization from performance of a legal obligation so as to avoid an unreasonable or disproportionate burden or obstacle.

Exam Probability: **Low**

57. *Answer choices:*

(see index for correct answer)

- a. The Burke Group
- b. Course of employment
- c. Victimisation
- d. Worker director

Guidance: level 1

:: Marketing ::

__________ is the marketing of products that are presumed to be environmentally safe. It incorporates a broad range of activities, including product modification, changes to the production process, sustainable packaging, as well as modifying advertising. Yet defining __________ is not a simple task where several meanings intersect and contradict each other; an example of this will be the existence of varying social, environmental and retail definitions attached to this term. Other similar terms used are environmental marketing and ecological marketing.

Exam Probability: **Medium**

58. *Answer choices:*

(see index for correct answer)

- a. Azerbaijan Marketing Society
- b. Green marketing
- c. Private label
- d. Marketing communications

Guidance: level 1

:: Progressive Era in the United States ::

The Clayton Antitrust Act of 1914 , was a part of United States antitrust law with the goal of adding further substance to the U.S. antitrust law regime; the __________ sought to prevent anticompetitive practices in their incipiency. That regime started with the Sherman Antitrust Act of 1890, the first Federal law outlawing practices considered harmful to consumers . The __________ specified particular prohibited conduct, the three-level enforcement scheme, the exemptions, and the remedial measures.

Exam Probability: **Medium**

59. *Answer choices:*

(see index for correct answer)

- a. Clayton Antitrust Act
- b. Clayton Act
- c. Mann Act

Guidance: level 1

Accounting

Accounting or accountancy is the measurement, processing, and communication of financial information about economic entities such as businesses and corporations. The modern field was established by the Italian mathematician Luca Pacioli in 1494. Accounting, which has been called the "language of business", measures the results of an organization's economic activities and conveys this information to a variety of users, including investors, creditors, management, and regulators.

:: Financial markets ::

__________ s are monetary contracts between parties. They can be created, traded, modified and settled. They can be cash , evidence of an ownership interest in an entity , or a contractual right to receive or deliver cash .

Exam Probability: **Medium**

1. *Answer choices:*

(see index for correct answer)

- a. Pfandbrief
- b. Financial instrument
- c. Price-weighted index
- d. Real-time economy

Guidance: level 1

:: Accounting terminology ::

In accounting/accountancy, _________ are journal entries usually made at the end of an accounting period to allocate income and expenditure to the period in which they actually occurred. The revenue recognition principle is the basis of making _________ that pertain to unearned and accrued revenues under accrual-basis accounting. They are sometimes called Balance Day adjustments because they are made on balance day.

Exam Probability: **Medium**

2. *Answer choices:*

(see index for correct answer)

- a. Capital expenditure
- b. Adjusting entries
- c. Share premium
- d. Accounts receivable

Guidance: level 1

:: Password authentication ::

A _________ , or sometimes redundantly a PIN number, is a numeric or alpha-numeric password used in the process of authenticating a user accessing a system.

Exam Probability: **High**

3. *Answer choices:*

(see index for correct answer)

- a. Password strength
- b. Pre-shared key
- c. Password authentication protocol
- d. Personal identification number

Guidance: level 1

:: Types of business entity ::

A sole __________, also known as the sole trader, individual entrepreneurship or __________, is a type of enterprise that is owned and run by one person and in which there is no legal distinction between the owner and the business entity. A sole trader does not necessarily work `alone`—it is possible for the sole trader to employ other people.

Exam Probability: **Low**

4. *Answer choices:*

(see index for correct answer)

- a. Private company limited by shares
- b. Proprietorship
- c. Unlimited liability corporation
- d. Holding company

Guidance: level 1

:: Accounting terminology ::

__________ are liabilities that reflect expenses that have not yet been paid or logged under accounts payable during an accounting period; in other words, a company`s obligation to pay for goods and services that have been provided for which invoices have not yet been received. Examples would include accrued wages payable, accrued sales tax payable, and accrued rent payable.

Exam Probability: **Low**

5. *Answer choices:*

(see index for correct answer)

- a. Cash flow management
- b. Basis of accounting
- c. revenue recognition principle
- d. Accrued liabilities

Guidance: level 1

:: Management ::

The _________ is a strategy performance management tool – a semi-standard structured report, that can be used by managers to keep track of the execution of activities by the staff within their control and to monitor the consequences arising from these actions.

Exam Probability: **Medium**

6. *Answer choices:*

(see index for correct answer)

- a. Project cost management
- b. Balanced scorecard
- c. Critical path method
- d. Control

Guidance: level 1

:: ::

_________ or accountancy is the measurement, processing, and communication of financial information about economic entities such as businesses and corporations. The modern field was established by the Italian mathematician Luca Pacioli in 1494. _________, which has been called the "language of business", measures the results of an organization`s economic activities and conveys this information to a variety of users, including investors, creditors, management, and regulators. Practitioners of _________ are known as accountants. The terms " _________ " and "financial reporting" are often used as synonyms.

Exam Probability: **Low**

7. *Answer choices:*

(see index for correct answer)

- a. corporate values
- b. Accounting
- c. surface-level diversity
- d. levels of analysis

Guidance: level 1

:: Tax credits ::

A __________ is a tax incentive which allows certain taxpayers to subtract the amount of the credit they have accrued from the total they owe the state. It may also be a credit granted in recognition of taxes already paid or, as in the United Kingdom, a form of state support.

Exam Probability: **High**

8. *Answer choices:*

(see index for correct answer)

- a. Pennsylvania Film Production Tax Credit
- b. Child tax credit
- c. Tax credit
- d. Paradigm Partners

Guidance: level 1

:: Accounting systems ::

In accounting, the controlling account is an account in the general ledger for which a corresponding subsidiary ledger has been created. The subsidiary ledger allows for tracking transactions within the controlling account in more detail. Individual transactions are posted both to the controlling account and the corresponding subsidiary ledger, and the totals for both are compared when preparing a trial balance to ensure accuracy.

Exam Probability: **High**

9. *Answer choices:*

(see index for correct answer)

- a. Purchase ledger
- b. Waste book
- c. Inflation accounting
- d. Counting house

Guidance: level 1

:: Inventory ::

_________ is a system of inventory in which updates are made on a periodic basis. This differs from perpetual inventory systems, where updates are made as seen fit.

Exam Probability: **High**

10. *Answer choices:*
(see index for correct answer)

- a. Buffer stock
- b. Inventory control problem
- c. Periodic inventory
- d. Stock demands

Guidance: level 1

:: United States Generally Accepted Accounting Principles ::

In a companies` financial reporting, _________ "includes all changes in equity during a period except those resulting from investments by owners and distributions to owners". Because that use excludes the effects of changing ownership interest, an economic measure of _________ is necessary for financial analysis from the shareholders` point of view

Exam Probability: **Medium**

11. *Answer choices:*
(see index for correct answer)

- a. GASB 34
- b. Working Group on Financial Markets
- c. Asset retirement obligation
- d. Comprehensive annual financial report

Guidance: level 1

:: Commercial crimes ::

__________ is the act of withholding assets for the purpose of conversion of such assets, by one or more persons to whom the assets were entrusted, either to be held or to be used for specific purposes. __________ is a type of financial fraud. For example, a lawyer might embezzle funds from the trust accounts of their clients; a financial advisor might embezzle the funds of investors; and a husband or a wife might embezzle funds from a bank account jointly held with the spouse.

Exam Probability: **Medium**

12. *Answer choices:*

(see index for correct answer)

- a. Monopolization
- b. Embezzlement
- c. Copyfraud
- d. Offshore leaks

Guidance: level 1

:: Generally Accepted Accounting Principles ::

__________ is a small amount of discretionary funds in the form of cash used for expenditures where it is not sensible to make any disbursement by cheque, because of the inconvenience and costs of writing, signing, and then cashing the cheque.

Exam Probability: **High**

13. *Answer choices:*

(see index for correct answer)

- a. Shares outstanding
- b. Petty cash
- c. Construction in progress
- d. Standard Business Reporting

Guidance: level 1

:: United States Generally Accepted Accounting Principles ::

In the United States, a _________ is one of the five governmental fund types established by GAAP. It is classified as a restricted true endowment fund for governments and non-profit organizations. Put simply, a _________ may be used to generate and disburse money to those entitled to receive payments by qualification or agreement, as in the case of Alaska citizens or residents that satisfy the rules for payment from their _________ from State oil revenues. It was first introduced through GASB Statement 34. The name of the fund comes from the purpose of the fund: a sum of equity used to permanently generate payments to maintain some financial obligation. Also, a fund can only be classified as a _________ if the money is used to report the status of a restricted financial resource. The resource is restricted in the sense that only earnings from the resource are used and not the principal. For example, a fund can be classified as a _________ if it is being used to pay for accounting services for a perpetual endowment of a government-run cemetery or financial endowments towards a government-run library.

Exam Probability: **Low**

14. *Answer choices:*

(see index for correct answer)

- a. Working Group on Financial Markets
- b. Impaired asset
- c. Single Audit
- d. Permanent fund

Guidance: level 1

:: Generally Accepted Accounting Principles ::

_________ is a measure of a fixed or current asset`s worth when held in inventory, in the field of accounting. NRV is part of the Generally Accepted Accounting Principles and International Financial Reporting Standards that apply to valuing inventory, so as to not overstate or understate the value of inventory goods. _________ is generally equal to the selling price of the inventory goods less the selling costs . Therefore, it is expected sales price less selling costs . NRV prevents overstating or understating of an assets value. NRV is the price cap when using the Lower of Cost or Market Rule.

Exam Probability: **Medium**

15. *Answer choices:*

(see index for correct answer)

- a. Operating statement
- b. Treasury stock
- c. Revenue
- d. Generally accepted accounting principles

Guidance: level 1

:: Accounting journals and ledgers ::

The subledger, or _________ , provides details behind entries in the general ledger used in accounting. The subledger shows detail for part of the accounting records such as property and equipment, prepaid expenses, etc. The detail would include such items as date the item was purchased or expense incurred, a description of the item, the original balance, and the net book value. The total of the subledger would match the line item amount on the general ledger. This corresponding line item in the general ledger is referred to as the controlling account. The _________ balance is compared with its controlling account balance as part of the process of preparing a trial balance.

Exam Probability: **High**

16. *Answer choices:*

(see index for correct answer)

- a. Subledger
- b. Subsidiary ledger
- c. General journal
- d. Sales journal

Guidance: level 1

:: Stock market ::

A _________ , securities exchange or bourse, is a facility where stock brokers and traders can buy and sell securities, such as shares of stock and bonds and other financial instruments. _________ s may also provide for facilities the issue and redemption of such securities and instruments and capital events including the payment of income and dividends. Securities traded on a _________ include stock issued by listed companies, unit trusts, derivatives, pooled investment products and bonds. _________ s often function as "continuous auction" markets with buyers and sellers consummating transactions via open outcry at a central location such as the floor of the exchange or by using an electronic trading platform.

Exam Probability: **Medium**

17. *Answer choices:*

(see index for correct answer)

- a. Common ordinary equity
- b. Ticker symbol
- c. Underweight
- d. Security

Guidance: level 1

:: Accounting terminology ::

_________ is a legally enforceable claim for payment held by a business for goods supplied and/or services rendered that customers/clients have ordered but not paid for. These are generally in the form of invoices raised by a business and delivered to the customer for payment within an agreed time frame. _________ is shown in a balance sheet as an asset. It is one of a series of accounting transactions dealing with the billing of a customer for goods and services that the customer has ordered. These may be distinguished from notes receivable, which are debts created through formal legal instruments called promissory notes.

Exam Probability: **Medium**

18. *Answer choices:*

(see index for correct answer)

- a. Capital appreciation
- b. Capital expenditure
- c. Accounts receivable

- d. profit and loss statement

Guidance: level 1

:: Budgets ::

An __________ is the annual budget of an activity stated in terms of Budget Classification Code, functional/subfunctional categories and cost accounts. It contains estimates of the total value of resources required for the performance of the operation including reimbursable work or services for others. It also includes estimates of workload in terms of total work units identified by cost accounts.

Exam Probability: **Low**

19. *Answer choices:*

(see index for correct answer)

- a. Energy budget
- b. Budget
- c. Railway Budget
- d. Participatory budgeting

Guidance: level 1

:: Legal terms ::

__________ is a state of prolonged public dispute or debate, usually concerning a matter of conflicting opinion or point of view. The word was coined from the Latin controversia, as a composite of controversus – "turned in an opposite direction," from contra – "against" – and vertere – to turn, or versus , hence, "to turn against."

Exam Probability: **Low**

20. *Answer choices:*

(see index for correct answer)

- a. Age of majority
- b. Arbitrariness
- c. Controversy
- d. Bench

Guidance: level 1

:: ::

The _________ of 1934 is a law governing the secondary trading of securities in the United States of America. A landmark of wide-ranging legislation, the Act of `34 and related statutes form the basis of regulation of the financial markets and their participants in the United States. The 1934 Act also established the Securities and Exchange Commission , the agency primarily responsible for enforcement of United States federal securities law.

Exam Probability: **Medium**

21. *Answer choices:*

(see index for correct answer)

- a. Securities Exchange Act
- b. functional perspective
- c. surface-level diversity
- d. co-culture

Guidance: level 1

:: Accounting in the United States ::

The _________ is the source of generally accepted accounting principles used by state and local governments in the United States. As with most of the entities involved in creating GAAP in the United States, it is a private, non-governmental organization.

Exam Probability: **Low**

22. *Answer choices:*

(see index for correct answer)

- a. Norwalk Agreement
- b. Revolving fund
- c. Accounting Today
- d. Governmental Accounting Standards Board

Guidance: level 1

:: Generally Accepted Accounting Principles ::

_________ , or non-current liabilities, are liabilities that are due beyond a year or the normal operation period of the company. The normal operation period is the amount of time it takes for a company to turn inventory into cash. On a classified balance sheet, liabilities are separated between current and _________ to help users assess the company`s financial standing in short-term and long-term periods. _________ give users more information about the long-term prosperity of the company, while current liabilities inform the user of debt that the company owes in the current period. On a balance sheet, accounts are listed in order of liquidity, so _________ come after current liabilities. In addition, the specific long-term liability accounts are listed on the balance sheet in order of liquidity. Therefore, an account due within eighteen months would be listed before an account due within twenty-four months. Examples of _________ are bonds payable, long-term loans, capital leases, pension liabilities, post-retirement healthcare liabilities, deferred compensation, deferred revenues, deferred income taxes, and derivative liabilities.

Exam Probability: **Medium**

23. *Answer choices:*

(see index for correct answer)

- a. Long-term liabilities
- b. Indian Accounting Standards
- c. Goodwill
- d. Insurance asset management

Guidance: level 1

:: Management accounting ::

_________ is the profit the firm makes from serving a customer or customer group over a specified period of time, specifically the difference between the revenues earned from and the costs associated with the customer relationship in a specified period. According to Philip Kotler,"a profitable customer is a person, household or a company that overtime, yields a revenue stream that exceeds by an acceptable amount the company`s cost stream of attracting, selling and servicing the customer."

Exam Probability: **Low**

24. *Answer choices:*
(see index for correct answer)

- a. Customer profitability
- b. Target costing
- c. Owner earnings
- d. Cost driver

Guidance: level 1

:: Finance ::

__________ is the ability of a bank customer in the United States and Canada to deposit a check into a bank account from a remote location, such as an office or home, without having to physically deliver the check to the bank. This is typically accomplished by scanning a digital image of a check into a computer, then transmitting that image to the bank. The practice became legal in the United States in 2004 when the Check Clearing for the 21st Century Act took effect, though not all banks have implemented the system.

Exam Probability: **Low**

25. *Answer choices:*
(see index for correct answer)

- a. Fine
- b. Replicating strategy
- c. Remote deposit
- d. Day trader

Guidance: level 1

:: International Financial Reporting Standards ::

__________ , usually called IFRS, are standards issued by the IFRS Foundation and the International Accounting Standards Board to provide a common global language for business affairs so that company accounts are understandable and comparable across international boundaries. They are a consequence of growing international shareholding and trade and are particularly important for companies that have dealings in several countries. They are progressively replacing the many different national accounting standards. They are the rules to be followed by accountants to maintain books of accounts which are comparable, understandable, reliable and relevant as per the users internal or external. IFRS, with the exception of IAS 29 Financial Reporting in Hyperinflationary Economies and IFRIC 7 Applying the Restatement Approach under IAS 29, are authorized in terms of the historical cost paradigm. IAS 29 and IFRIC 7 are authorized in terms of the units of constant purchasing power paradigm.IAS 2 is related to inventories in this standard we talk about the stock its production process etcIFRS began as an attempt to harmonize accounting across the European Union but the value of harmonization quickly made the concept attractive around the world. However, it has been debated whether or not de facto harmonization has occurred. Standards that were issued by IASC are still within use today and go by the name International Accounting Standards , while standards issued by IASB are called IFRS. IAS were issued between 1973 and 2001 by the Board of the International Accounting Standards Committee . On 1 April 2001, the new International Accounting Standards Board took over from the IASC the responsibility for setting International Accounting Standards. During its first meeting the new Board adopted existing IAS and Standing Interpretations Committee standards . The IASB has continued to develop standards calling the new standards " __________ ".

Exam Probability: **Medium**

26. *Answer choices:*

(see index for correct answer)

- a. Convergence of accounting standards
- b. IFRS 1
- c. IAS 16
- d. IFRS Foundation

Guidance: level 1

:: International taxation ::

A __________ tax, or a retention tax, is an income tax to be paid to the government by the payer of the income rather than by the recipient of the income. The tax is thus withheld or deducted from the income due to the recipient. In most jurisdictions, __________ tax applies to employment income. Many jurisdictions also require __________ tax on payments of interest or dividends. In most jurisdictions, there are additional __________ tax obligations if the recipient of the income is resident in a different jurisdiction, and in those circumstances __________ tax sometimes applies to royalties, rent or even the sale of real estate. Governments use __________ tax as a means to combat tax evasion, and sometimes impose additional __________ tax requirements if the recipient has been delinquent in filing tax returns, or in industries where tax evasion is perceived to be common.

Exam Probability: **High**

27. *Answer choices:*

(see index for correct answer)

- a. Common Reporting Standard
- b. Withholding
- c. Variable import levy
- d. Spahn tax

Guidance: level 1

:: ::

__________ are electronic transfer of money from one bank account to another, either within a single financial institution or across multiple institutions, via computer-based systems, without the direct intervention of bank staff.

Exam Probability: **Medium**

28. *Answer choices:*

(see index for correct answer)

- a. Electronic funds transfer
- b. information systems assessment
- c. surface-level diversity
- d. functional perspective

Guidance: level 1

:: Management accounting ::

_________ is an accounting methodology that traces and accumulates direct costs, and allocates indirect costs of a manufacturing process. Costs are assigned to products, usually in a large batch, which might include an entire month`s production. Eventually, costs have to be allocated to individual units of product. It assigns average costs to each unit, and is the opposite extreme of Job costing which attempts to measure individual costs of production of each unit. _________ is usually a significant chapter. It is a method of assigning costs to units of production in companies producing large quantities of homogeneous products..

Exam Probability: **Low**

29. *Answer choices:*

(see index for correct answer)

- a. Entity-level controls
- b. Certified Management Accountant
- c. Process costing
- d. Variable cost

Guidance: level 1

:: Banking ::

A _________ is a financial institution that accepts deposits from the public and creates credit. Lending activities can be performed either directly or indirectly through capital markets. Due to their importance in the financial stability of a country, _________ s are highly regulated in most countries. Most nations have institutionalized a system known as fractional reserve _________ ing under which _________ s hold liquid assets equal to only a portion of their current liabilities. In addition to other regulations intended to ensure liquidity, _________ s are generally subject to minimum capital requirements based on an international set of capital standards, known as the Basel Accords.

Exam Probability: **Low**

30. *Answer choices:*

(see index for correct answer)

- a. Short term deposit

- b. Banking software
- c. Origination fee
- d. Bank

Guidance: level 1

:: Accounting software ::

_________ is a freely available and global framework for exchanging business information. _________ allows the expression of semantic meaning commonly required in business reporting. The language is XML-based and uses the XML syntax and related XML technologies such as XML Schema, XLink, XPath, and Namespaces. One use of _________ is to define and exchange financial information, such as a financial statement. The _________ Specification is developed and published by _________ International, Inc. .

Exam Probability: **Low**

31. *Answer choices:*

(see index for correct answer)

- a. Sage 300 ERP
- b. XBRL
- c. Accounting software
- d. Kerridge Commercial Systems

Guidance: level 1

:: Accounting journals and ledgers ::

_________ is a daybook or journal which is used to record transactions relating to adjustment entries, opening stock, accounting errors etc. The source documents of this prime entry book are journal voucher, copy of management reports and invoices.

Exam Probability: **Medium**

32. *Answer choices:*

(see index for correct answer)

- a. Subledger
- b. Cash receipts journal
- c. Journal entry
- d. General journal

Guidance: level 1

:: Generally Accepted Accounting Principles ::

A _________ or reacquired stock is stock which is bought back by the issuing company, reducing the amount of outstanding stock on the open market .

Exam Probability: **Low**

33. *Answer choices:*

(see index for correct answer)

- a. Operating profit
- b. Trial balance
- c. Treasury stock
- d. Deferred income

Guidance: level 1

:: Classification systems ::

_________ is the practice of comparing business processes and performance metrics to industry bests and best practices from other companies. Dimensions typically measured are quality, time and cost.

Exam Probability: **High**

34. *Answer choices:*

(see index for correct answer)

- a. Systematized Nomenclature of Medicine
- b. Benchmarking
- c. Soil classification
- d. Genetypes

Guidance: level 1

:: ::

The ________ is a private, non-profit organization standard-setting body whose primary purpose is to establish and improve Generally Accepted Accounting Principles within the United States in the public`s interest. The Securities and Exchange Commission designated the FASB as the organization responsible for setting accounting standards for public companies in the US. The FASB replaced the American Institute of Certified Public Accountants` Accounting Principles Board on July 1, 1973.

Exam Probability: **High**

35. *Answer choices:*

(see index for correct answer)

- a. Financial Accounting Standards Board
- b. cultural
- c. surface-level diversity
- d. information systems assessment

Guidance: level 1

:: Costs ::

The ________ is computed by dividing the total cost of goods available for sale by the total units available for sale. This gives a weighted-average unit cost that is applied to the units in the ending inventory.

Exam Probability: **High**

36. *Answer choices:*

(see index for correct answer)

- a. Cost of poor quality
- b. Average cost
- c. Road Logistics Costing in South Africa
- d. Cost per paper

Guidance: level 1

:: ::

Accounts _________ is a legally enforceable claim for payment held by a business for goods supplied and/or services rendered that customers/clients have ordered but not paid for. These are generally in the form of invoices raised by a business and delivered to the customer for payment within an agreed time frame. Accounts _________ is shown in a balance sheet as an asset. It is one of a series of accounting transactions dealing with the billing of a customer for goods and services that the customer has ordered. These may be distinguished from notes _________ , which are debts created through formal legal instruments called promissory notes.

Exam Probability: **Low**

37. *Answer choices:*

(see index for correct answer)

- a. personal values
- b. Receivable
- c. process perspective
- d. hierarchical perspective

Guidance: level 1

:: Financial accounting ::

_________ is a financial metric which represents operating liquidity available to a business, organisation or other entity, including governmental entities. Along with fixed assets such as plant and equipment, _________ is considered a part of operating capital. Gross _________ is equal to current assets. _________ is calculated as current assets minus current liabilities. If current assets are less than current liabilities, an entity has a _________ deficiency, also called a _________ deficit.

Exam Probability: **Low**

38. *Answer choices:*

(see index for correct answer)

- a. Asset swap
- b. Financial Condition Report
- c. Capital account
- d. Holding gains

Guidance: level 1

:: Generally Accepted Accounting Principles ::

_________ s is an accounting term that refers to groups of accounts serving to express the cost of goods and service allocatable within a business or manufacturing organization. The principle behind the pool is to correlate direct and indirect costs with a specified cost driver, so to find out the total sum of expenses related to the manufacture of a product.

Exam Probability: **Low**

39. *Answer choices:*

(see index for correct answer)

- a. Treasury stock
- b. Revenue recognition
- c. Liability
- d. Cost principle

Guidance: level 1

:: Financial ratios ::

The _________ is a financial ratio indicating the relative proportion of shareholders` equity and debt used to finance a company`s assets. Closely related to leveraging, the ratio is also known as risk, gearing or leverage. The two components are often taken from the firm`s balance sheet or statement of financial position , but the ratio may also be calculated using market values for both, if the company`s debt and equity are publicly traded, or using a combination of book value for debt and market value for equity financially.

Exam Probability: **Low**

40. *Answer choices:*

(see index for correct answer)

- a. Return on event
- b. Bid-to-cover ratio
- c. Loan-to-value ratio
- d. K-factor

Guidance: level 1

:: ::

An _________ is a comprehensive report on a company`s activities throughout the preceding year. _________ s are intended to give shareholders and other interested people information about the company`s activities and financial performance. They may be considered as grey literature. Most jurisdictions require companies to prepare and disclose _________ s, and many require the _________ to be filed at the company`s registry. Companies listed on a stock exchange are also required to report at more frequent intervals .

Exam Probability: **Medium**

41. *Answer choices:*

(see index for correct answer)

- a. Annual report
- b. information systems assessment
- c. similarity-attraction theory
- d. imperative

Guidance: level 1

:: Taxation ::

_________ refers to the base upon which an income tax system imposes tax. Generally, it includes some or all items of income and is reduced by expenses and other deductions. The amounts included as income, expenses, and other deductions vary by country or system. Many systems provide that some types of income are not taxable and some expenditures not deductible in computing _________ . Some systems base tax on _________ of the current period, and some on prior periods. _________ may refer to the income of any taxpayer, including individuals and corporations, as well as entities that themselves do not pay tax, such as partnerships, in which case it may be called "net profit".

Exam Probability: **Medium**

42. *Answer choices:*

(see index for correct answer)

- a. Taxable income
- b. Taxpayer
- c. Inflation tax
- d. Sales tax token

Guidance: level 1

:: Financial statements ::

A Statement of changes in equity and similarly the statement of changes in owner`s equity for a sole trader, statement of changes in partners` equity for a partnership, statement of changes in Shareholders` equity for a Company or statement of changes in Taxpayers` equity for Government financial statements is one of the four basic financial statements.

Exam Probability: **Medium**

43. *Answer choices:*

(see index for correct answer)

- a. Statement of retained earnings
- b. Statement on Auditing Standards No. 70: Service Organizations
- c. Government financial statements
- d. Emphasis of matter

Guidance: level 1

:: Land value taxation ::

_________, sometimes referred to as dry _________, is the solid surface of Earth that is not permanently covered by water. The vast majority of human activity throughout history has occurred in _________ areas that support agriculture, habitat, and various natural resources. Some life forms have developed from predecessor species that lived in bodies of water.

Exam Probability: **High**

44. *Answer choices:*

(see index for correct answer)

- a. Harry Gunnison Brown
- b. Georgism
- c. Prosper Australia
- d. Land

Guidance: level 1

:: Retail financial services ::

A __________ is a prepaid stored-value money card, usually issued by a retailer or bank, to be used as an alternative to cash for purchases within a particular store or related businesses. __________ s are also given out by employers or organizations as rewards or gifts. They may also be distributed by retailers and marketers as part of a promotion strategy, to entice the recipient to come in or return to the store, and at times such cards are called cash cards. __________ s are generally redeemable only for purchases at the relevant retail premises and cannot be cashed out, and in some situations may be subject to an expiry date or fees. American Express, MasterCard, and Visa offer generic __________ s which need not be redeemed at particular stores, and which are widely used for cashback marketing strategies. A feature of these cards is that they are generally anonymous and are disposed of when the stored value on a card is exhausted.

Exam Probability: **High**

45. *Answer choices:*

(see index for correct answer)

- a. Dollar Financial Group
- b. Floor limit
- c. Antichresis
- d. Borro

Guidance: level 1

:: Debt ::

A __________ is a monetary amount owed to a creditor that is unlikely to be paid and, or which the creditor is not willing to take action to collect for various reasons, often due to the debtor not having the money to pay, for example due to a company going into liquidation or insolvency. There are various technical definitions of what constitutes a __________ , depending on accounting conventions, regulatory treatment and the institution provisioning. In the USA, bank loans with more than ninety days` arrears become "problem loans". Accounting sources advise that the full amount of a __________ be written off to the profit and loss account or a provision for __________ s as soon as it is foreseen.

Exam Probability: **Low**

46. *Answer choices:*
(see index for correct answer)

- a. Bad debt
- b. Paid outside closing
- c. Bailout
- d. Troubled Debt Restructuring

Guidance: level 1

:: Partnerships ::

Articles of partnership is a voluntary contract between/among two or more persons to place their capital, labor, and skills into business, with the understanding that there will be a sharing of the profits and losses between/among partners. Outside of North America, it is normally referred to simply as a _________ .

Exam Probability: **High**

47. *Answer choices:*
(see index for correct answer)

- a. Partnership agreement
- b. Limited partner
- c. Revised Uniform Partnership Act

Guidance: level 1

:: Management accounting ::

_________ is a professional business study of Accounts and management in which we learn importance of accounts in our management system.

Exam Probability: **High**

48. *Answer choices:*
(see index for correct answer)

- a. Cost driver
- b. Extended cost
- c. Accounting management
- d. Process costing

Guidance: level 1

:: Payment systems ::

A _________ or cheque, also called an image cash letter , clearing replacement document , or image replacement document , is a negotiable instrument used in electronic banking systems to represent a physical paper cheque . It may be wholly digital from payment initiation to clearing and settlement or it may be a digital reproduction of an original paper check.

Exam Probability: **High**

49. *Answer choices:*

(see index for correct answer)

- a. Adyen
- b. Scrip
- c. Ready Financial
- d. Substitute check

Guidance: level 1

:: ::

A _________ is a fund into which a sum of money is added during an employee's employment years, and from which payments are drawn to support the person's retirement from work in the form of periodic payments. A _________ may be a "defined benefit plan" where a fixed sum is paid regularly to a person, or a "defined contribution plan" under which a fixed sum is invested and then becomes available at retirement age. _________ s should not be confused with severance pay; the former is usually paid in regular installments for life after retirement, while the latter is typically paid as a fixed amount after involuntary termination of employment prior to retirement.

Exam Probability: **High**

50. *Answer choices:*

(see index for correct answer)

- a. similarity-attraction theory
- b. levels of analysis
- c. Pension
- d. empathy

Guidance: level 1

:: Generally Accepted Accounting Principles ::

Paid-in capital is capital that is contributed to a corporation by investors by purchase of stock from the corporation, the primary market, not by purchase of stock in the open market from other stockholders . It includes share capital as well as additional paid-in capital.

Exam Probability: **High**

51. *Answer choices:*

(see index for correct answer)

- a. deferred revenue
- b. Access to finance
- c. French generally accepted accounting principles
- d. Contributed capital

Guidance: level 1

:: Business ethics ::

In accounting and in most Schools of economic thought, _________ is a rational and unbiased estimate of the potential market price of a good, service, or asset. It takes into account such objectivity factors as.

Exam Probability: **High**

52. *Answer choices:*

(see index for correct answer)

- a. Salad Oil Scandal
- b. Conspiracy of Fools
- c. Marketing ethics
- d. Minority business enterprise

Guidance: level 1

:: ::

_________ is a process whereby a person assumes the parenting of another, usually a child, from that person`s biological or legal parent or parents. Legal _________ s permanently transfers all rights and responsibilities, along with filiation, from the biological parent or parents.

Exam Probability: **Medium**

53. *Answer choices:*

(see index for correct answer)

- a. corporate values
- b. Adoption
- c. similarity-attraction theory
- d. Character

Guidance: level 1

:: Free accounting software ::

A _________ is the principal book or computer file for recording and totaling economic transactions measured in terms of a monetary unit of account by account type, with debits and credits in separate columns and a beginning monetary balance and ending monetary balance for each account.

Exam Probability: **High**

54. *Answer choices:*

(see index for correct answer)

- a. JFin
- b. Ofuz
- c. HomeBank
- d. JGnash

Guidance: level 1

:: Internal Revenue Code ::

The _________ , formally the _________ of 1986, is the domestic portion of federal statutory tax law in the United States, published in various volumes of the United States Statutes at Large, and separately as Title 26 of the United States Code . It is organized topically, into subtitles and sections, covering income tax , payroll taxes, estate taxes, gift taxes, and excise taxes; as well as procedure and administration. Its implementing agency is the Internal Revenue Service.

Exam Probability: **Low**

55. *Answer choices:*

(see index for correct answer)

- a. Internal Revenue Code section 132
- b. Internal Revenue Code of 1986
- c. 475 fund
- d. Rollovers as Business Start-Ups

Guidance: level 1

:: Legal terms ::

A _________ is a gathering of people who have been invited by a host for the purposes of socializing, conversation, recreation, or as part of a festival or other commemoration of a special occasion. A _________ will typically feature food and beverages, and often music and dancing or other forms of entertainment. In many Western countries, parties for teens and adults are associated with drinking alcohol such as beer, wine, or distilled spirits.

Exam Probability: **Medium**

56. *Answer choices:*

(see index for correct answer)

- a. Party
- b. Harmless error
- c. Possession proceedings
- d. As is

Guidance: level 1

:: ::

The __________ of 1938 29 U.S.C. § 203 is a United States labor law that creates the right to a minimum wage, and "time-and-a-half" overtime pay when people work over forty hours a week. It also prohibits most employment of minors in "oppressive child labor". It applies to employees engaged in interstate commerce or employed by an enterprise engaged in commerce or in the production of goods for commerce, unless the employer can claim an exemption from coverage.

Exam Probability: **Medium**

57. *Answer choices:*

(see index for correct answer)

- a. Character
- b. co-culture
- c. levels of analysis
- d. information systems assessment

Guidance: level 1

:: Finance ::

The __________ of a corporation is the accumulated net income of the corporation that is retained by the corporation at a particular point of time, such as at the end of the reporting period. At the end of that period, the net income at that point is transferred from the Profit and Loss Account to the __________ account. If the balance of the __________ account is negative it may be called accumulated losses, retained losses or accumulated deficit, or similar terminology.

Exam Probability: **Medium**

58. *Answer choices:*

(see index for correct answer)

- a. Farm
- b. Yield
- c. Retained earnings
- d. Debt rescheduling

Guidance: level 1

:: Taxation ::

__________ is an estimate of the market value of a property, based on what a knowledgeable, willing, and unpressured buyer would probably pay to a knowledgeable, willing, and unpressured seller in the market. An estimate of __________ may be founded either on precedent or extrapolation. __________ differs from the intrinsic value that an individual may place on the same asset based on their own preferences and circumstances.

Exam Probability: **Low**

59. *Answer choices:*

(see index for correct answer)

- a. Fair market value
- b. Tax basis
- c. Voluntary taxation
- d. Tax cap

Guidance: level 1

INDEX: Correct Answers

Foundations of Business

1. c: Marketing strategy

2. a: Federal Trade Commission

3. d: Bankruptcy

4. c: Risk

5. d: Creativity

6. a: Information systems

7. : Firm

8. a: Negotiation

9. : Description

10. a: Publicity

11. d: Dimension

12. : Logistics

13. : Trade

14. c: Shareholders

15. : Brand

16. : Property rights

17. d: Internal control

18. : ITeM

19. b: Market research

20. a: Gross domestic product

21. b: Buyer

22. b: Best practice

23. b: Business

24. a: Market value

25. a: Franchising

26. b: Social security

27. b: Globalization

28. d: Number

29. d: American Express

30. a: Manufacturing

31. c: Document

32. b: Incentive

33. c: Demand

34. d: Price

35. d: Capital market

36. c: Resource management

37. b: Sustainability

38. a: Arthur Andersen

39. b: Revenue

40. c: Decision-making

41. d: Loan

42. a: Credit

43. d: Diagram

44. d: Threat

45. : Exercise

46. a: Outsourcing

47. b: Opportunity cost

48. b: Cash

49. d: Information technology

50. a: Regulation

51. b: Partnership

52. : Inflation

53. d: Human resources

54. d: Bias

55. c: Balanced scorecard

56. : Empowerment

57. c: Feedback

58. c: Sony

59. d: Efficiency

Management

1. b: Collaboration

2. c: Research and development

3. a: Pension

4. b: Synergy

5. d: Socialization

6. c: Project manager

7. d: E-commerce

8. a: Organizational culture

9. c: Product life cycle

10. a: Reinforcement

11. d: Product design

12. a: Feedback

13. a: Wage

14. d: Frequency

15. a: Management

16. c: Total cost

17. b: Entrepreneur

18. d: Social loafing

19. c: Strategy

20. c: Transformational leadership

21. d: Mass customization

22. a: Accounting

23. : Tariff

24. a: Property

25. b: International trade

26. c: Learning organization

27. d: Job design

28. b: Integrity

29. a: Patent

30. c: Bounded rationality

31. b: Subsidiary

32. d: Supply chain

33. : Organizational structure

34. b: Trade agreement

35. : Recruitment

36. a: Proactive

37. a: Vendor

38. d: Employee stock

39. b: Human resources

40. b: Customs

41. b: Leadership style

42. : Vertical integration

43. b: Job analysis

44. d: Affirmative action

45. d: Balanced scorecard

46. a: Market research

47. b: Inventory

48. c: Checklist

49. a: Brand

50. a: Profit sharing

51. a: Best practice

52. a: Training

53. d: Gantt chart

54. : Social capital

55. c: Decentralization

56. c: Project team

57. b: Statistic

58. a: Chief executive officer

59. a: Distance

Business law

1. c: Broker

2. d: Insurable interest

3. a: Fair use

4. d: Intellectual property

5. a: Affirmative action

6. d: Lien

7. c: Policy

8. a: Utilitarianism

9. a: Misappropriation

10. : Contributory negligence

11. : Public policy

12. b: Parol evidence

13. a: Operation of law

14. c: Anticipatory repudiation

15. c: Clayton Act

16. : Duty

17. d: Procedural law

18. c: Sexual harassment

19. : Executory contract

20. c: Real property

21. a: Writ

22. a: Insolvency

23. b: Option contract

24. c: Economy

25. d: Jurisdiction

26. d: Precedent

27. c: Consumer credit

28. : Secured transaction

29. c: Voidable

30. b: Condition precedent

31. : Commercial speech

32. a: Limited partnership

33. d: Market value

34. c: Testimony

35. b: Collective bargaining

36. d: Trade

37. d: World Trade Organization

38. b: Negotiable instrument

39. b: Requirements contract

40. c: Breach of contract

41. d: Delegation

42. a: Independent contractor

43. c: Stock

44. b: Accord and satisfaction

45. a: Enron

46. : Technology

47. a: Adoption

48. b: Shareholder

49. b: Personal property

50. d: First Amendment

51. : Brand

52. a: Contract law

53. a: Charter

54. d: Commerce

55. b: Utility

56. d: Uniform Electronic Transactions Act

57. : Computer fraud

58. d: Auction

59. b: Consumer Good

Finance

1. b: Double taxation

2. : Bank reconciliation

3. a: Current ratio

4. a: Accelerated depreciation

5. b: General journal

6. : Historical cost

7. : Dividend

8. d: Normal balance

9. b: Social security

10. a: Current asset

11. b: Promissory note

12. b: Stock exchange

13. b: Net profit

14. c: Liquidation

15. d: Return on investment

16. : Buyer

17. d: Accounting method

18. d: Activity-based costing

19. b: Accounting period

20. a: Balanced scorecard

21. : Stock

22. : Worksheet

23. : Periodic inventory

24. c: Convertible bond

25. : Payback period

26. : Cost of capital

27. d: Restructuring

28. d: Income

29. : Capital budgeting

30. c: Working capital

31. c: Primary market

32. a: Receipt

33. b: Limited liability

34. b: Variable cost

35. : Bond market

36. c: Certified Public Accountant

37. : Customer

38. b: Strategy

39. : Annuity

40. d: Net asset

41. a: Accrued interest

42. d: Preferred stock

43. d: Perpetual inventory

44. c: Revenue recognition

45. : Incentive

46. b: Monetary policy

47. b: Conservatism

48. : Aging

49. d: Budget

50. a: Asset turnover

51. b: Bank statement

52. b: Commercial paper

53. d: Capital structure

54. d: Competition

55. a: Source document

56. c: Interest rate risk

57. : Partnership

58. c: Advertising

59. a: Amortization

Human resource management

1. a: Self-actualization

2. a: Performance improvement

3. c: Control group

4. b: Ricci v. DeStefano

5. d: Cover letter

6. c: Agency shop

7. a: Open shop

8. : Living wage

9. c: Strategy map

10. a: Piece rate

11. a: Theory Z

12. a: Union shop

13. b: Training

14. a: Professional association

15. d: Public administration

16. : Cultural intelligence

17. c: Trainee

18. a: Job enlargement

19. b: Work ethic

20. a: Behavior modification

21. a: Organizational chart

22. a: Enforcement

23. c: Selection ratio

24. b: Interactional justice

25. a: Problem solving

26. d: Tacit knowledge

27. : Asbestos

28. d: Right-to-work law

29. : Supply chain

30. c: Employee surveys

31. a: Career management

32. : Mergers and acquisitions

33. b: Balance sheet

34. : Substance abuse

35. d: Aggression

36. b: Closed shop

37. : On-the-job training

38. c: Social media

39. : Layoff

40. d: Sexual harassment

41. d: Job rotation

42. : Vertical integration

43. d: Construct validity

44. b: Employee Polygraph Protection Act

45. b: Workforce management

46. a: E-HRM

47. b: Flextime

48. d: Aptitude

49. a: Works council

50. b: Person Analysis

51. : International Brotherhood of Teamsters

52. b: Onboarding

53. b: Unemployment benefits

54. a: Faragher v. City of Boca Raton

55. : Employee Free Choice Act

56. c: Affirmative action

57. d: Merit pay

58. c: Proactive

59. b: Age Discrimination in Employment Act

Information systems

1. d: Backbone network

2. b: Government-to-business

3. b: Interaction

4. b: Text mining

5. b: PayPal

6. d: Password

7. a: Authorization

8. c: Viral marketing

9. : Global Positioning System

10. b: Total cost of ownership

11. d: Information privacy

12. c: Information flow

13. b: Spyware

14. a: Mobile computing

15. : American Express

16. d: Worm

17. d: Web server

18. d: Google Maps

19. d: Network management

20. c: Geocoding

21. b: QR code

22. c: Reputation management

23. c: Analytics

24. d: Authentication

25. a: Virtual team

26. d: Big data

27. c: Encryption

28. c: Payment card

29. b: Asset

30. d: Transaction processing

31. c: Mobile payment

32. d: Data security

33. d: Disaster recovery plan

34. : Economies of scale

35. b: Change control

36. b: Manifesto

37. b: Data integration

38. c: Automation

39. a: Business analytics

40. b: Chart

41. b: Content management system

42. a: Virtual world

43. : Data element

44. d: Information governance

45. a: Carnivore

46. b: Data governance

47. a: Virtual reality

48. d: Information technology

49. a: PeopleSoft

50. d: Common Criteria

51. : System

52. c: Enterprise search

53. c: Search engine optimization

54. d: Expert system

55. a: Payment system

56. : World Wide Web

57. b: Affiliate marketing

58. a: Authentication protocol

59. : Consumer-to-business

Marketing

1. d: New product development

2. b: Price

3. b: Industry

4. c: Mass customization

5. d: Total cost

6. d: American Express

7. a: Strategic planning

8. d: Firm

9. b: Convenience

10. c: Economies of scale

11. c: Universal Product Code

12. : Competitive intelligence

13. d: Demand

14. b: Dimension

15. a: Merchant

16. d: Target market

17. : Brainstorming

18. b: Research and development

19. : Standing

20. a: Persuasion

21. d: Marketing mix

22. : Direct selling

23. d: Competitor

24. b: Credit

25. b: Interactive marketing

26. c: Inflation

27. b: Services marketing

28. d: Wall Street Journal

29. c: Resource

30. d: Star

31. c: Corporation

32. a: Interest

33. c: Product concept

34. b: Brand management

35. a: Social media

36. a: Merchandising

37. : Mass marketing

38. b: Advertising agency

39. b: Market share

40. : Manufacturing

41. d: Mobile marketing

42. a: Bottom line

43. d: Trial

44. : Commerce

45. a: Appeal

46. c: Shopping

47. b: Franchising

48. d: Marketing plan

49. d: Advertising

50. a: Public

51. c: Sponsorship

52. a: Asset

53. a: Pricing

54. c: Empowerment

55. : Expense

56. a: Marketing management

57. a: Presentation

58. : Management

59. c: Cooperative

Manufacturing

1. b: Dimension

2. : Inventory

3. d: Reflux

4. a: Process control

5. b: Consortium

6. a: Cost reduction

7. c: Knowledge management

8. : Service level

9. c: Project

10. a: Third-party logistics

11. a: New product development

12. a: Performance

13. c: Management process

14. c: Property

15. b: Authority

16. b: Project team

17. d: Reverse auction

18. d: Kaizen

19. c: Sales

20. a: Electronic data interchange

21. b: Expediting

22. c: Distillation

23. c: Initiative

24. a: Strategy

25. b: Mary Kay

26. d: Schedule

27. b: Cost estimate

28. d: Control chart

29. a: Design of experiments

30. d: Bill of materials

31. c: Time management

32. d: Quality function deployment

33. a: Indirect costs

34. d: Financial plan

35. c: Resource management

36. : Extended enterprise

37. : Total quality management

38. d: Consensus

39. a: Heat treating

40. c: Catalyst

41. d: Heat exchanger

42. b: Poka-yoke

43. a: Planning

44. b: Scheduling

45. : Credit

46. c: Vendor relationship management

47. d: Process capability

48. c: Ishikawa diagram

49. c: Malcolm Baldrige National Quality Award

50. b: Natural resource

51. : Global sourcing

52. : Solution

53. : DMAIC

54. c: Request for quotation

55. : Supply chain

56. a: Supply chain risk management

57. a: Remanufacturing

58. : Prize

59. d: Perfect competition

Commerce

1. d: Market structure

2. a: Cooperative

3. a: Fraud

4. a: English auction

5. d: International trade

6. b: Disney

7. d: Stock

8. a: Walt Disney

9. d: GeoCities

10. b: Total cost

11. b: Consultant

12. : Authentication

13. a: Consideration

14. : Market share

15. a: Reverse auction

16. c: Outsourcing

17. d: Advertisement

18. d: Bottom line

19. b: American Express

20. b: Pizza Hut

21. d: Front office

22. d: Jury

23. : Shareholder

24. : Trial

25. : Hearing

26. b: Minimum wage

27. : Human resources

28. : Purchasing

29. b: Security

30. b: Monopoly

31. : Merchant

32. : European Union

33. c: British Airways

34. d: Complaint

35. a: Joint venture

36. d: Collaborative filtering

37. b: Pop-up ad

38. d: Quality control

39. b: Tangible

40. a: Contribution margin

41. : E-procurement

42. d: Hospitality

43. b: Dutch auction

44. : Frequency

45. : Competitive advantage

46. c: Economies of scale

47. : E-commerce

48. a: Transaction cost

49. : Semantic

50. a: Inventory

51. b: Interest

52. b: Leadership

53. b: Shares

54. b: Management

55. c: Free market

56. a: Statutory law

57. b: Utility

58. a: Argument

59. a: Audit

Business ethics

1. c: Madoff
2. : Micromanagement
3. c: Tobacco
4. d: East Germany
5. d: Cultural relativism
6. c: Catholicism
7. c: Greenwashing
8. a: Foreign Corrupt Practices Act
9. d: Fair trade
10. c: Copyright
11. b: Qui tam
12. a: Marketing
13. c: Disclaimer
14. c: Business model
15. b: Organic food
16. b: Sustainability
17. b: Pyramid scheme
18. : Price fixing
19. : Utopian socialism
20. : Better Business Bureau
21. d: Parental leave
22. d: ExxonMobil
23. b: Utilitarianism
24. c: Biofuel
25. : Global reach
26. d: Great Depression
27. a: Workplace politics
28. b: Nepotism

29. c: Kyoto Protocol

30. d: Cause-related marketing

31. : European Commission

32. a: Fair Trade Certified

33. d: Global Fund

34. b: Fraud

35. b: Natural gas

36. a: Ethics Resource Center

37. c: Model Rules of Professional Conduct

38. c: Volcker Rule

39. : Solar power

40. c: Habitat

41. b: Pollution

42. a: Stanford International Bank

43. b: Vigilance committee

44. d: Exxon Valdez

45. a: Veil of ignorance

46. d: Federal Trade Commission

47. b: Social networking

48. a: Medicare fraud

49. a: Lead paint

50. a: Lanham Act

51. a: Coal

52. a: Guerrilla Marketing

53. a: Greenpeace

54. : Social responsibility

55. a: Medicaid

56. a: Transformational leadership

57. : Undue hardship

58. b: Green marketing

59. b: Clayton Act

Accounting

1. b: Financial instrument

2. b: Adjusting entries

3. d: Personal identification number

4. b: Proprietorship

5. d: Accrued liabilities

6. b: Balanced scorecard

7. b: Accounting

8. c: Tax credit

9. : Control account

10. c: Periodic inventory

11. : Comprehensive income

12. b: Embezzlement

13. b: Petty cash

14. d: Permanent fund

15. : Net realizable value

16. b: Subsidiary ledger

17. : Stock Exchange

18. c: Accounts receivable

19. : Operating budget

20. c: Controversy

21. a: Securities Exchange Act

22. d: Governmental Accounting Standards Board

23. a: Long-term liabilities

24. a: Customer profitability

25. c: Remote deposit

26. : International Financial Reporting Standards

27. b: Withholding

28. a: Electronic funds transfer

29. c: Process costing

30. d: Bank

31. b: XBRL

32. d: General journal

33. c: Treasury stock

34. b: Benchmarking

35. a: Financial Accounting Standards Board

36. b: Average cost

37. b: Receivable

38. : Working capital

39. : Cost pool

40. : Debt-to-equity ratio

41. a: Annual report

42. a: Taxable income

43. a: Statement of retained earnings

44. d: Land

45. : Gift card

46. a: Bad debt

47. a: Partnership agreement

48. c: Accounting management

49. d: Substitute check

50. c: Pension

51. d: Contributed capital

52. : Fair value

53. b: Adoption

54. : Ledger

55. : Internal Revenue Code

56. a: Party

57. : Fair Labor Standards Act

58. c: Retained earnings

59. a: Fair market value

CPSIA information can be obtained
at www.ICGtesting.com
Printed in the USA
LVHW100206301019
635715LV00011B/999/P

9 781538 855768